€ 39,-
'18.
Vana

Quality of Secondary Education in India

Charu Jain · Narayan Prasad

Quality of Secondary Education in India

Concepts, Indicators, and Measurement

 Springer

Charu Jain
National Council of Applied Economic
    Research
New Delhi, Delhi
India

Narayan Prasad
School of Social Sciences
Indira Gandhi National Open University
    (IGNOU)
New Delhi, Delhi
India

ISBN 978-981-10-4928-6   ISBN 978-981-10-4929-3   (eBook)
https://doi.org/10.1007/978-981-10-4929-3

Library of Congress Control Number: 2017945684

Printed on acid-free paper

This Springer imprint is published by Springer Nature
The registered company is Springer Nature Singapore Pte Ltd.
The registered company address is: 152 Beach Road, #21-01/04 Gateway East, Singapore 189721, Singapore

Quality is never an accident;
It is always the result of high intention,
Sincere effort, intelligent direction and
skillful execution;
It represents the wise choice of many
alternatives.

—William A. Foster

This book is dedicated to our families.

Foreword

Improvement in the quality of education is becoming increasingly important in the contemporary world. In the Indian context, both the 11th and 12th Five-Year Plans have accorded high priority to greater accessibility, equal opportunities, and improved quality of education to all segments of the society. In this direction, the centrally sponsored scheme *Rashtriya Madhyamik Shiksha Abhiyan* (*RMSA*, lit. National Secondary Education Programme) was launched in March 2009 with the objective of making secondary education of good quality available, accessible, and affordable to all young persons in the 14–15 year age group. The scheme envisages enhancing enrolment in Classes IX–X (senior secondary) by providing a secondary school within a reasonable distance of every habitation to enable universal access to secondary education by 2017 and universal retention by 2020; improving the quality of education through making all schools conform to prescribed norms; and removing gender, socio-economic, and disability barriers. Though vast progress has been made during the past few years, there still remain serious concerns that need to be addressed.

The available data reveal that both gross and net enrolment ratios are low at 78.5% and 48.5% at secondary level and 54.2% and 32.7% at higher secondary level of education in 2014–15. Although, transition from elementary to secondary has improved, transition from secondary to higher secondary level of education is quite low at 67.7% in 2013–14, which is also evident in the low pass percentage at the secondary level. Despite significant accomplishments, gender and regional disparities continue to persist. The enrolment of girls as a percentage of total enrolments in secondary education was 47.3% in 2014–15. Out-of-school children and dropout rates have reduced substantially over the years, but not evenly across all social groups. Dropout rates and unsatisfactory student learning levels continue to cause concern. Lower numbers of female teachers, quality of teaching–learning processes, and learning outcomes are the new challenges that the schooling system is facing, given the sharp increase in enrolments over a short period of time.

In view of the above, the present book entitled *Quality of Secondary Education in India: Concept, Indicators, and Measurement*, is a serious attempt in examining issues related to the overall progress and quality of secondary education in India covering both quantitative and qualitative aspects, making comparative assessments at other levels of school education, and providing key recommendations for policy makers. At the macro level, it covers national- and state-level progress, disparities, and challenges; whereas at the micro level, it covers first-hand qualitative information from schools, teachers, and students through primary surveys conducted in Delhi. The analysis presented in the book may not cover all possible issues related to secondary education in a comprehensive manner, but it does offer penetrating insights into quality-related issues in secondary education.

The book is divided into five parts. Each part is unique in terms of its focus and coverage, viz. theoretical concepts and existing literature; research methodology and measurement of variables; national- and state-level issues of growth; disparities in secondary education in India; determinants of quality education emerging from the empirical findings using primary survey results from schools, teachers, and students; and finally, policy discussions and recommendations. This will be essential reading for academics, students, and researchers interested in educational studies, research, and planning, and a useful reference source for others wishing to know about this highly topical subject.

I appreciate the effort put in by the authors towards conducting research in this area and bringing out this volume and hope that this volume is able to provide useful and feasible solutions for improving the quality of secondary education in India. I wish them success in this and all such forthcoming academic endeavors!

April 2017   Prof. Sushma Yadav
                                                        Member, University Grants Commission
                                                   Professor of Public Policy and Governance
                                                     Indian Institute of Public Administration
                                                                            New Delhi, India

Preface

Being one of the strongest links between elementary and higher education, secondary education is emerging as one of the important educational sectors in India. In order to reap its maximum benefits, it is of utmost importance for policy makers to now address the dual challenge of quantity expansion and quality enhancement. This book not only provides useful insights into quality related concepts of secondary education in India but also answers questions on why there is need to improve quality of education, how one can measure quality of education and the ways to improve quality. This book reviews the present status of quality of secondary education in schools at the national and state level in India, thereby identifying inequalities that exist at various levels and evaluating the factors that determine student outcomes and efficient teaching abilities in India. It also seeks to understand the extent to which school resources and infrastructural facilities, teachers and teaching methods, family characteristics, self-motivational factors, and exposure to mass media affect the performance of students. Along with this, perceptions of students and teachers on various issues related to enhancement of quality education and efficient learning environment in schools are also presented in this book.

For this, the analysis in this volume is conceptually designed at three levels: (i) national level performance and linkages; (ii) state level progress, disparities and linkages; and (iii) school level: measurement and improvement of learning outcomes of students and efficient teaching practices. While, first two approaches simply provide answers to research questions on why measuring the quality of secondary education is important in India; the third approach identifies various determinants for measuring the quality of secondary education. Both quantitative and qualitative methods have been used to probe the various issues related to the quality of secondary education at the micro and macro levels.

The book is divided into five parts. While the first part introduces the topic and gives a theoretical and conceptual framework, the second part describes the study area and research design used in the study. The third part presents the growth and linkages of secondary education at national and state levels. The key highlights of this section are that it provides answers to questions like: Why is it important to shift focus on secondary education? Why is there a need to improve quality? Given the fact that quality of education needs improvement, the fourth part gives empirical evidence on how quality of education can be measured, the factors that determine student outcomes, and the quality of teaching practices in schools. The last part concludes and gives policy implications and recommendations.

This book provides a methodological framework to scholars interested in measuring and evaluating the quality of secondary education in various settings. We hope that educational institutions, research scholars, students, policy makers, and many others find these findings useful and beneficial for strengthening and delivering the quality education in South Asia, Southeast Asia, and other developing regions. A major part of this study is based on the doctoral thesis, approved and awarded by School of Social Sciences, Indira Gandhi National Open University, to the first author.

The conduct of this research and writing of this book was an enriching experience for us. We would like to take this opportunity to thank all the people whose help has been valuable in writing this book. Firstly, we are grateful to the National Council for Applied Economic Research (NCAER) and IGNOU for not only providing us with an expert platform and infrastructural support, but also for facilitating us with various research material and references required for conducting this study. We express our deep gratitude to the faculty members and other staff members of both of these institutions for their guidance and support throughout. We are thankful to the National Book Trust (NBT), India and the National Action Plan for Readership Development of the Trust for granting us permission to use the National Youth Readership Survey (NYRS) primary data. We are also grateful to the board of the *Journal of Educational Planning and Administration*, published by the National University of Educational Planning and Administration, New Delhi for granting us the permission to republish some regression results and literature from the paper entitled 'Evidences of Linkage between Secondary Education and Socio-Economic Outcomes in India' published in Jan 2016 issue. We acknowledge the support of both these institutions.

Since this research work has undertaken primary survey from senior secondary schools in Delhi, we would like to give our special thanks to all those principals, teachers, students, and other key stakeholders in surveyed schools in Delhi who volunteered and participated in this study. Without their support this analysis would not have been completed. We are grateful to Dr. Vichar Das, Mr. Mehta, Mr. Vijay Thakur and Mr. Deepak for providing us with necessary input during the translation and printing of questionnaires, data collection and data entry. We want to acknowledge all our friends and colleagues for their great support during the study.

Last, but not the least, we are profoundly grateful to our family members, who have always been a true source of inspiration for us, for keeping up our morale, for being continuing source of help and encouragement, for their love, patience and understanding throughout the period. Their creative ideas and enduring support have helped a lot in completing this book. Finally, we would like to mention that the views expressed in this book are our own and do not necessarily reflect the opinion of the affiliated organizations.

New Delhi, India   Charu Jain
                                                                                      Narayan Prasad

Contents

About the Authors

Charu Jain is an Associate Fellow at National Council of Applied Economic Research (NCAER), New Delhi. Prior to this, she has worked at various other reputed organizations like TNS India and PHD Chamber of Commerce and Industry. Her areas of research interest include socio-economic studies, gender and educational studies, developmental changes and consumer studies. She has extensively worked in the area of large scale consumer studies, industrial surveys, housing studies, agriculture and macro-economic policy issues. Her current research focuses on educational issues, handloom sector and agricultural outlook. She has also contributed few research papers and articles in reputed national journals and has also presented papers in international conferences. She received top rank and gold medal from Guru Jambeshwar University for her Post Graduate program in Business Economics. She received her Ph.D. in Economics from School of Social Sciences, Indira Gandhi National Open University (IGNOU), New Delhi in the area of education sector, particularly looking at the quality issues of secondary education in India.

Narayan Prasad is presently Director, Research Unit and Professor of Economics in School of Social Sciences, IGNOU. He has been associated with this institution since 1992. Prior to joining IGNOU, he has worked in several reputed organizations like Monopolies and Restrictive Trade Practices (MRTP) Commission, Association of Indian Universities (AIU) etc. He was awarded post-doctoral fellowship by UGC and visited France under the scheme Indo-French Cultural Exchange Program. He has completed advanced course in Vedanta and Shrimad Bhagwat Geeta from Chinmay International Foundation. He was invited to deliver lectures on Vedanta at various places including New York, Washington and Los Angeles in USA. He has completed three research projects and wrote three books which have been published by reputed publishers like SAGE publications and Springer Publications. Recently, he has completed another major research project entitled "Assessment of Human Well-being in India" financially sponsored by ICSSR. He has contributed 25 research papers and three review articles to the reputed National and International journals. Ten students have been awarded Ph.D. and 9 M.Phil. degrees under his supervision. His areas of research interest are: Human Well-Being, Human Development, Spiritual Economics and Philosophical Foundation of Economics. He teaches research methodological course to M.Phil. and Ph.D. students.

Glossary

Absence rate is defined as number of days students go to school as percentage of total number of school days in a month.

An average year of schooling is the years of formal schooling received, on average, by students (total, male, female).

Completion rate is the total number of students (total, male, female) regardless of age in the last grade of secondary school, minus the number of repeaters (total, male, female) in that grade, divided by the (total, male, female) number of children of official graduation age. Note that when repetition rates are high, this indicator is not always a reliable measure of primary completion.

Drop-out rate (%), secondary is the percentage of a cohort of pupils (total, male, female) enrolled in the VIII grade, and is not expected to reach the first grade of lower secondary education. It is calculated as 100% minus the survival rate to the last grade of middle level education (VIII).

Education levels are broadly classified into four categories at school level of education; primary (upto Grade V), middle (Grade VI–VIII), lower secondary (Grade IX–X) and senior secondary (Grade XI–XII). At some places in this study, we have used the term 'elementary education' to indicate school education upto grade VIII and term 'secondary education' to indicate grade IX–XII.

GDP (constant at FC) is the sum of gross value added by all resident producers in the economy plus any product taxes and minus any subsidies not included in the value of the products. It is calculated without making deductions for depreciation of fabricated assets or for depletion and degradation of natural resources.

Gender parity index (GPI), gross enrollment ratio in secondary education is the ratio of the female-to-male values of the gross enrollment ratio in secondary education. A GPI of 1 indicates parity between sexes.

Girls' enrollment share (%), secondary is the number of girls enrolled in secondary school, expressed as a percentage of the total number of students in secondary school.

Gross enrollment rate (%), secondary is the number of pupils (total, male, female) enrolled in secondary, regardless of age, expressed as a percentage of the population (total, male, female) in the theoretical age group for secondary education.

HIV prevalence (% of adults) is the percentage of people ages 15–49 who are infected with HIV.

Indicators are data points that are predictive. This is contrasted with evidence of accomplishment, which demonstrates success.

Inputs are the essential elements that comprise the development and delivery of a course or school, such as textbooks, instructional materials, teaching, and technology. Quality assurance based on inputs often takes the form of standards or qualifications that apply to the inputs.

Labor force with secondary education (% of total) is the proportion of the (total, male, female) labor force that has a secondary education, as a percentage of the (total, male, female) labor force.

Labor force, female (% of total) is the percentage of females that are active in the labor force.

Labor force, total comprises people who meet the ILO definition of the economically active population. It includes both the employed and the unemployed. The labor force also includes the armed forces, the unemployed and first-time job-seekers, but excludes homemakers and other unpaid caregivers and workers in the informal sector.

Literacy rate, adult (% of people 15+) is the percentage of people (total, male, female) ages 15 and older who can, with understanding, both read and write a short, simple statement about their everyday life out of the whole population (total, male, female) ages 15 and older.

Literacy rate, youth (% aged 15–24) is the percentage of people ages 15–24 who can, with understanding, both read and write a short, simple statement about their everyday life.

Mortality rate, under 5 (per 1,000) is the probability that a newborn baby will die before reaching age five, if subject to current age-specific mortality rates. The probability is expressed as a rate per 1,000.

Outcomes measure the knowledge, skills, and abilities that students have attained as a result of their involvement in a particular set of educational experiences. They measure the effectiveness of the learning process, are more longitudinal in nature than outputs, and measure more than just academic achievement at a point in time. Ideally they are based on a common assessment, not one that is specific to the school or course.

Out-of-school children, secondary are the number of children in the official secondary-age range who are not enrolled in secondary education.

Passing rates are proportion of students appeared among the enrolled and proportion of successful students in the students appeared for the Board Examinations.

Percentage of repeaters, secondary (%) is the number of pupils (total, male, female) enrolled in the same grade of secondary education as in the previous year, expressed as a percentage of the total enrollment in that grade.

Population growth (annual %) is the exponential change of the population for the period indicated.

Presence rate is the percentage share of classes attended by students each day out of total number of periods allotted in a day.

Promotion rate is transfer/promotion of students between various secondary levels of education. Since the data on number of repeaters was not available year-wise hence ratios of enrolments at various levels were considered.

Public current education expenditure (% of current education expenditure), secondary is defined as the share of public current expenditure on education that is devoted to secondary education.

Public education expenditure as % of GDP is the current and capital expenditures on education by local, regional and national governments, including municipalities (household contributions are excluded), expressed as a percentage of the gross domestic product.

Pupil–teacher ratio, secondary is the average number of pupils per teacher in secondary education in a given school-year, based on headcounts for both pupils and teachers.

Sampling fraction is the ratio of total number of schools in each stratum divided by required number of schools.

School life expectancy (years) is the number of years a child (total, male, female) of school entrance age is expected to spend at school, or university, including years spent on repetition.

Secondary education, teachers (% trained) is the number of teachers (total, male, female) who have received the minimum organized teacher-training (pre-service or in service) required for teaching at the secondary level of education in the given country, expressed as a percentage of the total number of teachers (total, male, female) at the secondary level of education.

Student enrollment is defined as the number of students (total, female) enrolled in a particular level of education (primary, secondary, tertiary). For secondary education, student enrolment includes enrolment in general programs as well as enrolment in technical and vocational programs.

Transition rate refers to percent of students joining from one level to the next level of education. So far as computation of transition rates is concerned, first the repeaters are taken out from the enrolments in first grade of secondary education (Grade IX) which is divided by the terminal grade of previous cycle (Class VIII) that is middle level.

Abbreviations

ABE	Analysis of Budgeted Expenditure
AEP	Adolescence Education Programme
AISES	All India School Education Survey
AISSCE	All India Senior School Certificate Examination
AIU	Association of Indian Universities
ASER	Annual Status of Education Report
BCG	Boston Consulting Group
BE	Budget Estimates
B.Ed	Bachelor of Education
BPL	Below Poverty Line
CABE	Central Advisory Board of Education
CBSE	Central Board of Secondary Education
CIET	Central Institute of Education Technologies
CISCE	Council for Indian School Certificate Examination
CSO	Central Statistical Organisation
CTSA	Central Tibetan Schools Administration
DCB	Delhi Cantonment Board
DPT	Diphtheria, Pertussis and Tetanus
DT	Diphtheria and Tetanus
EBBs	Educationally Backward Blocks
EDI	Educational Development Index
EFA	Education For All
EPI	Education Performance Index
FICCI	Federation of Indian Chambers of Commerce and Industry
GBSSS	Government Boys Senior Secondary Schools
GDP	Gross Domestic Product
GEI	Gender Inequality Index
GER	Gross Enrolment Ratio
GGSSS	Government Girls Senior Secondary Schools
GPI	Gender Parity Index

GSDP	Gross State Domestic Product
HDI	Human Development Index
HPAE	High Performing Asian Economies
HRD	Human Resource Development
IAMR	Institute of Applied Manpower
IBO	International Baccalaureate Organisation
ICT	Information and Communication Technology
IEDC	Inclusive Education for Disabled Children
IEDSS	Inclusive Education for Disabled at Secondary Stage
IHDS	Indian Human Development Survey
IIM	Indian Institutes of Management
IIT	Indian Institutes of Technology
IMR	Infant Mortality Rates
JNV	Jawahar Navodaya Vidyalaya (Jawahar Navodaya Schools)
KGBV	Kastrurba Gandhi Balika Vidyalayas (Kasturba Gandhi Girl's School)
KMO	Kaiser-Meyer-Olkin Measure of Sampling Adequacy
KVS	Kendriya Vidyalaya Sangathan (Central School Organisation)
MCD	Municipal Corporation of Delhi
MDM	Mid-Day Meal scheme
MHFW	Ministry of Health and Family Welfare
MMR	Maternal Mortality Rates
MPCE	Monthly per Capita Consumption Expenditure
NACO	National Aids Control Organisation
NAEP	National Assessment of Educational Progress
NAS	National Accounts Statistics
NBT	National Book Trust
NCAER	National Council for Applied Economic Research
NCERT	National Council of Educational Research and Training
NCT	National Capital Territory of Delhi
NCTE	National Council of Teacher Education
NDMC	New Delhi Municipal Council
NFHS	National Family Health Survey
NIH	National Institute of Health
NIHFW	National Institute of Health and Family Welfare
NIOS	National Institute of Open Schooling
NIT	National Institutes of Technology
NMMSS	National Merit-cum Means Scholarship Scheme
NSHIE	National Survey of Household Income and Expenditure
NSSO	National Sample Survey Organisation
NUEPA	National University of Educational Planning and Administration
NVS	Navodaya Vidyalaya Samiti (Navodaya School Committee)
NYRS	National Youth Readership Survey
OECD	Organization for Economic Co-operation and Development
PCA	Principal Component Analysis

PGT	Post Graduate Teachers
PPP	Public Private Partnership
PTM	Parents Teacher Meeting
PTR	Pupil Teacher Ratio
QEDC	Quality Education in Developing Countries
RBI	Reserve Bank of India
RCH	Reproductive and Child Healthcare
RIE	Regional Institute of Education
RMSA	Rashtriya Madhyamik Shiksha Abhiyan (National Secondary Education Programme)
ROC	Receiver Operating Characteristic Curve
RTE	Right to Education
SBV	Sarvodaya Bal Vidyalaya (Sarvodaya Boy's School)
SCV	Sarvodaya Co-ed Vidyalaya (Sarvodaya Co-educational School)
SDP	State Domestic Product
SIET	State Institute of Education Technologies
SKV	Sarvodaya Kanya Vidyalaya (Sarvodaya Girl's School)
SQM	Strategic Quality management
SRS	Sample Registration System
SSA	Sarva Shiksha Abhiyan (Education for All Scheme)
SUCCESS	Universal Access and Quality at Secondary Education Scheme
SV	Sarvodaya Vidyalaya (Sarvodaya Schools)
TFR	Total Fertility Rates
TGT	Trained Graduate Teacher
TLM	Teaching Learning Material
TQM	Total Quality Management
UGC	University Grants Commission
UNDP	United Nations Development Programme
UNESCO	United Nations Educational, Scientific and Cultural Organization
UNICEF	United Nations Children's Educational Fund

List of Figures

List of Tables

List of Boxes

Chapter 1
Quality Improvement of Secondary Education in India: An Overview

Abstract Education is widely recognized as one of the fundamental factors contributing to the process of development. No country can achieve sustainable development without making sustainable investment in human capital. It raises people's productivity and creativity and promotes entrepreneurship and technological advances. Further, it plays a crucial role in securing economic and social progress and improving income distribution. An effective and innovative education system opens enormous opportunities for individuals, whereas a weak system can result in declining standards of living, social exclusion, and unemployment. Hence, there is a strong need to strive for excellence and quality in education. Even the Eleventh Five Year Plan has recognized the fact that higher growth rates would require a large quantitative and qualitative expansion of formal education and skill formation. Right to education (RTE) also ensures quantitative expansion so that all eligible school-going students are brought within the folds of formal education at the elementary level (GOI 2005). However, evidences show that presently the key problems at school-level education are high dropout rates and low retention rates. It's not just years of education that matter, the issue of quality of education provided at the school level is equally important. To reap the benefits of education to the extent possible, policymakers need to address the dual challenge of increasing the quantity of education and maintaining high quality of education. To achieve high standards of quality, the nation requires both: establishing quality assurance and evaluation system as well as promoting a quality culture within institutions or schools.

Keywords Secondary education · Quality assurance · Conceptual framework · Approaches

1.1 Background

In developing nations, where public resource is scarce, education has to compete with other urgent needs such as healthcare or infrastructure; hence, obtaining sufficient public resource is a major challenge. In India, a large part of the resources for education comes from the state governments thereby creating much pressure on the state funds. Apart from the fact that financing of education needs to be analysed and effective measures undertaken, it is also important to understand that successful learning outcomes, to a significant extent, depends on enabling environments at school, home, work, etc. Cognitive skills may be developed through formal schooling but also in many instances a child acquires such skills from the family, peers, his/her surrounding culture, and so forth. However, the returns to quality education vary from situation to situation. The disparity in the quality of education across states and different types of schools within a state is enormous. It is recognized that for growth to be inclusive, access to quality education need to be broadened so that the fruits of development in terms of productive employment, higher wages accompanied with higher standards of living can be made available to all sections of society. Although secondary education and its expansion have gained importance in India since the Eleventh Five Year Plan, efforts on quality enhancement are still lacking. Globally, immense research has been conducted to determine how quality of secondary education can be improved, but in India, this area has still not gained much attention among research scholars. Thus, there is a strong need to undertake intensive research work in this area that can probe these issues and offer policy recommendations. This book is an attempt to fill up this gap and provide insights into the quality issues of secondary education in India.

The unique feature about this study is that it covers the issues of secondary education in India from quantitative and qualitative perspectives. Through this study, an attempt has been made to provide clarity on the concept of the quality of education, its origin, and various models/approaches adopted so far. In addition to this, it will also provide detailed discussion on the literature available worldwide and also what has been achieved in India so far. This book not only discusses quality concepts but also provides answers to questions on why there is need to improve quality of education in India, how one can measure the quality of education, and how quality can be improved.

To answer these questions, the methodological conceptual framework in this book is designed using three approaches: (i) national level growth, performance and linkages; (ii) state level performance, disparities and linkages; and (iii) identifying the determinants of quality indicators and measuring its impact on student outcomes. While, the analysis in first two approaches is based on information gathered from renowned secondary data sources, the third approach is entirely based on the primary survey data collected from sample schools. The entire analysis in this book is presented from both macro and micro perspective.

The analysis presented in this book may not provide comprehensive analysis of all the possible issues but it does offer a penetrating insight into the qualitative issues of secondary education in India.

1.2 Why Focus on Secondary Education?

The book specifically looks at quality concerns in secondary education in India. This section will more precisely provide an answer to the question on why is it necessary now to focus on secondary education. The specific reasons may be outlined as: firstly, secondary level of education provides the strongest link between primary and higher education that prepares the human capital base for the country. Considering its importance, the Eleventh Five Year Plan has also included this level of education in their agenda. Secondly, few international studies have found that among all levels of education, secondary education has strongest impact on reducing income inequality and improving health perspectives as with broader educational base, low-income people are able to seek out better socio-economic opportunities. Bourguignon and Morrison (1990) found that one percent increase in the labor force with at least secondary education would increase the share of income of the bottom 40 and 60% by between 6 and 15%. Similar evidences have been reported in another study that finds significant relation between secondary enrollment rates and determinants of income distribution in 36 countries (Bourguignon 1995). On health perspective, a study of fourteen African countries for the mid-eighties showed that secondary education has invariably reduced fertility level (Birdsall et al. 1995; Behrman and Wolfe 1987). Another study by Ainsworth et al. (1995) showed that the three successful countries in terms of reduced fertility i.e. Kenya, Botswana, and Zimbabwe, had the highest levels of female schooling and lowest child mortality rates. Thirdly, according to recent World Bank reports on World Development Indicators, India has been now classified under lower-middle income economy. In one of the study, it has been found that for middle-income countries, although the expanding primary education continues to remain socially profitable, secondary education would yield the highest social returns if developed well, therefore, investing in secondary education will boost the economic growth of developing countries (Mingat and Tan 1996). Fourthly, it has already been proved by many economists that higher the level of education, greater will be the productivity. For example, in Thailand, farmers with four or more years of schooling were three times more likely to adopt fertilizer and other modern inputs than less educated farmers (Birdsall 1993). Similarly, in Nepal, the completion of at least seven years of schooling increased productivity in wheat by over a quarter, and in rice by 13% (Jamison and Moock 1994). According to Lucas (1998), for example, the higher the level of education of the work force the higher the overall productivity of capital because the more educated are more likely to innovate, and thus affect everyone's productivity. In other models a similar externality is generated as the increased education of individuals raises not only their own productivity but also that of others with whom they interact, so that total productivity increases as the average level of education rises (Perotti 1993). Finally, students' enrollment in schools was forecasted to grow at 3.2% during 2006–2014. Out of every eight schools in India, only one caters to secondary education while the remaining seven caters to elementary education. Nearly 77% of the total student enrolments were for elementary level of education, while secondary schools accounted for only 23% of the total school enrolments in 2013–14. Despite being one of the strongest links between elementary and higher education in providing inputs, the number of secondary level schools is low. Not only this, students enrolled in secondary schools were substantially lesser than in elementary schools due to the fact that the dropout rate after elementary education was approximately 47.4%, as reported in 2013–14. Thus, one needs to decipher whether it is a problem of low access to secondary schools or of low quality standards in these schools? In this context, it is utmost important to find out the quality standards of education in secondary schools, highlighting issues that need to be addressed for sustainable growth.

1.3   Overview of the Book

This book is precisely divided into five parts.

Part I Theoretical and Conceptual Framework: This section includes three chapters. First chapter provides a brief understanding on the theoretical issues concerning the concept and phenomenon of quality of education. The second chapter reviews the relevant research studies undertaken in this area. The third chapter throws light on conceptual framework of the study. The need for conducting research study, outlining objectives and hypotheses, etc., has also been covered in this chapter.

Part II Research Methodology and Study Methods: This section comprises two chapters. The first chapter introduces the study area and research design. The next chapter briefly discusses the study methods, survey procedure, measurement of indicators incorporated in the study and further talks about the processing and analysis of data.

Part III Secondary Education in India: Growth, Disparities, and Linkages: This section comprises three chapters. The first chapter explains the structure of Indian education system and its key challenges. This chapter also provides brief scenario of secondary education and its benchmarks at the global level. The second chapter reviews the trends in development and performance of secondary education at national level particularly looking at the pattern of enrolments, dropouts, financing and management of secondary education in India. The chapter also tries to evaluate why secondary education is important from the national perspective. The third chapter under this section presents inter-state disparities in educational indicators in terms of their capabilities and inefficiencies, emphasizing thereby the point that states the need to re-evaluate their education policies. It also elaborates the importance and need for investment in secondary education in terms of its strong socio-economic linkages. The findings presented under this part of the book are based on the data gathered from renowned secondary sources for e.g., Census of India, National Sample Survey, Analysis of Budgeted Expenditure, Economic Surveys, Ministry of HRD, Educational Statistics at a Glance, NUEPA, SRS etc.

Part IV Determinants of Quality of Education: Empirical Results and Discussion: This part includes three chapters each giving the findings of empirical analysis for identifying the quality determinants of education in India. The first chapter discusses the characteristics of the sample schools and respondents particularly students and teachers in a more comprehensive way. The next chapter presents survey findings on various factors that influence the performances of students affecting their overall development and learning skills. On the basis of these factors, this chapter further discusses the development of quality model for secondary education and throws light on how it differs according to the socio-economic-demographic and school profiles of different students. The chapter also presents the perceptions of students on various issues related to their performance, schools, teachers, and teaching methods. The last chapter of this section discusses the role of teachers in students' learning process and the methods used by them for teaching, as well as the part played by performance-related indicators. The perceptions on various issues related to school facilities and development from teacher's point of view have also been presented here.

Part V Summary and Suggestions: This part provides the summary of all the major findings of the study, policy implications, and suggestions.

We hope that this book can play a great role in providing the useful and implementable suggestions/ solutions for improving the overall quality of education system in India. This book is useful for all those involved in educational studies, educational research, social science research, research institutions, educational institutions and policy makers. We believe that for policy makers, the findings of the book will bring clear insights on various issues that need attention on priority basis.

References

Ainsworth, M., Beegle, K., & Nyamete, A. (1995). The impact of female schooling on fertility and contraceptive. *World Bank: Washington DC. LSMS working paper,* (110).

Behrman, J. R., & Wolfe, B. L. (1987). How does mother's schooling affect the family's health, nutrition, medical care usage and household?. *Journal of Econometrics, 36.*

Birdsall, N. (1993). *Social Development in Economic Development.* World Bank Policy research working Papers, WPS 1123, Washington DC.

Birdsall, N., Ross, D., & Sabot, R. (1995). Inequality and growth reconsidered: Lessons from East-Asia. *World Bank, Economics Review, 93,* 477–508.

Bourguignon, F. (1995). *Equity and Economic Growth: Permanent questions and Changing Answers.* Prepared for the Human Development Report, UNDP.

Bourguignon, F., & Morrison, C. (1990). Income distribution, development and foreign trade: A cross-sectional analysis. *European Economic Review, 34.*

Government of India. (2005). Right to education bill. August 25, 2005. http://www.education.nic.in/htmlweb/RighttoEducationBill2005.pdf.

Jamison, D., & Moock, P. (1994). Farmer education and farmer efficiency in the Nepal: The role of schooling. *World Development, 12.*

Lucas, R. (1998). On the mechanics of economic development. *Journal of Monetary Economics, 22*(1).

Mincer, J. (1974). *Schooling, Earnings, and Experience*. New York: Colombia University Press.
Mingat, A., & Tan, J. P. (1996). *Full social returns to education: Estimates based on countries economic growth performance*. Working Paper World Bank: Washington, D.C.
Perotti, R. (1993). Political equilibrium income distribution, and growth. *Review of Economic Studies, 60*.

Part I
Theoretical and Conceptual Framework

Chapter 2
Quality in Education—Concept, Origin, and Approaches

Abstract Being instrumental in bringing about the economic development of a country, education and is one of the basic services offered by government and stakeholders to society. However, as mere quantitative expansion would not generate the desired results unless a particular standard of quality is maintained, it is essential that policies shift their focus from increasing enrolments to quality improvement in all spheres—beginning from making school facilities available to students, developing their learning skills which is not just limited to curriculum knowledge, and initiating efficient teaching practices. The concept of quality in the field of education is not new; therefore, it is even important to understand how the quality debate has evolved over the years and how it has come to be linked with the provision of education. This chapter describes the theoretical aspect of quality concept, its historical origin in the field of education, various related models and approaches. It is being argued that the concept of quality in education is multi-faceted; it does not possess any specific definition; different scholars have interpreted the concept differently. The differences lie not only in the way this concept is defined, but is also reflected in the manner in which quality is measured. Although, worldwide, research initiatives has been undertaken to identify the quality indicators, measuring the educational outcomes, in the Indian context, little evidence is available, particularly in case of secondary education.

Keywords Quality · Concept · Secondary education · Approaches

2.1 Historic Origin of Quality Concept in Education

The available literature asserts that quality debate evolved with the advent of industrialization as the need to ensure that products conformed to specifications escalated and customers began to demand value for money (Sallis 1996). Wadsworth et al. (2002) argued that at this stage the focus was more on products rather than on quality. Slowly industrialization led to mass production and division of work into small repetitive tasks, thus shifting the quality checking responsibility

© Springer Nature Singapore Pte Ltd. 2018
C. Jain and N. Prasad, *Quality of Secondary Education in India*,
https://doi.org/10.1007/978-981-10-4929-3_2

from workers to processes and systems in organizations. The concept of quality control, which was under inspection till 1940, soon started dominating production lines to detect defective products and stop them from reaching customers. Post World War II, that is, in the 1960s, there was a shift from statistical process control to quality assurance. The thrust was now to avoid producing defective products in the first place. This focus intensified further leading to the emergence of the concept of Total quality management (TQM) in the 1980s.

As social services like education, health, defense expanded and took in high portions of public funds, government and communities started asking for quality improvement in terms of value addition of money. Education was not spared as schools competed with other schools for students. Thus, issues of quality transcended the boundary between the corporate world and public sector and quality and service concepts adapted themselves to meet the specific environments of educational institutions, thereby opening up possibilities of it being reformed in the next century (Linston 1999).

2.2 Defining Quality of Education

In spite of the fact that the debate on quality has been prevailing for a long time, there has been no universally acceptable definition of quality. This section reviews the definitions given in various contexts by different scholars. There are two aspects of quality in education: *Quality* of the education system as a whole (including schools and related bodies, teaching and learning environment, policies etc) and *Quality* of what the system offers to the students/learners (i.e. quality of teaching and learning process, curriculum etc). Terms like efficiency, effectiveness, equity, and quality have often been used synonymously (Adams 1993). It is therefore not easy to define quality in the context of education.

According to Hoy et al. (2000), quality in education is an evaluation process of education, which enhances the need to achieve and develop the talents of the customers and, at the same time, meet the accountability standards set by the clients who pay for the process. Goddard and Leask (1992) highlighted the definition of quality as simply meeting the requirements of customers. They have included different customers for education—parents, government, students, teachers, employers, and institutions—who look for different characteristics of quality.

Education being a service and not a product, its quality cannot lie exclusively in the final output. Its quality should also be manifested in the delivery process. Quality of education should also take into account determinants such as provision of teachers, building, curriculum, equipment, textbooks, and teaching processes (Grisay and Mahlck 1991). For them, quality of education has a three-dimensional approach comprising quality of human and material resources available for teaching (inputs), teaching practices (process), and results (outcomes). Further, according to them, there are some indicators—repetition, dropouts, promotion, and transition rates—which are frequented by planners to arrive at an approximate measurement of quality.

In 1990, *the World Conference on Education for All held at Jomtien*, Thailand, identified that to achieve the fundamental goal of equity, quality of education was instrumental in assuring children's cognitive development. UNESCO's education quality definition emphasized more on 'lifelong learning' and 'relevance' as most important factors (Delors et al. 1996). Accordingly, education is based upon four pillars—learning to know, learning to focus on the practical application of what is learned, learning to live together where all have an equal opportunity to develop, and learning to emphasize the skills needed for individuals to develop their full potential.

In addition to this, UNICEF also strongly emphasized the desirable dimensions of quality, as identified in the Dakar Framework. Its paper 'Defining Quality in Education' recognizes five dimensions of quality: learners, environment, content, processes, and outcomes, founded on 'the rights of the whole child, and all children, to survival, protection, development and participation' (UNICEF 2000). The *Communiqué of the World Conference on Higher Education 2009* states that 'Quality criteria must reflect the aim of cultivating in students critical and independent thought and the capacity of learning throughout life. They should encourage innovation and diversity' (UNESCO 2009). Thus, it is clear that quality is not a unitary concept but involves multiple perspectives.

2.3 Why is Quality of Education Important?

Earlier, greater emphasis was being placed on ensuring free and compulsory primary education for all children. However, with the tremendous growth in school enrolments throughout the world, the need for shifting priority on increasing access to higher quality of schooling was felt. In fact, many international organizations now believe that access and quality are not sequential elements, rather they visualized the role of quality being instrumental in improving access. Due to the current state of education in both developing as well as industrialized countries, this issue of quality has become the focus of concern. The Jometian Declaration in 1990 and more particularly, the Dakar Framework of Action, 2000, through its sixth goal has also emphasized on quality of education.

UNESCO's Global Monitoring Report UNESCO 2005 highlights the importance of quality of education provided in schools in terms of the teaching–learning processes. It relates quality schooling with higher life-time incomes. According to the report, higher quality of schools enhances students' cognitive skills which directly influence their performance in the labour market in terms of individual earnings, greater productivity, and economic growth. Schools are also instrumental in developing desirable non-cognitive outcomes among students such as honesty, reliability, determination, etc. It affirmed that the achievement of universal participation in education will be fundamentally dependent upon the quality of education available. The instrumental roles of schooling—helping individuals achieve their own socio-economic and cultural objectives and helping society to be better served and protected by its leaders and more equitable in important ways—will be strengthened if education is of higher quality (UNESCO 2005a, b).

The European Union in its report on the Quality of School Education highlighted that its highest political priority and concern of all member states was quality of education. According to the report 'High levels of knowledge; competencies and skills are considered to be the very basic condition for active citizenship, employment and social cohesion' (European Commission 2000). A study by Reddy (2007) shows that world over, school effectiveness or quality has been viewed in terms of cognitive outcomes attained by students i.e., achievement that is easily measured by standardized tests. Though this is indeed the primary concern of schooling, it needs to be stressed that school quality should be defined not only in terms of the cognitive achievement of children, but also by non-cognitive/affective outcomes such as attitudes and values which are so critical for the all-round development of every child.

One of the famous educationists, Erick Hanushek (2002), while pointing out that typical studies relate the number of educated individuals with economic growth rates of a country, considers such a measure of knowledge and cognitive skills of people crude because schooling might not be the actual cause of growth but may reveal other attributes of the economy that are beneficial to growth. According to him, research underscores the importance of student's achievement and lays more stress on individual productivity and earnings and associates it with faster growth of the nation's economy. Hence, according to him, an economy's ability to grow over time is in part related to the quality of its education system.

In the Indian context, there is an increasing concern about the quality of education that the education system is able to provide (NUEPA 2014). The disparity at various levels is proving to be cancerous for the nation. According to Education for All (EFA) 2014 report, one of the key challenges facing the Indian education system is the quality-related deficiencies at each stage of education resulting in unsatisfactory level of student learning. The phenomenon of under-achievement among pupils depicts the quality-related deficiencies of the education system. Various studies show that children do not have school-readiness competencies in cognitive and language domains, thereby revealing the poor quality of the curriculum, deficiencies of the teaching–learning process, and lack of quality teachers. If the basic foundation of children at the school level is weak, there are possibilities that benefits from later educational interventions get reduced, therefore, it is important that appropriate interventions need to be formulated and implemented to remove quality-related deficiencies at school-level education. It is seen that there is wide gap between quality education and quality students. A large cross-section of unresponsive students hailing from the affluent class makes their way into good schools whereas children from poor families cannot avail admission to such good schools. It is important to understand that the facilities for education should be equal for all. Quality Education is the right of every quality student.

2.4 Quality Models

Review of literature identifies eight models for quality of education which are discussed here in detail.

Quality Control: This is a regulatory process through which we measure quality performance, compare it with standards, and act on the difference (Wadsworth et al. 2002). It is basically an after-the-event process concerned with detecting and rejecting defective items. Such a strategy for measuring education quality is inadequate and inherently flawed owing to two reasons: firstly, the checking is done only at the end of the process by inspectors who are not involved in teaching practices and secondly, efforts need to be taken to assure quality rather than merely detecting it.

Quality Assurance: Wadsworth et al. (2002) defined it as a system of activities which assures that the overall quality control is done effectively. It is a before and during-the-event process. Here the focus is prevention of defects rather than just detecting them. Stephens (2003) argues that it is a process of evaluating the extent to which the institution is delivering on its promises. However, quality assistance is a process of preventing defects which is not an end in itself rather a means towards satisfying customers.

JJ Bonsting's Creating Quality Community of Learners by Quality Management: This model draws from TQM thinking and proposes the four pillars of TQM that constitute quality. These four pillars are: Customer–supplier focus, personal dedication by everyone for improvement, process/systems, and management accountability to TQM. The customer–supplier focus believes that each individual is a customer as well as a supplier who has a clear role to play to ensure quality. Team work and collaboration must be emphasized if schools are to create high quality benefits for the maximum.

Malcolm Baldridge Quality Criteria: The Baldridge framework consists of a leader setting values, systems and level of accountability; a system that comprises four building blocks of education and business management processes, human resource development, strategic planning, and information and analysis; measurement of progress which uses quantitative indicators of performance; and the goal, that is, the student's focus. Baldridge holds the view of accelerating improvement efforts by serving as a framework to align institutional activities to achieve ever-improving outcomes.

Philip B. Crosby's Zero Defect Approach: This approach believes in elimination of defects to reduce cost. It makes the work team responsible for quality assurance although inspectors also play a critical role.

Joseph Juran's Project Management: Juran viewed quality as a fitness requisite to achieve a purpose. As per his 85/15 rule, 85% of the organization's quality problems are a direct result of poorly structured processes.

Deming's Total Quality Management: The concept of TQM was propounded by Deming (1986). Deming viewed quality as a continuous improvement of processes and services to keep pace with changing demands of customers. He argued that quality is the ability to meet customers' needs at all times and the urge to excel.

Shewhart Cycle: Shewhart came with a four-phase cyclic approach to quality improvement. The phases include: Plan–Do–Check–Act. From an analysis of the entire process, a single aspect is isolated for improvement. A plan how to improve the aspect is drawn up and once the plan is clarified and accepted, it is implemented on a small scale. The effects of implementing plans are scrutinized closely. Depending on the results, action is taken to implement the plan on a larger scale, refine, or discard it for a new one.

2.5 Approaches to Quality of Education

While defining quality of education, it is useful to distinguish between educational outcomes and the processes leading to them. Several educational approaches have tried to analyse the concept of quality though they differ from each other in ideology, epistemology, and disciplinary composition (EFA Global Monitoring Report 2005).

Quality in Humanist Approach: According to this approach, learning is emphasized as a process of social practice rather than the result of individual intervention. Standardized and controlled curricula are rejected. Educational programmes remain responsive to individual learners' circumstances and needs. Self-assessment and peer assessment are welcomed as ways of developing deeper awareness of learning. The teacher's role is more that of a facilitator than an instructor.

Quality in Behaviourist Approach: According to this approach, standardized and controlled curricula, based on prescribed objectives are endorsed. Assessment is seen as an objective measurement of learned behaviour against preset assessment criteria. Tests and examinations are regarded as the central features of learning. The teacher directs learning, and is considered as the expert who controls stimuli and responses.

Quality in Critical Approach: Sociologists and critical pedagogues tend to equate good quality education as one that prompts social change; includes a curriculum and teaching methods which encourage critical analysis of social power relations and ways in which formal knowledge is produced and transmitted; and involves the active participation by learners in the design of their own learning experience.

Quality in Indigenous Approach: Indigenous approaches reassert the importance of education's relevance to the socio-cultural circumstances of the nation and learner. They believe that all learners have rich sources of prior knowledge, accumulated through a variety of experiences, which educators should draw out and nourish. Learners should play a role in defining their own curriculum. Learning should move beyond the boundaries of the classroom through non-formal and lifelong learning activities.

Quality in Adult Education Approach: In the adult education tradition, experience and critical reflection on learning is an important aspect of quality.

Radical theorists see learners as socially situated with the potential to use their experience and learning as a basis for social action and social change.

To conclude, it may be stated that this chapter provides a conceptual perspective on quality of education by examining the various ways in which it has been understood and addressed in various parts of the world. There is a great deal of diversity in the way quality concept in education originated and its models and approaches have been defined. Though multiple meanings have been ascribed to the term education quality, as it has been viewed in myriad ways by educators, the most practical definition of educational quality would include a combination of inputs, processes and outcomes and their inter-relationships. Therefore, despite viewing quality of education mostly in terms of learning outcomes of students, the quality of inputs and processes to achieve better learning outcomes are equally important.

References

Adams, D. (1993). Defining educational quality. *Improving Educational Quality Project Publication*, 1.

Delors, J. (1996). *Learning, the treasure within*. Report to UNESCO of the international commission on education for the twenty-first century: Highlights, UNESCO Publications.

Deming, D. W. (1986). *Out of crisis*. London: Cambridge University Press.

European Commission. (2000). *Report on the quality of education 16 quality indicators*.

Goddard, D., & Leask, M. (1992). *The search for quality: Management in education*. London: Paul Chapman.

Grisay, A., & Mahlck, L. (1991). *The quality of education in developing countries*. IIEP, Paris: A Preview of Some Research Studies and Policy Documents.

Hanushek, E. A. (2002). *The importance of school quality*. (pp. 141–173). Stanford, CA: Hoover Institution Press. http://hanushek.stanford.edu/publications/importance-school-quality.

Hoy, C., Bayne-Jardine, C., & Wood, M. (2000). *Improving quality in education*. London: Falmer Press.

Kumar, K., & Sarangapani, P. M. (2005). *History of the quality debate*. Paper commissioned for the EFA global monitoring report 2005, the quality imperative, UNESCO.

Linston, C. (1999). *Managing quality and standard*. Buckhingam: Open University Press.

NUEPA. (2014). *Education for all: Towards quality with equity India* (1st ed.) Ministry of Human Resource Development, GOI, August 2014.

Reddy, S. (2007). *School quality: Perspectives from the developed and developing countries*, AzimPremji Foundation. http://www.azimpremjifoundation.org/pdf/ConsolidatedSchool Qualityreport.pdf.

Sallis, E. (1996). *Total quality management in education*. London: Kogan Page.

Stephens, D. (2003). *Quality of basic education*. Background paper for education for all global monitoring report 2003–04, Gender and education for all: The leap to equality.

UNESCO. (1990). *World declaration on education for all: Framework for action to meet basic learning needs*, Jomtein, Thailand from March 5–9, 1990. http://unesdoc.unesco.org/images/0012/001275/127583e.pdf.

UNESCO. (2005). *Understanding education quality*. EFA global monitoring report 2005.

UNESCO. (2005). *The importance of good quality: What research tells us*. EFA global monitoring report.

UNESCO. (2009). *World conference on higher education: The new dynamics of higher education and research for societal change and development* held in Paris, 5–8 July 2009. Draft Communique (1st Draft 26 June 2009), ED.2009/CONF.402/2.

UNICEF. (June 2000). *Defining quality in education.* A paper presented by UNICEF at the meeting of the international working group on education florence, Italy, Working Paper Series, Education Section, Programme Division, United Nations Children's Fund UNICEF, USA.

Wadsworth, H. M., Stephens, K. S., & Godfrey, A. B. (2002). *Modern methods for quality control and improvement.* New York: Wiley.

Chapter 3
Literature on School Education, Quality, and Outcomes: A Review

Abstract To understand why it is essential to invest in education and at what level of education, various research scholars across the globe have conducted research studies and have tried to analyse the relationship between educational performance indicators and socio-economic outcomes in developing the methods of measuring quality of education and identification of its determinants. This chapter reviews the literature of such noteworthy studies. However, it has been noted that in the absence of qualitative indicators of education, most researchers have used quantitative indicators as a base for doing these analyses. Although most of the research work in this area has been conducted at global level, we have tried to present a few Indian cases as well to identify what has already been done and what needs to be done.

Keywords Secondary education · Educational outcomes · Economic · Health · Social · Quality

3.1 Studies Linking Educational Performance with Socio-Economic Outcomes

Economic analysis has followed two lines of inquiry: micro and macro analysis. While, micro-economic analyses have looked at the impact of education on individual earnings and social outcomes; macro-economic analyses have attempted to estimate the contribution of education to country's economic growth performance. Findings of the two approaches have traditionally been inconsistent. Micro-economic evidence suggests that the private returns to education are substantial (Psacharopolous and Patrinos 2004) and the impact on social outcomes are significant. But growth researchers have had great difficulty finding statistically significant and economically plausible impacts of educational variables in global growth regression models (Pritchett 2001; Ndulu and O'Connell 2006; Glewwe 2002; Glewwe and Kremer 2008). New patterns have recently emerged in the findings of both types of analysis which are beginning to reconcile microeconomic and growth evidence via better measurement of educational attainment and greater

© Springer Nature Singapore Pte Ltd. 2018
C. Jain and N. Prasad, *Quality of Secondary Education in India*,
https://doi.org/10.1007/978-981-10-4929-3_3

care in the statistical procedures. Most importantly, attempts to move beyond the traditional measurement of human capital by considering the number of years of schooling completed or enrolment ratios and assessing the impact of quality of education and distribution of educational opportunities on countries' economic performance have begun to bear fruit. They are of considerable interest for this study as they affect the role of secondary education and may trigger re-examination of current resource allocation priorities. At the same time, there also remains little doubt that the benefits of secondary education extend beyond purely economic factors, because they affect health, fertility, democratic participation, and social cohesion. The findings of few such studies that have tried to examine the benefits of educational attainments in terms of health outcomes, economic growth, social and demographic transitions have been discussed here in detail.

3.1.1 Educational and Economic Outcomes

Pritchett (2001) points out that the belief that expanding education promotes economic growth has been a fundamental theory of development strategy for at least 40 years. Many studies have been done so far to estimate the relationship between economic growth and education (Hanushek and Wobbmann 2007; Hanushek 2005; Chatterji 2008). Some of these have been able to find relationship, while some fails to find any evidences of relationship. In fact, education was not even considered as major input for production and hence was not included in growth models in the earlier neoclassical theories. The seminal work by Schultz (1961) and Denison (1962) led to a series of growth accounting studies pointing to education's contribution to the unexplained residuals in the economic growth of western economies. A survey of growth accounting studies in 1984, covering 29 developing countries found estimates of education's contribution to economic growth ranging from less than 1% in Mexico to as high as 23% in Ghana (Psacharopoulos 1984). In one of the speeches in a conference held in Paris in 2007, Angel Gurría, the Secretary-General of the Organization for Economic Cooperation and Development (OECD) addressed that 'one extra year to the average years of schooling increases GDP per capita by 4–6%'. Using time series data from 1951 to 87 to examine the relationship between public spending on education and growth, a particular study shows that there is no long-run relationship between the two (Ansari and Singh 1997). However, they do find a direct causal link from public spending in education to private capital formation, hence, indirectly to growth. Barro (1991) in his cross-country study found that once other factors were controlled, human capital did indeed have a positive influence on growth. Barro's analysis was focused on the positive impact of education variables—primary and secondary schooling—on growth. Chatterji (1998) extended this to tertiary education and found similar positive impacts. Using Indian data, one study tested the impacts of all levels of education on Indian growth performance (Self and Grabowski 2004). This study finds that primary education has the strongest impact, followed by secondary education, while there is no evidence to show that tertiary education has affected growth. Temple (2001) in an OECD study shows that between 1971 and 98, economic performance and human capital have been positively correlated in OECD countries. Recently, Bloom et al. (2006) find that an additional year of general schooling can increase the rate of growth by 0.6%. Barro and Lee (1993 and 2001) also find positive relation between secondary education and economic growth. Hence, it is quite clear that the exact nature of casual link between the two still remains undetermined.

3.1.2 Education and Social Outcomes

Different scholars have tried to link educational performances with various social outcomes in terms of income generation, employment patterns, poverty reduction, etc. One of the research studies reflecting on cross-country analyses showed weak and elusive evidences to support a possible correlation between higher education and economic growth; however, there were evidences to infer that there was a strong link between average earnings of individuals and their educational attainment (Macerinskiene and Vaiksnoraite 2006). Another study suggested that 1% increase in the labour force with at least secondary education would increase the share of income of the bottom 40–60% by between 6 and 15%, respectively (Bourguignon and Morrison 1990). Positive feedback was observed from improved education to greater income equality, which, in turn, is likely to favour higher rates of growth. A study of the relation between schooling, income inequality, and poverty in 18 countries of Latin America in the 1980s found that one quarter of the variation in workers' incomes was accounted for by variations in schooling attainment (Psacharopolous 1993). Few studies provide direct and consistent estimate of impact of test performance on earnings (Mulligan 1999; Murname et al. 2000; Lazear 2003). These studies suggest that one standard deviation increase in mathematics performance to end of high schools translates into 12% higher annual earnings. This gives indication that higher school education does have an impact on the earnings of individuals. Many studies even show that rate of returns of educational attainments are higher in case of women compared to men despite their low education (Kingdon and Unni 2001; Duraisamy 2002; Self and Grabowski 2004).

3.1.3 Education and Health Outcomes

Many economists have analysed the relationship between educational attainment and health performances of individuals. A study of 14 African countries, conducted in the mid-1980s, showed a negative correlation between female schooling and fertility in almost all countries with primary education having a negative impact in about half the countries and no significant effects in the other half, while secondary education invariably reduced fertility (Behraman and Wolfe 1987; Birdsall et al. 1995). Empirical research by economists suggests that in India, women's education plays a vital role in the understanding of issues like health, fertility, child labour, mortality rates, etc. In this regard, one study shows that high female education act as a major factor in determining low fertility rates while general indicators like urbanization, poverty reduction, and male literacy have no impacts on female fertility (Dreze and Murthi 2001). It is mostly seen that educated women are more concerned for child health and diet. Moreover, studies have shown that education of women has a strong downward impact on fertility rates. This evidence is mirrored in other African countries, where condom use is rising sharply among both men and women with higher levels of schooling (UNESCO EFA 2005). The level of education in a society has also been found to be positively correlated to decline in fertility, reduced infant mortality and maternal mortality rates (World development Indicators, World Bank 2012). In a study it is found that in Guinea, 50% of uneducated mothers suffer from growth retardation, this is 36% in case of primary educated women and further down to 25% in case of secondary educated ones (UNESCO BREDA 2005). The secondary education has serious implications on HIV/AIDS infections as well. In Uganda, though, clear evidence exists that those with some secondary education had much lower HIV/AIDS prevalence rates than those with less schooling (De Walque 2004).

3.2 Studies Identifying Determinants of Educational Outcomes

According to Ross (2002), as the economies of nations compete for strong positions within competitive global markets; many governments have become increasingly inclined to view the relative performance of their education systems as way of enhancing national economic development. With the advent of globalization, the rapid technological development is also going on which further imposes pressures to meet quality standard in education while ensuring that schools adapt to the demands of new technology. Moreover, if education is planned in a way that ensures quality then resources may also be allocated in efficient ways to reduce cost and wastages. So far, there is a lack of consensus on whether the quality of education system can be improved simply by increasing education spending, or does school resources, teaching quality or family background help in improving the educational performances? In this context, various studies have been conducted. Most of these research studies have been conducted at the international level, though at the national level there are quite a few. The findings of some of these studies have been presented here.

3.2.1 School Resources

One of the research study conducted to analyse the panel data on education expenditures and results of NAEP test in USA concluded that increase in spending has led to slight increase in students' scores (Kruger 2000), however, another study with similar dataset found that there was no clear and robust relation (Hanushek 1998). Hanushek and Kimko (2000) tried to test the relation between educational variables and scores taking into consideration data of 39 countries. Again, they concluded that no relation was found between them. A similar research was conducted which concluded that though school resources had a significant impact on students' performance, size of the class had negative effect (Lee and Barro 2001). Further research to test the extent to which school resources influence education performance concluded that educational expenditure had no effect on test scores. Teachers' pay had a negative and significant effect on the quality of education for developing countries (Nadir Altinok 2007). This study also showed that for OECD countries, class size had positive effect, while for non-OECD countries it had negative effect. Further, repetition rates had a negative impact on developing countries. There are studies which have measured the impacts of school management on students' achievement levels. One such study suggests that in order to improve students' performance, head teachers are required to first improve the management of schools (Wekesa 1993). Schools can bring difference to students' achievement level through factors like the amount of emphasis given to teaching and academics; the extent and nature by which abilities were grouped; the extent of teacher expectations; styles of teaching and classroom management; size of school; pattern of discipline and characteristics of school climate (Rutter et al. 1979). Although, most studies showed that school resources and quality do have an impact on student outcomes the magnitude varies from region to region and from country to country.

3.2.2 Teaching Quality

Along with the studies discussed earlier, there are many evidences that show that teaching quality affects pupils' achievements. A study revealed that a teacher holding a graduation or post graduation degree in mathematics statistically has a significant and positive impact a student's performance in mathematics (Goldhaber and Brewer 1997). Another study showed that there is positive relationship between teacher's preparation of the content that he/she teaches and student's achievement (Monk 1994). However, the magnitude of positive effect varies according to subject matter and grade level. One study estimates that the difference in annual achievement between an average and a good teacher is large. Within one academic year, a good teacher can move a typical student up at least four percentiles in overall distribution, thus concluding that a series of good teachers can dramatically improve achievement of students (Rivkin et al. 2005). Another study (Aslam and Kingdon 2011) suggests that training of teachers is often used as a measure to determine teacher's quality which has no bearing on students' achievements. It further reveals that girls benefit from being taught by female teachers and that usually un-measured teaching processes like lesson planning, teacher student interaction, etc., benefit pupil learning substantially. Thus, literature shows that various characteristics of teachers in terms of their qualification, teaching methods, lesson planning, attitudes, training and interaction with students have different implications on the achievement level of students.

3.2.3   Family Background

Apart from schools and teaching quality, socio-economic background of the students also play an important role. One study shows that parents from high social background are likely to invest more and better in human capital (Becker 1964). According to a well-known sociological approach, socio-economic inequalities in education persist because highly educated parents give their children a better understanding of the dominant culture and an ability to act within it (Bourdieu 1984 and Bourdieu 1977). Another study reveals that school quality and family socio-economic background are substitutes in the production of human capital in Italy (Brunello and Checchi 2005). Schools with better results are those with students from a favourable socio-economic background (Coleman et al. 1966; Summers and Wolfe 1977; Zimmer and Toma 2000).

3.2.4   Quality Education Barriers

Hill and Chalaux (2011) has clearly highlighted major shortcomings in the way of achieving higher educational attainments and improved learning outcomes as high dropouts, lower student attendance, gender disparities, need to enhance teacher effectiveness by strengthening accountability and incentives and reducing high teacher-student ratio. Apart from the factors discussed earlier, UNICEF (UNICEF 2002a, b) identifies five categories of barriers to education. These are: household barriers; policy barriers; infrastructure barriers; community beliefs and practices; and educational barriers. Each of these barriers has a high potential of compromising efficiency of the school system, thereby eroding the quality of education offered. *Household barriers* refer to levels of family resource available to bear both direct and indirect costs towards education. *Political barriers* include budget allocations for crafting implementation of policy issues required to improve quality of education. Lack of policy on how to deal with dropouts or infrastructural issues or curriculum development can affect quality efforts in schools. *Infrastructural barriers* play an important role in providing access to schools and physical facilities in form of classrooms, laboratories, etc., which in turn affect the quality of education. *Community beliefs and practices*, for example, gender discrimination, may restrict availability of resources for female students. With low educational levels, especially in rural areas, communities are bound to have poor knowledge of social and private benefits of education. Finally, *educational barriers*, which include qualifications and performance of teachers, school climate and management, etc., impact the quality of education provided to students. Thus, if efforts are put into control all of these barriers, it can positively enhance the quality of education.

3.3 Indian Literature in Quality Context

Since mid-1960s, economics of education has emerged as one of the most prominent research area in economics discipline. Although on universalization of education, some progress has been made by increasing accessibility and ensuring provision of free education to students, as far as quality is concerned, not much has been achieved till now. The Eleventh and Twelfth Five Year Plans have articulated the need for improving quality of education at all levels. The targets set in the Twelfth Five Year Plan (FYP) for secondary education also include: (a) assurance of quality secondary education with relevant skills, including required competency in mathematics, science, language, and communication; (b) implementation of common curricula and syllabi of nationally accepted standards for Science, Mathematics, and English in all schools in the country; and (c) development of life skills, including skills of critical and constructive thinking, use of information and communication technology (ICT), organization and leadership, and community services. The strategic framework for ensuring quality of secondary education envisages the following—measures to conform to minimum standards with regard to available facilities and quality; renewal of curriculum, improvement of the teaching–learning process, and reform of examination pattern; betterment of school leadership; institutionalization of the use of ICT and other technologies for upgrading school management; and development of a school quality assessment and accreditation system. This covers all aspects of school functioning, including scholastic and co-scholastic domains, physical infrastructure, teacher management, school leadership, learning outcomes, and satisfaction of pupils and their parents. With all these schemes, although accessibility and enrolments have increased over a period of time, as far as quality and learning outcomes are concerned not much is visible at the ground level. Therefore, the need for research on how to determine the quality of education continues to be extremely important with an explicit aim to better understand how education is acquired, how it affects economic and social outcomes of individuals, and how it can perform public policy. In this section, we have attempted to discuss a few such studies that have covered quality issues in school education, focusing on secondary education in the Indian context.

Several research studies have been conducted to measure quality of education or educational development at the primary level of education. However, very few studies have examined the issues related to secondary and senior secondary education in India. For instance, NUEPA has done immense work on both qualitative and quantitative issues in education in India. Considering various quality indicators, they have developed an all-India level *educational development index* (*EDI*) projecting the development of primary and upper primary level of education in India (NUEPA 2006; Barnwal 2008). However, no such index is available to depict the situation of secondary education. NUEPA has also published a few books particularly looking at secondary education. The book titled *Quality in Secondary Education: Secondary Education and Education Boards* deals with the role of education boards in managing change and quality of secondary education in four states in India—Himachal Pradesh, Madhya Pradesh, West Bengal, and Andhra Pradesh (Narula 2006). Another book named as *Development of Secondary Education in India: Access, Participation, Delivery Mechanism and Financing* examines the development of secondary education covering different aspects like access, participation, gender, financing, and equity in India, amongst states and districts, and includes a case study of schools covering four states—Andhra Pradesh, Uttar Pradesh, Maharashtra, and Kerala (Sujatha and Geetha 2011a). The third book titled *Management of Secondary Education in India: Quality, Performance and Administration* studies the quality, performance, and administration of secondary education by examining the availability of infrastructure facilities for secondary schools, transition, dropouts, and retention, and provides critical analysis of secondary education management by initiating an all India analysis, as well as through a case study of schools from four states—Andhra Pradesh, Uttar Pradesh, Maharashtra, and Kerala (Sujatha and Geetha 2011b).

Another study has examined the development and performance of secondary education in India and across 17 major states using the methodology of the United Nations Development Programme (UNDP) (Rani 2007). This index uses three critical inputs for education entailing both demand for (enrolment) and supply of (institutions and teachers) secondary education. However, this study excludes cost factor which is considered as one of the four factors for quality measurement of education as considered by Quality Education in Developing Countries (QEDC). Tyagi (2011) makes a comparative study of selected government, private, and private-aided senior secondary schools in Delhi, Chhattisgarh, and Uttarakhand, thereby emphasizing how academic supervision and support by educational authorities help improve the teaching–learning process and the professional development of teachers. The study examines how heads of government and private-aided institutions feel it is necessary to place emphasis on instructional supervision. It also investigates how they improve the teaching-learning process and provide effective professional development of teachers at the school level. It discusses the practices followed by principals when supervising instruction in different situations including classroom observation, meetings, conferences, and deliberations with teachers. Effective instructional leadership by heads of institutions encourages teachers to collaborate and be involved in school-based professional development activities.

The recent report on '*India: Education for All—Towards Quality with Equity*' prepared by National University of Educational Planning and Administration (2014) tracks the progress of Education for All goals which also includes quality as one of their agenda. According to the report, although huge progress has been made during the past few years, the education system in India still faces several challenges as it seeks to further enhance accessibility and quality of education at all levels of education. One of the key challenges facing the Indian education system is quality-related deficiencies at each stage of education resulting in unsatisfactory level of student learning. The slow progress in reducing the number of non-literates, dropout rates, enrolments, unsatisfactory student learning levels, gender and regional disparities, teacher shortage, poor quality of teaching–learning process, lower learning outcomes continue to be the key areas of concern. The report further argues that given the serious quality issues that persist in the education sector, further expansion of the school and higher education system without quality improvement at this stage would be counterproductive for future development of education in India.

There is another study conducted titled *Quality in Education* by the Institute for Studies in Industrial Development for Quality Council in India. This research work has tried to study the role played by four education boards (Central Board of Secondary Education, Council for Indian School Certificate Examination, State Boards, and International Baccalaureate Organisation) with special emphasis on the various components of the curriculum, namely, syllabus, pedagogy, examination and evaluation, and accreditation and affiliation standards. The major objectives of the study were: to analyse how the curriculum, syllabus, and pedagogy in these schools differ from one another; what is the actual compliance status of selected schools; how the affiliating bodies carry out inspection; what is the pattern of study evaluation conducted by the affiliating bodies; how to find out good practices in schools and make a comparative assessment; and how to measure the quality percentage achievement of studied schools through various quality indicators.

A case study on the Quality of Primary Education in Madurai and Villupuram districts in Tamil Nadu, was conducted by researchers at the Harvard Graduate School of Education under the aegis of the Center for International Development to assess the current state of primary education in the sample districts and to analyse the weaknesses that may be contributing to the lack of acceptable quality of education in primary schools (Grover and Singh 2002). The goal of this study is to identify and analyse the processes that impact attendance, completion, and repetition. Therefore, the focus of this study was on the learning environment, which encompasses the classroom, teacher–learning practices, teaching–learning materials, teachers, and students. Issues related to school governance and management was also examined as they affect learning outcomes. The study found that teachers lacked accountability; classrooms for instruction were ill maintained; number of toilets was inadequate which in turn affected students' attendance; drinking water was not easily available; most teachers were not using teaching learning materials (TLM) in classrooms.

Kingdon (2007) has presented an overview of school education in India. The study revealed that India's educational achievements in international perspective was relatively better than its South Asian neighbours, that is, Pakistan and Bangladesh while lagging behind other countries with which it is increasingly compared, such as the BRIC (Brazil, Russia, India and China) economies. The study concluded that learning achievements in both primary and secondary schooling are very low, signalling poor quality of schooling, thereby suggesting the need for evaluation of quality of education and relative cost-effectiveness for evidence-based policymaking. One of the contributors of the study, Govinda (2011), using secondary data, has done an in-depth analysis on government and private schools using factors like educational access, enrolment, dropouts, attendance, progression, social and gender equity in education, level of achievement, quality of education, teachers and teachers' education, local governance and community participation. Based on population norms, modification of traditional distance and opening of schools in small habitations has yielded positive results. The author found that in India government schools are more expensive than private schools with lower teacher accountability. However, because of poor quality and scarcity of public education, private education has become the necessity for India.

Govinda and Varghese (1993) have examined the quality of primary schooling in India through their work titled: 'A case study of Madhya Pradesh', and have shown that a trained teacher makes considerable difference in terms of teaching style and classroom management. The authors are of the opinion that several researchers and reports indicating improvement in learning level of children depend not only on the expansion of schooling provision but also on availability of ample instructional time and its effective use. It is the teacher who plays an important role in effective use of instructional time.

Khatoon and Mahmood (2010) have examined how achievement in a subject like mathematics is affected by factors like type of school, gender, or anxiety towards the subject. The study was conducted using a sample of 863 males and 789 females from 15 secondary schools of Uttar Pradesh in India. The results of the analysis showed that among the three independent variables: school type, mathematics anxiety and gender, school type had the greatest influence on mathematics achievement followed by mathematics anxiety. As per the study findings gender showed no significant influence on the achievement of the subject. It shows that school types do play an important role in students' learning levels.

3.4 What Is New in This Study-Identifying Gaps

The literature review indicates that educational performances and the structure of educational system strongly differ between different countries and economic levels. Even if few studies have tried to estimate the relationship between these variables particularly in the case of India, it shows that the extent of the impact varies from region to region. Available literature clearly indicates that that although a lot of research work has been conducted in measuring quality of education across the globe, very few studies have examined these issues from the Indian perspective. Although, no-one can deny the great contributions made by famous international economists like Hanushek, Kruger, Stephen, and Woessmann in the field of economics of education, yet, we found that although their analysis focused on worldwide comparisons using huge international data bases but it did not cover the issues of Indian education system that needs to be addressed in greater detail separately. Our research found that different economists have made attempts to explain the relation between educational attainments and various outcomes like health outcomes, educational spending, economic growth, individual earnings etc. but have reached to the conclusion that most of these studies underline the lack of consensus about the validity of correlation between educational performances and various outcomes, thereby creating more ambiguity in the major findings. Thus, there is a strong need to bring more clarity in the understanding of the exact nature of relationship between these variables and at the same time, identifying various quality indicators that can determine the students' outcomes and efficient teaching abilities. It is well recognized that secondary education provides the strongest link between elementary and higher education that prepares the human capital base for the country. Despite this fact, the whole system of secondary education in India is ruined by factors like low enrolments, low retention rates, high dropouts, and wide disparities at various levels that need to be pinpointed and addressed. Hence, a need was felt to reveal the true picture of the performance of secondary level of education in India both at the national and state levels to measure the disparities and progress. It is generally seen that most of the studies that have been conducted at the secondary level of education in India, either examines the progress or growth of secondary education in India in terms of enrolments, dropouts, attendance, and impacts of government policies or have tried to analyze their management or financing issues. Some of these studies have even tried to relate students' achievements with school quality. Most of the available literature so far only relates to issues such as: slow progress of secondary education, privatization and poor public financing, lower students learning levels, and need for quality improvement. There are hardly such studies (reflecting on the Indian context) that have empirically identified the indicators that could affect student learning outcomes, teachers' efficiencies, quality of teaching practices, or have tried to understand their perspectives on quality education. All these gaps underline the need to undertake intensive research work in this area that can probe such issues and offer policy recommendations.

Considering the vast educational system in India on one hand and the wide disparities in dissemination of education on the other, a strong need was felt to highlight the issues of secondary education in Indian context. This book may not be comprehensive in its approach but we have tried to cover up as many gaps as we could in the available literature, linking different variables and developing new models and indices for measurement of quality at secondary level of education. We have also highlighted the importance of secondary education particularly in India by linking educational outcome with socio-economic outcomes. Along with this, the factors affecting student learning outcomes and teachers' efficiencies have also been identified. Hence, this study not only answers why quality of secondary education is important but also answers to the question on how one can measure it. We strongly believe that the findings of this study will be useful in providing suggestions for improvement of overall quality and learning outcomes of the students.

References

Altinok, N. (2007). *Do school resources increase school quality? Institute for research in the sociology and economics of education*. Research papers.

Ansari, M. I., & Singh, S. K. (1997). Public spending on education and economic growth in India: Evidence from VAR modeling. *Indian Journal of Applied Economics, 6*(2), 43–64.

Aslam, M., & Kingdon, G. (2011). What Can Teachers do to Raise Pupil Achievement? *Economics of Education Review, Elsevier, 30*(3), 559–574.

Barnwal, S. K. (2008). *Educational development index in India*. http:/digitallearningeletsonline.com/2008.

Barro, R. J. (1991). Economic growth in a cross-section of countries. *Quarterly Journal of Economics, 106,* 407–443.

Barro, R. J., & Lee, J. W. (1993). International comparisons of Educational attainment. *Journal of Monetary Economics, 32,* 363–394.

Becker, G. S. (1964). *Human capital: A theoretical and empirical analysis with special reference to education* (3rd ed.) Chicago: University of Chicago (1993).

Behrman, J., & Wolfe, B. (1987). How does mother's schooling affect the family's health, nutrition, medical care usage and household sanitation? *Journal of Econometrics, 36,* 185–204.

Birdsall, N., Ross, D., & Sabot, R. (1995). Inequality and growth reconsidered: Lessons from East-Asia. *World Bank, Economics Review, 93,* 477–508.

Bloom, D., Canning, D., & Chan, K. (2006). *Higher education and economic development in Africa*. Washington D.C.: World Bank.

Bourdieu, P. (1977). *Cultural reproduction and social reproduction*. In J. Karabel & A. H. Halsey (Eds.), Power and ideology in education, (pp. 487–511). New York: Oxford University.

Bourdieu, P. (1984). *Distinction: A Social critique of the judgment of taste*. London: Routledge.

Bourguignon, F., & Morrison, C. (1990). Income distribution, development and foreign trade: A cross sectional analysis. *European Economic Review, 34,* 1113–1132.

Brunello, G. A., & Checchi, D. (2005). School quality and family background in Italy. *Economics of Education Review, 24,* 563–577.

Chatterji, M. (1998). Tertiary education and economic growth. Regional Studies. *Taylor & Francis Journals, 32*(4), 349–354.

Chatterji, M. (2008). *Education and economic development in India*. Dundee Discussion papers in economics, Working Paper No 210.

Coleman, J., et al. (1966). *Equality of educational opportunity*. Washington D.C.: Government Printing Office.

De Walque, D. (2004). *How does the impact of an HIV/AIDS information campaign vary with educational attainment: Evidence from rural Uganda?*. Washington D.C.: World Bank, Development Research Group.

Denison, E. F. (1962). *The sources of economic growth in the United States and the alternatives before* (pp. 13–15). NY: Committee for Economic Development.

Dreze, Jean, & Murthi, Mamta. (2001). Fertility, education, and development: Evidence from India. *Population and Development Review, 27*(1), 33–63.

Duraisamy, P. (2002). Changes in returns to education in India 1983–94: By gender, age-cohort and location. *Economics of Education Review, 21*(6), 609–622.

Glewwe, P. (2002). Schools and skills in developing countries: Education policies and socioeconomic outcomes. *Journal of Economic Literature, 40*(2).

Glewwe, P., & Kremer, M. (2008). Schools, teachers, and education outcomes in developing countries. *Handbook of the economics of education*, Chapter 16 (Vol. 2, pp. 945–1017). Amsterdam: North Holland.

Goldhaber, D., & Brewer, D. (1997). Why don't schools and teachers seem to matter? Assessing the impact of unobservable on educational productivity. *Journal of Human Resources, 32*(3), 505–523.

Govinda, R. (2011). *Who goes to school? Exploring exclusion in Indian education* (pp. 22–77). Oxford: Oxford University Press.

Govinda, R., & Varghese, N. V. (1993). *Quality of primary schooling in India—A case study of Madhya Pradesh*. New Delhi: International Institute of Educational Planning and NIEPA.

Grover, S., & Singh, N. H. (2002). *The quality of primary education: A case study of Madurai and Villupuram districts in Tamil Nadu*. India report.

Hanushek, E. A. (1998). Conclusions and controversies about the effectiveness of school resources. *Economic Policy Review, 4*, 11–28.

Hanushek, E. A. (2005). *Economic outcomes and school quality*. Report jointly published by the International Institute for Educational Planning (IIEP) and the International Academy of Education (IAE). Education Policy Series, UNESCO. http://www.unesco.org/iiep.

Hanushek, E. A., & Wobmann, L. (2007). *The role of education quality in economic growth*. World Bank policy research working paper 4122.

Hanushek, E. A., & Kimko, D. D. (2000). Schooling, labor-force quality, and the growth of nations. *American Economic Review, 90*(5), 1184–1208.

Hill, S., & Chalaux, T. (2011). *Improving access and quality in the Indian education system*. OECD economics department working papers, No. 885. OECD Publishing.

Khatoon, T., & Mahmood, S. (2010). Mathematics anxiety among secondary school students in India and its relationship with achievement in mathematics. *European Journal of Social Sciences, 16*(1), 75–86.

Kingdon, G. G. (2007). The progress of school education in India. *Oxford Review of Economic Policy, 23*(2), 168–195. https://ssrn.com/abstract=1151127.

Kingdon, G., & Unni, J. (2001). Education and women's labour market outcomes in India. *Education Economics, Taylor & Francis Journals, 9*(2), 173–195.

Krueger, A. B. (2000). *An economist's view of class size research*. Mimeo, July 29, 2000.

Lazear, E. A. (2003). Teacher incentives. *Swedish Economic Policy Review, 10*(3), 179–214.

Lee, J. W., & Barro, R. J. (2001). Schooling quality in a cross-section of countries. *Economica, 38* (272), 465–488.

Macerinskiene., I. & Vaiksnoraite, B. (2006). The role of higher education to economic development. *ADYBA/Management, 2*(11), 82–90.

Monk, D. H. (1994). Subject area preparation of secondary mathematics and science teachers and student achievement. *Economics of Education Review, 13*, 125–145.

Mulligan, C. B. (1999). Galton versus the human capital approach to inheritance. *Journal of Political Economy, 107*(6), S184–S224.

Murname, R. J., Willet, J. B., Duhaldeborde, Y., & Tyler, J. H. (2000). How important are the cognitive skills of teenagers in predicting subsequent earnings? *Journal of Policy Analysis and Management, 19*(4), 547–568.

Narula, M. (2006). *Book on quality in secondary education: Secondary education and education boards*. Shipra Publications.

Ndulu, B., J.& O'Connell, S. (2006). *Policy plus: African growth performance 1960–2000*. Synthesis volume of the African Economic Research Consortium's Explaining African Economic Growth Project.

NUEPA. (2006). *Education development index*. Part V, analytical report on elementary education in India.

NUEPA. (2014). *Report on education for all: Towards quality with equity.* (1st ed.) August 2014.
Pritchett, L. (2001). Where has all the education gone?. *World Bank Economic Review, 15*(3), 367–391.
Psacharopoulos, G. (1984). The contribution of education to economic growth: international comparisons. In J. W. Kendrick (Ed.), *International comparisons of productivity and causes of the slowdown.* Cambridge, MA: Ballinger/America Enterprise Institute.
Psacharopoulos, G. (1993). *Returns to investment in education: A global update.* PPR working paper No. WPS 1067, World Bank, Washington D.C.
Psacharopoulos, G., & Patrinos, H. (2004). Returns to investment in education: A further update. *Education Economics, 12*(2), 111–134.
Quality of school education. *Report by institute for studies in industrial development for quality council in India.* http://www.qcin.org/PDF/Comman/Quality-in-School-Education.pdf.
Rani, G. (2007). *Secondary education in India: Determinants of development and performance.* Repec, online paper https://www.researchgate.net/publication/23778564.
Rivkin, S. G., Hanushek, E. A., & Kain, J. F. (2005). Teachers, Schools and Academic Achievement. *Econometrica, 73*(2), 417–458.
Ross, K. N. (2002). Monitoring the quality of education. *IIEP Newsletter, 10*(1).
Rutter, M., Maugham, B., Mortimer, P., & Smith, A. (1979). *Fifteen thousand hours in secondary schools and their effects on children.* USA: Cambridge Harvard University.
Schultz, T. W. (1961). Investment in human capital. *American Economic Review, 51,* 1–17.
Self, S., & Grabowski, R. (2004). Does education at all levels cause growth in India, a case study. *Economics of Education Review, 23,* 47–55.
Sujatha, K., & Geetha, R. P. (2011a). *Book on development of secondary education in India: Access participation.* Delivery Mechanism and Financing: Shipra Publications.
Sujatha, K., & Geetha, R. P. (2011b). *Book on management of secondary education in India: Quality.* Performance and Administration: Shipra Publications.
Summers, A., & Wolfe, B. (1977). Do schools make a difference? *American Economic Review, 67,* 639–652.
Temple, J. (2001). *Growth effects of education and social capital in the OECD countries.* OECD economic studies No. 33, 2001/II. https://www.oecd.org/eco/growth/18452154.pdf.
Tyagi, R. S. (2011). *Academic supervision in secondary schools:School-based approach for quality management,* NUEPA
UNESCO. (2005). *EFA global monitoring report.* http://portal.unesco.org/education/en/ev.php-URL_ID=34850&URL_DO=DO_TOPIC&URL_SECTION=201.html.
UNESCO BREDA. (2005). *EFA: Paving the way for action: Education for all in Africa.* Dakar, Senegal.
UNICEF. (2002). *Quality education for all: From a girl's point of view.* UNICEF: New York.
UNICEF. (2002). *Barriers to girl's education: Strategies and interventions.* https://www.unicef.org/teachers/girls_ed/barriers_02.htm.
Wekesa, G. W. (1993). *The impacts of head teachers' instructional leadership on student academic achievement in Kenya.* Columbia: Columbia University.
World Bank. (2012). *World development indicators.*
Zimmer, R. W., & Toma, E. F. (2000). Peer effects in private and public schools across countries. *Journal of Policy Analysis and Management, 19,* 75–92.

Chapter 4
Conceptual Framework of the Study

Abstract This study has been conceptualized that the study proceeds in three steps: *firstly,* it examines the performance of secondary education at the national level; *secondly*, it evaluates the performance of educational indicators at the state level, identifies inter-state disparities, and also sees how educational indicators are linked to various outcomes. *Thirdly*, identifies the determinants of quality indicators and measures its impact on student outcomes in sample schools in Delhi. In addition to this, the chapter also discusses research questions, objectives, hypothesis, and significance of the study.

Keywords Conceptual framework · Inputs · Process · Output · Research objectives · Hypothesis

4.1 Conceptual Framework

The three approaches are discussed here in detail.

Approach I—Examining the Present Situation Related to the Development and Performance of Secondary Education: National-Level Analysis

This approach evaluates the present status of development and performance of secondary education at the national level. Within development indicators, enrolments, institutions' growth, number of teachers, and so on, are being covered. In analyzing performance, trends related to dropouts, transition rates, passing rates have been captured. The overall idea of this approach is to have complete understanding of how this sector of education is performing at the national level and what are its deficiencies that need to be addressed. Another major objective of this approach was to identify the relationship between secondary education and various socio-economic and demographic outcomes at the national level, while comparing it with elementary level educational attainments to see the impacts.

© Springer Nature Singapore Pte Ltd. 2018
C. Jain and N. Prasad, *Quality of Secondary Education in India*,
https://doi.org/10.1007/978-981-10-4929-3_4

Approach II—Identifying Relationship Between Attainments from Secondary Education and Various Other Outcomes: State-level Analysis

Educational inputs affect processes which, in turn, lead to outcomes that are linked with the national goals for education and positive participation in society. Various studies have discussed that improved level of quality of education have in return higher private benefits, economic benefits, and social benefits. Therefore, it is a kind of loop where improved economic conditions of a nation support quality education which, in turn, promotes economic growth, health and overall human development of a nation. Within this, various educational indicators at the state level have been studied while pointing out the huge level of disparities existing between states. Under this approach, an exploratory model has been developed to explore the impacts of secondary educational outcomes at both the state and household levels. While, macro-model considers data from various renowned secondary sources, the micro-model considers NBT-NCAER National Youth Readership Survey unit level primary data set for all major states. This approach has highlighted how educational outcomes vary among states and has identified the states which need improvement.

Approach III—Identification and Measuring Quality of Education in Sample Schools in Delhi

This approach is based on the primary data collection in sample schools in Delhi. It was conceptualized around the proposition that quality of education is basically a three-dimensional composition comprising inputs, processes, and outcomes (Grisay and Mahlck 1991). While thinking about the quality of education, it is useful to distinguish between educational outcomes and processes leading to them with respect to the types of inputs which are put into the system. These interlinked three dimensions are given as follows:

- *Inputs* further divided into internal efficiencies and external influences affect the learning abilities of students. These determine and comprise the schooling environment and individuals' educational experience which in turn impact processes.
- *Processes* through which trained teachers use student-centric teaching approaches in well-managed classrooms and schools and skilful assessment to facilitate learning and reduce disparities, leading to final outcome.
- *Outcomes* which represent the 'ultimate end' that encompass knowledge, skills, and attitudes, and can be measured in the form of their academic scores, students' participation, and health performances.

High academic achievement or performances are influenced by a combination of various variables, namely, infrastructure and resources of the school, teachers and teaching methods, family characteristics, external influence of friends/peer group, impact of information and communication technology (ICT), health issues, accessibility to various facilities, students' self-motivation, learning abilities and their participation in various academic activities.

The main focus is given on school facilities and teachers which are the central independent variables. School environments and teachers ability eventually determine the kind of results. An effective teacher ensures that he/she employs organizational skills which lead to effective teaching resulting into high academic achievement. Apart from these two broad variables, students and their family characteristics have also been given due importance. Impacts of other external factors have also been taken into consideration in identifying students' achievement level. Given the overall framework, the study has resorted to three approaches as described in the model (See Box A1 in Appendix).

4.2 Research Questions

In the light of the foregoing discussion, this book addresses various research questions. At the onset we have emphasized that mere quantitative expansion is not sufficient and maintaining a minimum standard of quality in education is equally important. But why is quality improvement important and why at the secondary level of education? For seeking answers to some of these questions, one has to see what is the present status of school education (in both qualitative and quantitative terms) at national and state levels in India and how do quality indicators vary across various levels of school education, by school types, across gender, and between states? This kind of analysis of school education at the national and state levels can only answer half of the above-raised question on quality loopholes in the education system; however, what is essential to understand here is why do we need to focus on secondary education only? For finding an answer to this, it is important to see if there are any linkages between secondary education and various socio-economic outcomes and thus evaluating how these linkages vary between different levels of school education. Once we find the answers to these questions, the next important question may arise on the design methodology used for measuring the quality of education, that is, the indicators of educational outcomes and students' performance at the secondary level of education. At the same time, one might also be interested to seek whether there is any inter-connection between students' achievement level and school or students' characteristics; students' parental backgrounds and classroom practices. It is equally interesting to know how teachers and teaching practices are related to students' performance.

4.3 Objectives of the Study

This book aims to fulfill following objectives: (a) to study the growth and performance of secondary education at national and state levels, identifying various gaps and underlying issues existing in the system; (b) to understand why there is a need for improving the quality of secondary education by evaluating its linkages with various socio-economic outcomes at both national and state levels, while having comparative assessments with other levels of school education; (c) to develop indexes for linking educational accomplishments with economic, social, health, and demographic performances at the national and state levels respectively, from both macro and micro perspectives; (d) to analyze how these outcomes varies between different states with different socio-economic and demographic profiles; (e) to identify various determinants affecting the performance and learning outcomes of students and understanding their perspectives on quality of education including schools, teachers, and learning environment; (f) to measure the extent to which school resources, family characteristics, and teachers play roles in students' learning processes; and finally, (g) to understand teachers' perspectives on overall quality improvement in education and identifying various factors that affect the teaching practices in schools.

4.4   Hypotheses

In the process of deeper analysis of the issues involved in the quality of education, the following hypotheses have been formulated and tested:

- Positive association exists between educational and economic development at the state and national levels. Improvement in the development of secondary education leads to rise in economic performance.
- The level of earnings rises with increase in attainment of school-level education.
- Educational development and health performances are interrelated. Improvement in secondary education performance brings positive changes in health performance.
- Improvement in educational development at the secondary and senior secondary levels improves the performance of demographic indicators.
- As the quality of school infrastructure improves, students perform better.
- Higher the education background of students' mothers, better is the performance of students at the secondary and senior secondary levels.
- The more friendly teachers are towards students, the probability of better students' performance increases.

4.5   Significance of the Study

The study will help in identifying various factors that strongly influences the overall performance and achievement level of students. These factors need to be considered by the researcher, academicians, and policymakers for the overall development of learning and cognitive skills of students. This study can play a great role in providing suggestions for improving the overall quality of education system in India at the state level by considering state-specific socio-economic issues. The research findings will enable us to understand the key obstacles to quality dissemination of secondary education in Delhi, the capital city of India, and will highlight the issues that need to be addressed from the perspectives of students, teachers, and school authorities. It will also bring clarity on the linkages between education attainment and educational outcomes for the country.

Reference

Grisay, A., & Mahlck, L. (1991). *The quality of education in developing countries: A preview of some research studies and policy documents.* Paris: IIEP.

Part II
Research Methodology and Study Methods

Chapter 5
Secondary Education: Sampling Procedure and Design

Abstract This chapter is broadly divided into two parts. The first part provides a detailed description of the study area covering its geographical, economic, demographic, and educational background. The second part introduces the research methodology adopted to answer the research questions raised. This includes selection of target respondents, sample size, and its fixation procedure and sampling design covering sources of data, survey procedure, and tools used in data collection. A two-stage stratified systematic random sampling technique was adopted for collection of primary data.

Keywords Research methods · Sampling design · Secondary education · Sample size · Random sampling · Stratification

5.1 Description of the Study Area

For the purpose of this study, Delhi, capital city of India, has been chosen; located along the west bank of the river Yamuna, it is one of the fastest growing cities in India. Delhi has a vibrant history, having been the capital of several empires in ancient India and has over 60,000 recognized monuments built over several millennia, making it an important cultural and intellectual centre. This section of the chapter will elaborate some of the key socio-economic and educational characteristics of Delhi.

5.1.1 Geography and Administration

The National Capital Territory of Delhi is spread over an area of 1,484 km^2, accounting about 0.05% of the India's total geographical area. With the rapid urbanization and growth of urban population, the rural population is continuously decreasing as confirmed by successive Census Reports from 9.5 lakh in 1991 to 4.2

lakh in 2011. Number of villages in rural areas has declined from 209 in 1991 to 165 in 2001, and to 112 in 2011, while urban villages are increasing. New Delhi today is one of the fastest growing cities in both India and the world and is also considered as the governmental, commercial, and financial centre of India. The climate of New Delhi is considered as humid subtropical and it is highly influenced by the seasonal monsoon. It has long, hot summers and cool, dry winters. As of July 2007, the National Capital Territory of Delhi comprises nine districts, 27 tehsils, 59 census towns, 300 villages and three statutory towns, the Municipal Corporation of Delhi (MCD), the New Delhi Municipal Council (NDMC), and the Delhi Cantonment Board (DCB). In July 2011, the districts have been increased from nine to 11. Delhi has four major satellite cities, which lie outside the National Capital Territory of Delhi—Gurgaon, Faridabad, Noida and Ghaziabad. Delhi is divided into nine major districts: Central Delhi, New Delhi, West Delhi, East Delhi, North Delhi, North East Delhi, North West Delhi, South Delhi, and South West Delhi.

5.1.2 Demographics

As per Census 2011, population of Delhi, as on 1 March 2011, was 16.7 million (1.38% of India's population) as against 13.8 million as on 1 March 2001. According to Census 2011, about 97.5% of the population of Delhi lives in urban areas and the remaining 2.5% in rural areas. The decadal growth rate of population during 2001–11 was recorded at 21%, thereby registering the sharpest drop of 26% points from 1991–01 to 2001–11. The sex ratio of Delhi increased from 821 as reported in 2001 to 866 in 2011. Density of population in Delhi in 2011 was the highest amongst all states and union territories at 11,297 persons per km^2 as against the national level of 382 persons per km^2 in 2001. More than 80% of the people living in Delhi practice Hinduism, but there are also other large communities in the city. Census shows that there were 33,40,538 households in Delhi with the average household size being 5.02. Hindi constitutes the mother tongue followed by Urdu and Punjabi. According to the economic survey of Delhi 2011–12, the literacy rate has increased from 81.7% in 2001 to 86% in 2011.

5.1.3 Economy

Delhi is the most prosperous state with highest per capita income in India. The gross state domestic product (GSDP) of Delhi at current prices during 2014–15 was Rs. 4,51,154 crore, which recorded growth of 15.3% over the previous year and nearly 78% growth in the last five years from Rs. 2,52,753 crore in 2010–11. The per capita income (PCI) of Delhi is almost three times higher than the per capita income of India. The average PCI in Delhi remained more than Rs. 2 lakh in two consecutive years—2013–14 and 2014–15. In real terms, PCI of Delhi has registered an annual growth of 6.25% from 2013–14 to 2014–15. As per the Economic Survey of Delhi (2014–15), the tertiary sector contributes the most for Delhi's GSDP at 87.5% during 2014–15, followed by contribution of industries and agriculture sectors. The tertiary sector plays a pivotal role in the state economy both in terms of employment generation and contribution to state income. The growth rate of Delhi is likely to achieve 8.2% during 2014–15 compared to 7.4% growth at the national level during the same period. During 2001–11, the proportion of working population to the total population in Delhi increased at the rate of 0.46% with female workers constituting 14% of workers in Delhi. The proportion of persons below poverty line during 2011–12 was estimated at 9.9% of the total population of Delhi. The key service industries in Delhi are information technology, telecommunications, hotels, banking, media, and tourism. Construction, power, health and community services, and real estate are also important to the city's economy. Delhi has one of India's largest and fastest growing retail industries.

5.1.4 Educational Background of Delhi

Delhi Government is persistently thriving to develop a 'knowledge economy' by way of enhanced budgetary allocation for improving the infrastructure and quality of education. In Delhi, educational facilities are provided in stages, that is, pre-primary, primary, middle, lower secondary, senior secondary, and university level. Primary education is the responsibility of three civic bodies of Delhi—Delhi Municipal Corporations, New Delhi Municipal Council, and Delhi Cantonment. However, Delhi government has also introduced primary classes in Sarvodaya Vidyalayas. It looks after secondary, higher secondary, technical, and professional education. The overall network of educational institutions in Delhi is being run by local bodies, Central Government, Government of Delhi and private sector agencies.

As per Census 2011, the literacy rate of male youth increased from 91.8% in 2001 to 98.3% and for females from 85.1 to 96.4%. Delhi is very close in attaining the universal literacy rate among youth with a gender parity of 1. However, more important than achieving the target is to sustain the achieved target. Overall, Delhi constitutes 1.3 crore literates in 2011 as compared to 96 lakh in 2001, showing a growth rate of 3.2%. The continuous increase in literates in Delhi is the outcome of significant investments made in the education sector. The planned expenditure of the education sector in Delhi has increased from 8.5% in 2007–08 to 9.5% in 2011–12 and further to 15.7% in 2014–15. The expenditure on education to the gross state domestic product (GSDP) of Delhi was highest at 1.9% in 2009–10 but over the years it has been declining and has reached 1.7% in 2011–12 and further down to 1.5% in 2014–15.

According to the Economic Survey of Delhi 2014–15, the total number of schools run by various agencies, including the Government of Delhi, are 5,798 (2,806-primary, 933-middle, 385-secondary, and 1,674-senior secondary schools)

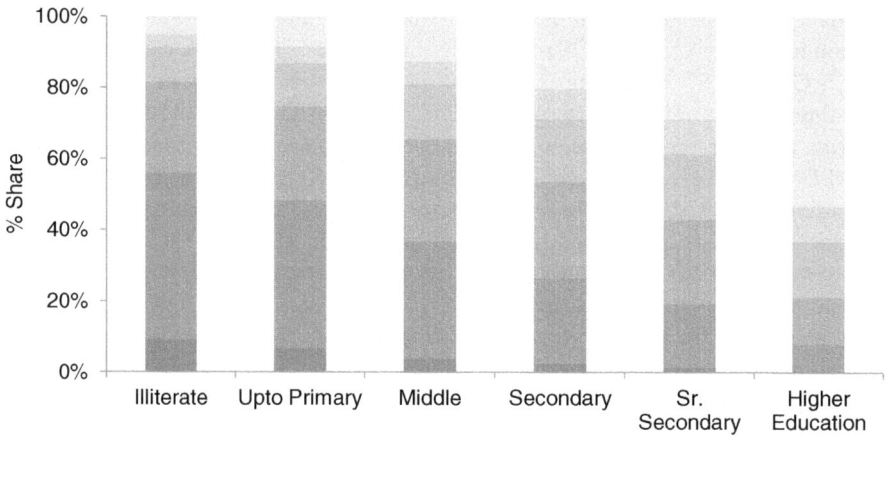

Fig. 5.1 Number of schools, enrolments, teachers and PTR: Delhi

up from 5,122 as recorded in 2011–12 (Fig. 5.1). The gross enrolment of students, both in private and government sectors, increased from 41.5 lakh in 2011–12 to 44.1 lakh 2014–15. Of the total enrolments, around 32 lakh enrolled students were in the primary and middle levels and 12 lakh were at the secondary and senior secondary level in 2014–15. Simultaneously, it also indicates that the number of teachers increased from 94 thousand in 2004–05 to 1.2 lakh in 2011–12 and further to 1.4 lakh in 2014–15. On the other hand, the student–teacher ratio has declined from 36 in 2005–06 to just 32 in 2014–15. Further, the appointment of teachers through all these years has not been consistent with the increase in students' enrollment. This has affected to a large extent the overall quality of education in schools.

The share of private sector schooling in Delhi is 27.3% in case of secondary and senior secondary in 2013–14; while in primary and middle together, it is 38.3% during the same period. As far as higher education is concerned, Delhi had 207 higher educational institutions in 2014–15, of which about 181 were colleges of general and professional education, 11 universities, and 12 deemed to be universities.

5.1.4.1 Secondary Education in Delhi

Secondary education is characterized by transition from primary education to higher education. The secondary school education in Delhi consists of two years of lower secondary education and two years of senior secondary education after eight years of compulsory elementary education. Delhi has made considerable educational progress over the years with high literacy rate, improved access to educational facilities, and high enrolment rate. Secondary education has seen expansion in Delhi, with nearly three times increase in both lower/senior secondary schools and enrolments between 1980–81 and 2014–15. In 1980–81, Delhi had 704 secondary schools, which increased from 1,890 in 2011–12 to 2,059 schools in 2014–15. Student enrolment for the lower secondary and senior secondary levels has also increased from 2.54 lakh in 1980–81 to 11.69 lakh in 2011–12 and 12.14 lakh in 2014–15.

Although, in comparison to the last 30 years the situation has improved a lot, yet if we look at the prevailing situation within various levels of education during all these years, we will find that there are huge discrepancies which are further affecting the overall quality of education, hence have huge implications on the learning levels of students. The number of educational institutions in Delhi during the last seven years was more than 5,000. Of these, more than 50% are in the category of primary education, while senior secondary schools that further link up to higher education constitute only one-fourth of the total strength. The situation of lower secondary schools in Delhi is even worse. Among all levels of education, the number of lower secondary schools is lowest with 385 schools that constitute only 6.6% of the total schools. This is even lower than middle-level schools that hold the strength of 16% of schools in Delhi. One reason could be that more and more of lower secondary schools are now being converted into senior secondary schools.

The available data shows that although the number of lower secondary schools in Delhi has declined in the last decade, student enrolments have increased during these years, thereby creating pressure on the available resources and causing infrastructural constraints (Table 5.1). Hence, due to the high growth rate of Delhi's population and student enrolments, as well as the simultaneous shortage of infrastructure facilities, majority of the Sarvodaya Vidyalayas has been asked by the Directorate of Education in Delhi to operate in two different shifts—morning for girls and evening for boys. Due to poor infrastructural facilities, the lower secondary and senior secondary levels have also marked the lowest enrolment rates as compared to other levels of education. Out of 44.1 lakh students enrolled in 2014–15, senior secondary schools shows the lowest enrolment rates with only 5.6 lakh students followed by

Table 5.1 Level-wise number of schools and students enrolments in Delhi

Years	Schools (in numbers)				Enrolments (in lakh)			
	Primary	Middle	Lower secondary	Senior secondary	Primary	Middle	Lower secondary	Senior secondary
2005–06	2668	645	483	1267	18.5	8.9	4.1	2.8
2010–11	2613	588	480	1392	18.8	9.8	6.3	4.2
2011–12	2632	600	463	1427	19.7	10.1	6.8	4.9
2012–13	2629	564	458	1504	19.8	10.6	6.4	5.8
2013–14	2709	728	389	1627	20.2	11.2	6.4	6.0
2014–15	2806	933	385	1674	20.8	11.2	6.5	5.6

Source Economic Survey of Delhi 2012–13, 2014–15 and Delhi Statistical Handbook 2013

6.5 lakh of students in lower secondary level of education. Further, female enrolments are also lower in the secondary level of education in Delhi.

However, as far as number of teachers is concerned, there were about 10.8 thousand teachers employed in lower secondary schools, while this was even higher at 88.6 thousand teachers at the senior secondary levels. The lower secondary and senior secondary levels of education together holds much better strength of teachers as compared to primary and middle levels of education. Hence, the pupil–teacher ratio was also better at these two levels of education as compared to the primary/middle one. The proportion of students passing the lower secondary and senior secondary levels of education has improved over the last seven years. Private institutions contribute significantly to secondary schooling facilities in Delhi. About 38.4% students in primary and middle level of education in Delhi attended private schools in 2013–14. In case of secondary education, nearly 27.3% students were in private schools.

Though, a large number of educational institutions exist in Delhi, participation at secondary levels still remains low as reflected by enrolment ratios. Among those, who complete elementary education, very few have been able to transit to secondary level of education. The reason behind the same is the high dropout rates. The passing percentage of students in the Twelfth Class has improved from 81.9% in 2007 to 86.8% in 2013, while in case of the Tenth Class examinations, the percentage has gone up from 77% in 2007 to 98.4% in 2013. This clearly reflects that students in Delhi have talent but need to be nurtured further with adequate resources and infrastructural facilities at both lower secondary and senior secondary levels of education.

5.2 Research Design

5.2.1 Target Respondents

To fulfill the objective of exploring quality issues in senior secondary schools in Delhi, three types of target respondents were considered for conducting survey—students, teachers, and school authorities. *First* set of target respondents were school students studying in lower and senior secondary levels of education in selected government/ private schools all over Delhi, covering both male and female students from science and non-science streams. The *second* set of target respondents were teachers teaching various subjects in the Ninth and Twelfth classes of the sample schools. Along with this, information on school resources and quality aspects was also considered through interviews of key informants. This constituted the *third* set of target respondents. These key informants could have been a senior teacher or administrative staff member, nevertheless well informed about the overall functioning of the school.

5.2.2 Coverage Area

The geographical coverage for the study included collection of primary information from the secondary and senior secondary schools located all over Delhi. According to the Directorate of Education, the total registered senior secondary schools (up to the Twelfth Standard) in Delhi were 2288 (as on 31st August 2013), of these, about 43.4% constituted government schools while the remaining 56.6% were public-recognized schools. These schools were distributed across 12 administrative districts and 28 administrative zones as per the Census of India 2011. The sample survey were selected from both private and government senior secondary schools registered with the Directorate of Education, except few categories of government schools like registered with Municipal Department Corporation (MDC), New Delhi Municipal Corporation (NDMC), Kendriya Vidyalaya (KVS), Delhi Cantonment Board (DCB), and Jawahar Navodaya Vidyalaya (JNV). In geographical terms, the survey excluded the NCR region of Delhi.

5.2.3 Sample Size

Generally, there is no definite recommendation for the appropriate sample size and researchers decide on the sample sizes based on their financial limitations and time available. However, it is important that besides these limitations, we should calculate the sample size with acceptable or reasonable precision. Literature shows that the sample size in most social science studies is calculated using confidence interval, confidence level, and degree of precision. Generally, wider the confidence interval, more certain a researcher is that the population answers would fall within that range. We have used the following methodology given by Daniel (1999) for sample size calculation:

$$n = \frac{Z^2 P(1 - P)}{d^2}$$

where

n sample size
Z   statistic for a level of confidence,
P   expected prevalence or proportion, and
D   precision or confidence interval expressed as decimal.

Using the above method, maximum sample size was selected at 95% confidence interval level that satisfied the assumption of normal approximation as well. Considering this methodology, about 41 sample schools were selected from all over Delhi from which 512 students and 160 teachers were selected for the purpose of personal interviews. The sample size for both students and teachers were also justified on grounds of limited resources available and time constraints.

5.2.4 Sampling Design and Technique

From the above discussion, it is clear that the primary survey was conducted to capture facts and viewpoints of students, teachers, and key informers from secondary levels of education in selected sample schools. This information was canvassed through a set of three well-designed questionnaires. For this, *Two-Stage Stratified Systematic Random Sampling Technique* was adopted. The first stage constituted selection of sample schools in each region followed by selection of students and teachers that constituted the second stage of selection (Box A.2 in Appendix).

5.2.4.1 First Stage of Sample Selection: Schools

Sample schools were selected in the first stage. To proceed, a sampling frame covering an updated list of nearly 2,288 public and government schools according to districts and zones in Delhi was taken from the Directorate of Education, Government of India. This frame provided the information about the school's name, address, ID, contact details, district name, and zone number. Since our aim was to look into quality perspectives, we found that schools in the same zones/districts had almost homogenous attributes in terms of services provided, that is, infrastructural facilities, study fields, curriculums, students' and teachers' profiles, and so on. The reason could be high competition in the education market within each district. Therefore, 12 administrative districts were reclassified into four broad regions—north, south, east, and west on the basis of their geographical locations. The re-classification signifies homogeneity within the regions and heterogeneity between them. To avoid any bias in selection of any particular region and to have a better representation of schools from all over Delhi, sample schools were selected from each of the four regions. The summary of distribution of schools district-wise and region-wise is given in Table 5.2.

Stratified systematic random sampling technique was applied for the final selection of schools. This method generally requires the sampling frame which was already available in this case. The sampling frame was divided into different strata on the basis of regions and type of school ownership. Based on this, it was decided to cover eight schools per region covering four private schools and four government schools in the sample. These quotas were fixed purposively for making comparisons based on regions and type of school ownership, which was not possible otherwise.

One major issue of concern during sample collection was that government schools were further divided into morning (for girls) and evening shifts (for boys) in Delhi due to infrastructural constraints.[1] In addition to these, there were few co-ed

---

[1]The point to note here is that each of these shifts, although operates in the same school premises, is considered as a separate school with separate identification code and working staff.

Table 5.2 Distribution of schools in Delhi as per districts and ownership-type

District name	No. of zones	No. of govt. schools	No. of public schools	Total no. of schools
East region				
East region	3	114	137	251
North east	3	125	234	359
East region total	6	239	371	610
North region				
North	2	61	28	89
North west A	2	108	94	202
North west B	3	119	180	299
North region total	7	288	302	590
West region				
West A	3	58	61	119
West B	2	77	183	260
South west A	2	47	60	107
South west B	2	87	158	245
West region total	9	269	462	731
Central region				
South	3	150	120	270
New Delhi	1	5	13	18
Central	2	41	28	69
Central region total	6	196	161	357
Total	28	992	1296	2288

Source Based on list of schools from Directorate of Education, GOI as on August 2013

Table 5.3 Distribution of sample schools

Regions	Public schools	Govt. schools	Total schools
North	4	4	8
South	4	6	10
East	4	8	12
West	4	7	11
Total	16	25	41

government schools. Ideally, four schools were selected from each stratum particularly in case of private schools, but in case of government schools it varied from four–8 eight within each region to address the above-mentioned issue. Overall, the total number of sample schools covered in the study was 41 covering 16 private and 25 government schools from all over Delhi. The summary of total number of sample schools covered in this study is given in Table 5.3.

5.2.4.2 Second Stage of Sample Selection: Students and Teachers

It involved selection of target respondents including students and teachers from the sample schools. For this, *Stratified Systematic Random Sampling Technique* was applied.

Students Sample Selection: Care was taken to depict the sample which provided a wider representation of male and female students of lower and senior secondary levels of education from government and private schools. The stratification technique adopted used the following criteria: level of study and gender. Hence, four strata were formed. These included male lower secondary, female lower secondary, male senior secondary, and female senior secondary. Using a systematic random sampling technique, four students from each stratum were selected. Based on this methodology, 16 students in total were selected from each sample private and co-ed government schools for personal interviews. In case of government schools with shift classes, eight students per school were selected from lower secondary and senior secondary levels. At senior secondary levels of education, efforts were made to cover students from both science–non-science fields, although no fixed quota was allocated for them. On the whole, 512 students were selected as target respondents for this study, where each stratum constituted at least 64 units, well enough for running any analysis (Table 5.4).

Teachers' Sample Selection: As far as teachers were concerned, five teachers from each school were selected randomly for various subjects teaching classes from Ninth–Twelfth standards (Table 5.4). In case of government schools with separate morning and evening shifts, it was decided to cover three female teachers from girls' government schools and two male teachers from boys' government schools. Although, it was a random process to select teachers from respective schools, yet their willingness to participate in this survey was also taken into consideration. In total, 160 teachers were covered in the sample.

Table 5.4 Distribution of teachers sample size as per school type

Regions	Students sample			Teachers sample		
	Public schools	Govt. schools	Total schools	Public schools	Govt. schools	Total schools
North	64	64	128	20	20	40
South	64	64	128	20	20	40
East	64	64	128	20	20	40
West	64	64	128	20	20	40
Total	256	256	512	80	80	160

References

Babbie, E. R. (1986). *The practice of social research.* Belmont: California.

Bartlett, J. E., Kotrlik, J. W., & Higgins, C. C. (2001). Organizational research: Determining appropriate sample size in survey research. *Information Technology, Learning, and Performance Journal, 19*(1), 43–50.

Bridget, S., & Cathy, L. (2005). *Research methods in the social sciences.* New Delhi: Book published by Vistaar Publications.

Chugh, S. (2011). *Dropout in secondary education: A study of children living in slums of Delhi.* Occasional papers No. 37, NUEPA.

Daniel, W.W. (1999). *Biostatistics: A foundation for analysis in the health sciences* (7th ed.). New York: Wiley.

Governmentof NCT of Delhi. (2008). *Statistical abstract.* GOI: Directorate of Economics & Statistics.

Government of NCT of Delhi. (2012–13). Delhi economic survey, Planning Department.

Government of NCT of Delhi. (2013). Delhi statistics handbook, Directorate of Economics and Statistics.

Government of NCT of Delhi. (2014–15). Delhi economic survey, Planning Department.

Gupta, S., Verhoeven, M., & Tiongson, E. (1999). *Does higher government spending buy better results in education and health care? International Monetary Fund (IMF).* Working paper 99/21, February, 1999.

Kothari, C. R. (1985). *Research methodology—methods and techniques.* New Delhi: Wiley Eastern Limited.

Krejcie, Robert V., & Morgan, Daryle W. (1970). Determining sample size for research activities. *Educational and Psychological Measurement, 30,* 607–610.

Mehrotra, S. (2005). The economics of elementary education in India: The challenge of public finance. In *private provision and household costs.* New Delhi: Sage.

Mehta, A. C. (2003). *Universalization of secondary education: Can it be achieved in the Near future.* NUEPA, *XVII*(4), 507–528.

Naing, L., Winn, T., & Rusli, B. N. (2006). Practical issues in calculating the sample size for prevalence studies. *Archives Orafacial Sciences,* 9–14.

Chapter 6
Quality Measurement: Tools and Techniques

Abstract Qualitative and quantitative research methods were adopted as complementary strategies for this study. While quantitative methods involved interviews through survey instruments, qualitative approach included key informers and observations attained thereof. Evaluation was carried out using both primary and secondary data sources. The description of various indicators used in the study, ways to measure them, econometric models applied, and the methodology used for the development of indexes has been also elaborated in this chapter. The limitations of the study have been mentioned in the last section of this chapter.

Keywords Qualitative research · Quantitative research · Logistics regression · Factor analysis · Principal component analysis

6.1 Study Methods

Qualitative research differs from quantitative research in that the latter is characterized by the use of large samples, standardized measures, deductive approach, and highly structured interview instruments to collect data for hypothesis testing (Marlow 1993). In contrast to qualitative research, quantitative research easily and typically generates quantifiable categories before the study and statistical techniques are used to analyse the data collected. In the quantitative approach, a structured questionnaire was put across 512 sample students and 160 sample teachers from secondary and senior secondary levels of education in private as well as government schools through face-to-face interviews. In the qualitative approach, findings were obtained through direct observation method and interview with key informer through a structured questionnaire. These findings supplemented the quantitative information.

© Springer Nature Singapore Pte Ltd. 2018
C. Jain and N. Prasad, *Quality of Secondary Education in India*,
https://doi.org/10.1007/978-981-10-4929-3_6

6.1.1 Quantitative Phase

This method involved predetermined instruments which yield statistical data. The data, thus collected, determined the quality gaps between government and private schools. Two sets of questionnaire were used for students and teachers to fulfill the objectives of study. The technique adopted here was in-depth face-to-face interviews with the respondents. Taylor and Bogdan (1998) define in-depth interviews as 'repeated face-to-face encounters between the researcher and informants directed toward understanding informants perspectives on their lives, experiences, or situations as expressed in their own words'. The broad coverage of these questionnaires is elucidated here.

Student Questionnaire: The questionnaire gathered overall information about students under eight broad sections—student particulars, household particulars, school resources and infrastructure, teachers and teaching practices, student performances and self-evaluation, exposure to mass media, general perceptions on various issues and future. The survey questionnaire comprised the following sections:

Section I contained information regarding respondents' background. It covered indicators like respondents' age; gender; religion; social group and type of family they belong to; native language; hobbies and interests; type of coaching classes attended. It also covered questions for those students who were involved in part-time jobs.

Section II included questions to assess information about household characteristics. It covered variables like household size, education and occupation of family members, major source of income of household, status of household with respect to ownership of durable commodities and facilities accessible at home which can affect learning skills. Responses on parents' involvement in their studies and school-related matters, support and help they provide to their child and their views on students' performance, etc., were also obtained. The main aim of this section was to know to what extent parents' involvement and family background affect student performances.

Section III contained information regarding school resources and infrastructure. It covered indicators like accessibility to school, availability of various facilities, condition of those facilities, and kind of activities organized by school, and rate of participation. It also covered ranking of the school on various issues from quality perspective. This part of the section explained the effects of the physical infrastructure of the school on student's performance.

Section IV captured information regarding teachers and the various teaching methods or aids used by them in their teaching practices. More in the nature of teachers' evaluation from students' points of view, it covered indicators like presence of teachers in class, attitude of teachers, their teaching methods, and how comfortable or friendly students feel themselves with their teachers. This section also depicted perceptions of students on various issues related to teachers.

Section V covered questions on students' performances and their self-evaluation. Questions were asked about their attendance in class, reasons for absence, their scores, participation level, awards or prizes received, chosen/expected field of study, and private tuitions taken by them. It also included questions related to their subjects, about their past performances/success/failures, their interests and satisfactions with various issues related to their performances.

Section VI explored the information related to their exposure to mass media and internet applications. The main idea was to identify respondent's interest in available technology, various applications, accessibility to those applications, and how they affected their learning skills.

Section VII captured the perceptions of students on various academic, health, general, economic, political and scientific issues. The aim of this section was to test the IQ level of students and to know their beliefs which could influence their overall performance.

Section VIII finally covered indicators related to future aspirations of students like what they would like to become in future, or till which level of education they wanted to study, and to what extent they thought they could achieve their targets.

Teachers Questionnaire: This questionnaire was designed to grasp information regarding teachers' perspectives on issues categorized under five sections: teachers' particulars, teaching background, school resources and infrastructure, teaching practices and aptitude, their opinion on various issues related to quality of education and self-development/satisfaction levels. The questionnaire was divided into five sections which are discussed below:

Section I covered indicators related to teachers' profile like age, gender, religion, marital status, social group, education level, area of specialization, and so on. The main idea was to obtain some information about socio-economic profile of teachers.

Section II contained information about teacher's background which included indicators on their experience, subjects/classes taught by them, their participation in academic and non-academic activities, and curriculum development and trainings attended.

Section III captured information about school and its resources. This section was included to gather responses from teachers regarding facilities or physical resources that they considered most important for students and for themselves and to what extent schools could assure providing the same.

Section IV included indicators related to teaching methods, aids, textbooks referred by teachers. Moreover, it also covered teachers' perceptions on issues related to students' levels of understanding and school performances.

Section V finally contained opinions of teachers on their own efficiencies, the factors that motivate or distract them, along with perceptions of their peer groups.

6.1.2   Qualitative Phase

In recent years, there has been an increase in the number of qualitative studies in the field of education as a way to collect information through the process of observations made by the researcher. As stated by Boeije (2002), the qualitative research method enables the researcher to approach the topic from the perspective of the subject. Qualitative research is also referred to as naturalistic research or inquiry into everyday living (Taylor 1977). Moreover, qualitative techniques could be used to examine social processes that might be missed out by traditional quantitative measures (Powers and Witmer 1951). As Meadows (2003) says qualitative research helps to understand the social phenomenon in a natural setting with emphasis on the views and experience of the respondents. The data for qualitative research is collected through interviews, field notes, observations, videos, personal journals, memos, or other types of pictorial or written material, though interviews form the most common data collection method (Creswell 1998; Marshall and Rossman 2006; Strauss and Corbin 1998). This study employs two approaches for qualitative analysis: observations and interview of the key informer.

Direct observation and field notes: As stated by Pope et al. (2000) 'in order to understand people's behaviour in a certain social environment, one must not only investigate the characteristics of this environment, but also how people give meaning to this'. The direct observation technique enabled researcher to learn about the behaviour of the people under study: students and teachers in the natural setting, in other words, the schools. The main idea behind adopting this technique was to understand the present status of the quality of education in selected schools and the level of participation and performances of both students and teachers. This method provided first-hand information and a qualitative perspective on the physical and facilities of the school, including the level of hygiene maintained in classrooms, toilets and overall school premises; availability of drinking water facilities; safety features undertaken; and working conditions for teachers. During each visit, the researcher went into all classes, labs, library, playground, and medical rooms to learn about the behaviours of students and teachers. The field notes taken were instrumental in analysing and interpreting the results.

Key informant interviews: The qualitative approach facilitated flexibility and an in-depth analysis of various aspects of a social situation (Babbie 1986). Interviews with the key informants were qualitative informal interactions conducted to obtain the insider's views of the community and first-hand knowledge about the overall functioning of the school. The key informers in the sample schools were selected using purposive sampling technique. Marshall (1998) says one form of purposive sampling is strategic informant sampling which is, 'selecting the people whom you think can give you the most information'. This strategy of purposeful sampling was used in this study to identify the key informer and it was felt that in this case the key informants were either senior teachers or senior administrative personnel. The questionnaire was made short and direct, and the interview was conducted face-to-face with the respondents. One respondent from each school was selected purposively for gathering this information. They were asked about the rules and regulations of the school, timings, admission procedures, fees structure, and school's ranking, kind of scholarships awarded for meritorious academic performances, and future development plans of the school. Specific questions related to facilities available in school were discussed with other key informants like lab assistants, librarians, health checkups, playgrounds, etc. The questionnaire also included the information about staff teachers and the promotional and growth strategies followed by the school management. Finally, suggestions were taken on how to improve the quality levels in the education system for both teachers and students. Apart from these formal interviews, the school guards/receptionists were also contacted informally to gather information on school timings for teachers and students, school transport facilities, and security issues. Driessen and Jansen (2013) have recently argued that the value of informal conversation is often underestimated. They emphasized the relevance of 'small talk' for learning specific expressions and words, understanding the sensitivities in a culture, and acquiring access to meaningful social and cultural details crucial for a 'thick description'.

6.2 Data Sources and Measurement

This section gives a brief description of all the variables used in the study and were collected either through primary survey in schools or through renowned secondary data sources. In addition to this, the methods of measurement and analysis techniques have also been discussed here.

6.2.1 Data Sources

Along with the primary survey, as mentioned earlier, there were few other sources which were considered in this study for an analysis both at the all-India and state levels. First was primary data on 'National Youth Readership Survey' which gave information on states and union territories in India covering both rural and urban sectors. Along with this, time-series data was prepared by referring various renowned sources. The description of both these data sets is given as follows:

6.2.1.1 National Youth Readership Survey Data (NYRS)—Primary Survey

Along with the collection of primary data, the study used the sub-sample of the National Youth Readership Survey (NYRS) undertaken by renowned organizations like NCAER and NBT in 2009–10 under the initiative of National Action Plan for Readership Development of the Trust. The information for most questions was collected primarily over 12 months since the date of reference period; for a few questions it was the last three months. This survey was conducted for the financial year April 2009 to March 2010. The target population of the study was in the age group 13–35 years. Relevant indicators from this data set were selected from this data set to fulfill the objectives of this study.

6.2.1.2 Secondary Data Sources

Along with the primary survey data, the study heavily relied on secondary data sources for national and state analyses. Several journals, websites, literature, and reports were referred for generating initial information on the subject and also for facilitating collection of information about the sample states. The most recent, accurate, and well-renowned sources were used as secondary data; few of them are summarized here as follows:

- **For Economic Parameters**: Economic Budgets, Economic Surveys, RBI database, Ministry of Finance, Centre for Monitoring Indian Economy (CMIE), Ministry of Commerce and Industry, Central Statistical Office (CSO), National Accounts Statistics (NAS).
- **For Demographic and Health Parameters**: National Family Health Survey (NFHS), Census of India, United Nations International Children's Emergency Fund (UNICEF), National Institute of Health (NIH), Ministry of Health and Family Welfare (MHFW), National Institute of Health and Family Welfare (NIHFW), National Health Profiles, and Sample Registration System (SRS).
- **For Household and Educational Parameters**: National Sample Survey Organization (NSSO), National Council of Applied Economic Research (NCAER), National University of Educational Planning and Administration (NUEPA), University Grants Commission (UGC), National Council for Educational Research and Training (NCERT), Planning Commission, Ministry of Human Resource Development (MHRD), Association of Indian Universities (AIU), India Human Development Survey(IHDS), National Survey of Household Income and Expenditure (NSHIE), Analysis of Budgeted Expenditure (ABE), Institute of Applied Manpower (IAMR), UNESCO (UIS Data). For understanding the status of education in Delhi, the data was taken from Economic Survey of Delhi (previous issues and latest 2014-15) and Statistical Handbook of Delhi 2013, Directorate of Economics and Statistics, Govt. of NCT of Delhi.

6.2.2 List of Indicators

Socio-Demographic Indicators: It included variables like age, gender, religion, caste of the respondents.

School Infrastructure and Facilities: It covered indicators like class size, class of study, stream/field of study, distance from school, mode of travelling to school, time taken to reach school, and medium of instructions. It also included variables on facilities available in schools in terms of library, playgrounds, science labs, canteen, toilet facilities, classroom types, and class facilities, provision of first aid, drinking water facility, etc., as well as types of activities organized by school.

Family Characteristics: Family characteristics play an important role in performance and learning of students. The variables covered under this category included parents' income and education level, social class, parents' occupation, household type and ownership pattern, family type, family assets ownership, number of siblings, time devoted by parents on their child's studies, as well as perception on what students felt about parents and their expectations.

Student Performance Measures: To analyze the student's achievement level, it was necessary to cover various indicators related to their performance in school in both academic and non-academic field. For this, the types of indicators covered were grades achieved in the last academic year, awards/scholarships/prizes received, extra classes/tuitions attended and their participation level in academic and non-academic activities organized by school or outside. They were also asked about their access to mass media resources like newspapers, television, books, internet etc., as they also have important place in overall learning process. The respondents were asked about their role models, their leisure time activities, future aspirations, health and absenteeism from schools.

Teachers' Performance Measures: To measure the abilities of teachers, indicators like education level, number of years of experience, specialization subjects, and teaching subjects were covered. Their performance was measured on the basis of students' satisfaction levels, passing percentage of students, trainings attended, awards received, teaching methods used, and teaching aptitude. Teacher's satisfaction level was also measured in terms of their own growth, salary increments, promotional strategies, school facilities, students' behaviour and scores, working environment, amount of work load, self-performance, peer group, etc.

Perceptions and Views: A number of indicators are included in the study so as to understand the various perceptions/views of both teachers and students on diverse issues, for example; self-performance, facilities provided at home and school, quality of teachers, school resources, curriculum, examination system, etc. These indicators cover the behavioural aspects of the respondents.

6.2.3 Construction of Indices

To measure the impact of secondary educational attainment on various socio-economic outcomes and comparing it with other levels of school education, separate indices have been developed. These indices are developed at both national and state levels using secondary data sources through *principal component analysis technique*. The main objective of developing these indices is to identify which level of school education is more important in terms of its socio-economic, demographic linkages. Although the methodology for the development of national-and state-level indices is the same, there is a difference in its approach. While, national indices are developed at the all-India level considering time series data, the state-level indices on the other hand are based on the latest information available. Moreover, there is also difference in the selection of indicators for developing composite indexes. The reason being that there are certain indicators that affect the growth of states and hence they need to be considered separately. The methodology for the development of indices is discussed here in details.

6.2.3.1 Construction of National-Level Indices

The national indices have been developed using time series data collected from renowned secondary sources at the all-India level, between the time period 1991–2011. The individual components of each of these composite indices are given as follows:

Secondary Education Development Index (SEDI): This index not only represents the 'quality' of secondary education but also the overall development of secondary education in India. The idea for index development has been taken from Hewlett Foundation's Global Development Program strategy which includes the Quality Education in Developing Countries (QEDC) initiative as one of its components to improve student learning and drive education reform efforts in East and West Africa and India. QEDC has identified four factors that contribute significantly in improving educational outcomes: Enrolments, Access, Quality, and Funding. For quality component, we have considered Pupil Teachers Ratio (PTR) as the proxy indicator defining quality of teaching in schools. PTR is a crude measure of school quality and found to have a negative and significant impact on student's test scores (Lee and Barro 2001). Overall, SEDI is based upon four components at the secondary level of education—gross enrolment ratios, expenditure on education as a percentage of GDP, pupil–teacher ratio, and number of schools with secondary education. The higher the index value, the better is the development of secondary education in India.

Elementary Education Development Index (EEDI): The formation of this index is similar to that of SEDI. The only difference is that this index represents the development of elementary education (First–Eighth standards) in India.

Economic Performance Index (EPI): This index is based on four components: GDP at factor cost, gross domestic savings, gross domestic capital formation, and per capita national income. Higher index value reflects better prospects for economy.

Demographic Performance Index (DPI): In order to measure the impact of education on demographic changes, a separate DPI has been developed using seven indicators: birth rate, death rate, natural growth rate, infant mortality rate, maternal mortality rate, sex ratio, and total fertility rate. The decline in all the seven components of the index ensures well-being of society.

Health Performance Index (HPI): Health Performance Index was developed using seven components: number of children immunized against Polio, number of children immunized against DPT, number of children immunized against BCG, number of children immunized against DT, life expectancy at birth rate, tetanus immunization for expectant mothers, and couples effectively protected due to all methods. The higher the value of the index, the better is the health performance of society.

6.2.3.2 Construction of State-Level Indices

To highlight the disparities between states in achieving secondary education and its impact on various outcomes, separate state-level indexes were developed. Although the methodology is similar to national level indexes in most of the cases, however, there are differences in indicators' selection. The construction of state-level indices are discussed here:

Secondary Education Index (SEI) and Elementary Education Index (EEI): These indices represent the development of secondary education (Ninth–Twelfth standards) and elementary education (First–Eighth standards) separately at aggregate state level. These indices are based upon five components: public expenditure on education as percent of gross state domestic product (GSDP), schools per 1000 population, pupil–teacher ratio (PTR), Gross Enrolment Ratio (GER), girls per 100 boys each at respective levels of education.

Economic Index (ECI): This index measures overall performance of economy and is based on four components: Per Capita net state domestic product (NSDP) at factor cost, public debt as percent of GSDP, real growth rate of states as percent of GSDP, FDI proposals approved.

Social Index (SCI): The social development index of states at an aggregate level is based on components like urban population, mean age at effective marriage, poverty rate, literacy rate, HIV prevalence rate adult, employment in organized sector.

Demographic Index (DMI): This index represents demographic transition and includes indicators like sex ratio, life expectancy at birth, and exponential growth of population.

Health Index (HLI): The educational attainment may also have serious implications on the health of society, therefore, to capture this relation, HLI is developed using the following components: full immunization of children, contraceptive use by any method, institutionalized deliveries, women with any anti natal care (ANC), and population served per government hospital.

Demographic-Health Index (DMHI): This includes indicators like crude birth rates, crude death rates, infant mortality rates, maternal mortality rates, and total fertility rates.

6.2.4   Scales and Ranking

The following ranking and scaling methods were applied to capture the perceptions and satisfaction level of students and teachers on various quality issues related to school facilities, etc.

Likert Scale: To measure the conditions of various types of facilities available in schools and also to measure performance and satisfaction level of the respondents, 5–7 point scale has been used. The responses are presented in percentage form.

Ranking: There were certain set of questions where preferences of the respondents were required and hence ranking method was applied, in which individuals were asked to rank their preferences from 1 to 9, where 1 means their highest and 9 means least preferred. In this case weights were assigned to frequencies and scores were calculated for ranks.

6.3   Data Analysis

Data analysis was carried out using both bivariate and multivariate techniques. While bivariate analysis includes tabulations, multivariate techniques include principal component analysis, binary logistic regression, and factor analysis. These techniques are elaborated here.

6.3.1   Binary Logistic Regression

When the dependent variable is a categorical variable having only two categories, the binary logistic regression is considered over the simple multiple regressions. In such cases, it seems preferable to fit some kind of sigmoid curve to the observed points.

The basic form of the logistic function is

$$P = \frac{1}{1 + e^{-z}} \tag{1}$$

where, 'z' is the predictor variable and 'e' is the base of the natural logarithm (Retherford and Choe 1993).

If the numerator and denominator of the right-hand side of (1) are multiplied by e^z, the logistic function in (1) can be written alternatively as

$$P = \frac{e^z}{1 + e^z} = \frac{\exp(z)}{1 + \exp(z)} \tag{2}$$

From (1), it follows

$$1 - P = 1 - \frac{1}{1 + e^{-z}}$$
$$= \frac{e^{-z}}{1 + e^{-z}} \tag{3}$$

Dividing (1) by (3) yields

$$\frac{P}{1 - P} = e^z \tag{4}$$

Taking natural logarithm of both sides of (4), we obtain

$$\log \frac{P}{1 - P} = z \tag{5}$$

The quantity $\frac{P}{1-P}$ is called the odds and the quantity $\log \frac{P}{1-P}$ is called the log odds or the logit of P. Thus

$$\text{Odds} = \frac{P}{1 - P} \tag{6}$$

Suppose that z is a linear function of a set of predictor variables:

$$z = b_0 + b_1 x_1 + b_2 x_2 + \cdots b_k x_k \tag{7}$$

where, $x_1, x_2 \ldots x_k$ are predictor variables.

Substituting (7) in (5), we obtain:

$$\log \frac{P}{1 - P} = b_0 + b_1 x_1 + b_2 x_2 + \cdots + b_k x_k \tag{8}$$

$$\log \text{it} P = b_0 + b_1 x_1 + b_2 x_2 + \cdots + b_k x_k \tag{9}$$

Equations (8) and (9) are in the familiar form of an ordinary multiple regression equation. The logit model is an additive model, as in ordinary multiple regression.

6.3.2 Factor Analysis

Factor analysis is based upon setting up a statistical model of the data. Each variable is modelled as a linear combination of a small number of 'factors' with the addition of a random component term, a little like regression analysis (Cooper and Weekes 1983). So the factor analysis model has the form:

$$X_1 = k_{11}F_1 + \cdots + k_{1m}F_m + u_1$$

$$X_2 = k_{21}F_1 + \cdots + k_{2m}F_m + u_2$$

where, m denotes the number of factors in the model and $m \leq$ number of variables. Unlike regression analysis, the factors F_1, F_2, ...F_m are hypothetical variables.

In the limiting case when the number of factors equals the number of variables, the random component terms disappear and the factor analysis model reduces to the principal component model.

6.3.3   Principal Component Analysis

Principal Components (PCs) are used as linear combinations of the variables selected to compose the social indicators. They have special statistical properties in terms of variances. The first PC is the linear combination, which accounts for maximum variance of the original variables. The second PC accounts for maximum variation of the remaining variations, and so on. Maximizing variances helps to maximize information involved among the sets of variables, hence, it is most appropriate for weighting these variables for the development of the Index.

The main reason for employing PCA is that it makes it possible to define a synthetic measure that is able to capture interactions and interdependence between the selected set of indicators making up the three indices. Principal Component constitutes a canonical form and helps to understand both the individual contri bution of each of the indicators to the Index and their aggregate contribution. An attractive feature of this methodology is that it permits calculation of statistical weights of the various components of the Index for the sample that thereby identifies what drive the results.

Let $x1$, $x2$, $x3$, ..., xp are variables under study, then first principal component may be defined as

$$z1 = a11\,x1 + a12\,x2 + \cdots + a1p\,xp$$

such that variance of $z1$ is as large as possible subject to the condition that

$$a112 + a122 + \cdots + a1p2 = 1$$

This constraint is introduced because if this is not done, then Var ($z1$) can be increased simply by multiplying any $a1$ is by a constant factor. The second principal component is defined as $z2 = a21$

$$x1 + a22\,x2 + \cdots + a2p\,xp \text{ such that}$$

Var ($z2$) is as large as possible next to Var ($z1$) subject to the constraint that

$$a212 + a222 + \cdots + a2p2 = 1 \text{ and } \mathrm{cov}(z1, z2) = 0 \text{ and so on.}$$

It is quite likely that the first few principal components account for most of the variability in the original data. If so, these few principal components can then replace the initial p variables in subsequent analysis, thus, reducing the effective dimensionality of the problem.

6.4 Limitations of the Study

Although we have tried to capture as many indicators and methods possible to present all aspects of secondary education and its quality issues, however, we understand that there are limitations to the study which are further elaborated here.

- **In terms of coverage area**: The study has been confined to Delhi only. The state of Delhi is divided into 12 administrative districts and 28 zones. Due to time and cost limitations, these 12 districts were clubbed together into four broad districts. The sample schools have been randomly selected from these four broad districts. The schools in the NCR region remained uncovered.
- **In terms of variables selection**: Quality of education in this study was strictly measured in terms of student performance and achievement level. Although efforts were taken to cover all aspects which affected student performance and their participation rates and achievements, there were certain factors which were not taken into consideration.
- **In terms of linking the relationship**: Educational outcomes had benefited the economy and its people in several ways. However, this study established the relationship between education and the four broad results: economic performances, individual earnings and employment, behavioural aspects, and social outcomes in terms of health performances and demographic changes.

References

Babbie, Earl R. (1986). *The practice of social research* (p. 1986). Belmont: Calif.

Boeiji, H. (2002). A purposeful approach to the constant comparative method in the analysis of qualitative interviews. *Quality & Quantity, 36,* 391–409.

Cooper, R. A., & Weekes, T. J. (1983). *Book on data*. New Jersey, USA: Models and Statistical Analysis. Barnes & Noble Books.

Creswell, J. W. (1998). *Qualitative Inquiry and research design: Choosing among five traditions*. London: Sage Publication.

Driessen, H., & Jansen, W. (2013). The hard work of small talk in ethnographic fieldwork. *Journal of Anthropological Research, 69*(2), 249–263.

Lee, J. W., & Barro, R. J. (2001). Schooling quality in a cross-section of countries. *Economica, 38* (272), 465–488.

Marlow, C. (1993). *Research methods*. Pacific Grove, CA: Brooks/Cole.

Marshall, C., & Rossman, G. B. (2006). *Designing qualitative research* (4th ed., p. 262). Sage Publication: Thousand Oaks (Social Science).

Marshall, P. (1998). *Quest for quality assessment*. Harare: ZIMSEC.

Meadows, K. A. (2003). So you want to do research? An overview of the research process. *British Journal of Community Nursing, 8*(8).

Pope, C., Ziebland, S., & Mays, N. (2000). Analyzing quantitative data. *British Medical Journal, 320,* 114–116.

Powers, E., & Witmer, H. (1951). *An experiment in the prevention of delinquency: The Cambridge-somerville youth study*. New York: Columbia University Press.

Retherford, Robert D., & Choe, Minja K. (1993). *Statistical models for causal analysis*. New York: John Wiley & Sons Inc.

Strauss, Anselm,& Corbin, Juliet M. (1998). *Basics of Qualitative Research: Techniques and Procedures for Developing Grounded Theory*. SAGE Publications, Social Science, p. 312.

Taylor, J. (1977). Toward alternative forms of social work research: The case for naturalistic methods. *Journal of Social Welfare, 4*(2–3), 119–126.

Taylor, S. J., & Bogdan, R. (1998). *In-depth interviewing*. In S. J. Taylor & R. Bogdan (Eds.), *Introduction to qualitative research methods: A guidebook and resource*. Wiley.

Part III
Secondary Education in India: Growth, Disparities, and Linkages

Chapter 7
Indian Education System: Structure and Key Challenges

Abstract The Indian education system has made significant progress in recent years. With more than 1.6 million schools and more than 290 million enrolments, India is home to one of the largest and complex school education systems in the world along with China. This chapter not only gives an overall picture of the vast and continuously changing Indian school education system, but also discusses the key challenges faced thereof with special focus on secondary education. The comparative assessment of Indian school education system at the global level is also discussed later in this chapter.

Keywords School education · Secondary education · Human development · Gender inequality

7.1 Understanding Indian School Education System

India has the most complex school education systems in the world along with China. With 35 diverse states and union territories, school education as per the constitution of India was originally a state subject, that is, states had complete authority on deciding policies and implementing them. The role of the government was limited to coordination and deciding on the standards of higher education. This was changed with a constitutional amendment in 1976, thereafter, education comes under the concurrent list. With this, school education policies and programmes are suggested by the Government of India at the national level, though the state governments have a lot of freedom in implementing programmes.

Education in India is provided by both the public and private sector, with control and funding coming from three levels—central, state, and local. Various organizations operate to regulate and manage the functioning of school educational system in India. The National Council of Educational Research and Training (NCERT) is the apex body for curriculum-related matters in school education in India. It provides support and technical assistance to a number of schools in India and overseas with respect to enforcement of education policies. Other curriculum bodies

© Springer Nature Singapore Pte Ltd. 2018

C. Jain and N. Prasad, *Quality of Secondary Education in India*,
https://doi.org/10.1007/978-981-10-4929-3_7

rning school education system are: State Government Boards; Central Board of Secondary Education (CBSE) which conducts examinations for the Tenth and Twelfth standards; the Council of Indian School Certificate Examination (CISCE) which conducts three examinations, namely, Indian Certificate of Secondary Education (ICSE–Tenth Class/Grade); Indian School Certificate (ISC–Twelfth Class/Grade), and Certificate in Vocational Education (CVE–Twelfth Class/Grade); National Institute of Open Schooling (NIOS) conducts two examinations, namely, Secondary Examination and Senior Secondary Examination (All India) and also some courses in vocational education; Islamic Madrasah schools; autonomous schools like Sri Aurobindo International Centre of Education, etc. In addition, while National University of Educational Planning and Administration (NUEPA) deals with capacity building and research on planning and management of education in India and South Asia, National Council of Teacher Education (NCTE) act as an advisory body to both central and state government on all matters pertaining to teacher's education.

Generally, central and most state boards uniformly follow the '10+2+3' pattern of education. In this pattern, study of 12 years is done in schools, and then three years of graduation for a bachelor's degree. Within 10+2 pattern, school education is further categorized in four stages—five years of primary schooling, three years upper primary, two years secondary and two years senior secondary. This pattern originated from the recommendation of the Education Commission of 1964–66. While, the minimum number of years required to complete general school education remain ten years throughout the country, about eighteen states and union territories have adopted the 5+3+2 pattern of general school education (Fig. 7.1).

India is undergoing a historic demographic transition where education will play a major role in the country for reaping the expected 'Demographic Dividend' over the next decades. In this background, the Tenth and Eleventh Five Year Plan periods corresponding to the last 10 years (2002–12) have witnessed a concerted effort to provide a thrust towards universalization of elementary education and significantly expanding access to secondary and higher education. The major developments during the Eleventh Five Year Plan period have been: expansion of Sarva Shiksha Abhiyan (SSA) as the vehicle of universal elementary education; extension of Mid-Day Meal scheme (MDM) to all elementary schools; enactment of the Right to Education (RTE) Act, 2009; establishment of Rashtriya Madhyamik Shiksha Abhiyan (RMSA); and enhancement of allocation for higher education through the establishment of Indian Institutes of Technology (IITs), Indian Institutes of Management (IIMs), and National Institutes of Technology (NITs). Although these schemes are successful in increasing the enrolments at the elementary level, quality education continued to be the issue of concern.

The Indian education system has made significant progress in recent years with more than 1.6 million educational institutions and more than 290 million enrolments in 2014–15 including primary, secondary, and tertiary levels of education. The Indian government has laid huge emphasis on primary education and has therefore even made it compulsory and free for children between 6 and 14 years of age or up to Eighth Standard under the Right of Children to Free and Compulsory

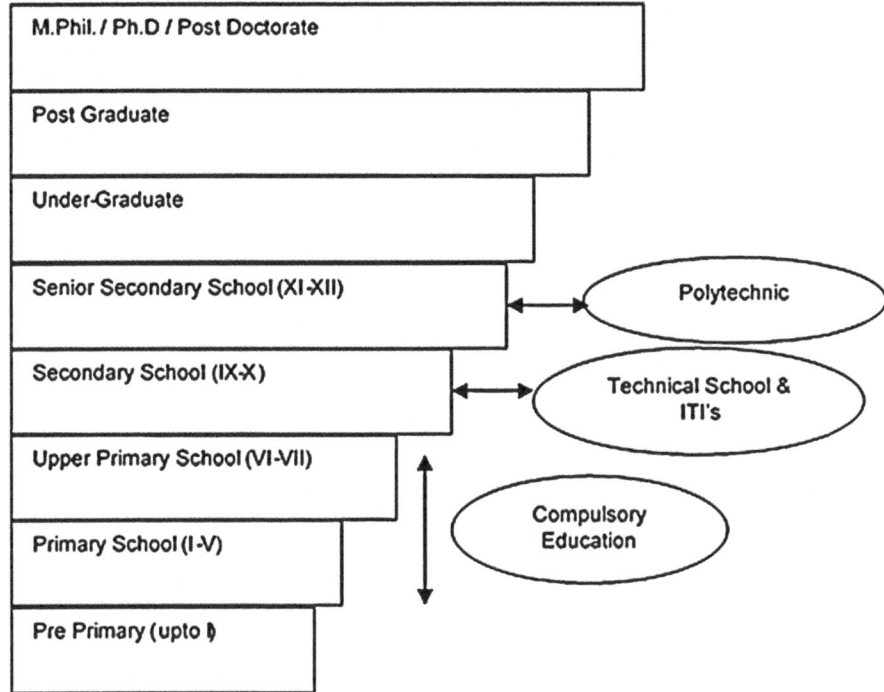

Fig. 7.1 Educational structure in India

Education Act 2009. With SSA, the enrolments in primary education picked up very fast. As of 2014–15, gross enrollment ratios are 100.1% for primary, 91.2% for upper primary, 78.5% for secondary, and just 54.2% for higher secondary. For higher education, GER is just at 24.3%. Although the country targeted towards devoting 6% share of the GDP towards the educational sector, the performance has definitely fallen short of expectations. Expenditure on education has steadily risen from 2.1% of GDP in 1970–71 to 4.14% in 2000–01. However, in the last one decade, it has remained almost stable at 4.13% of GDP in 2013–14.

As far as higher education is concerned, with nearly 34 million students and more than 51,534 institutions in 2014–15, India's higher education is the third largest in the world, after China and the United States. The main governing body at the tertiary level is the University Grants Commission (UGC), which enforces its standards, advises the government, and helps coordinate between the centre and the state. Higher education sector has witnessed a tremendous increase in the number of university-level institutions and colleges since independence. The number of universities has increased 35 times, from 20 in 1950 to 760 in 2014–15. The sector boasts of 43 central universities, 316 state universities, 181 state private universities, 122 deemed to be universities, 75 institutions of national importance under MHRD, including IITs, NITs, and IISERs, and three institutions established under various state legislations. The number of colleges has also registered manifold increase—77 times— from 500 in 1950 to 38,498 in 2014–15. Although higher education is the shared responsibility of both the centre and states, the coordination and determination of standards in universities and colleges are entrusted to the UGC and other statutory regulatory bodies.

Apart from these, India's emphasis was also to develop a pool of scientifically inclined manpower for which an apex body was provisioned by National Policy on Education (NPE) or regulation and development of higher technical/vocational education, which came into being as the All India Council for Technical Education (AICTE) in 1987 through an act of the Indian parliament. In 2013, there are more than 4,599 vocational institutions that offer degrees, diploma, and post-diploma in architecture, engineering, hotel management, infrastructure, pharmacy, technology, town services, and others with approximately 1.7 million students enrolled in these schools. Even at the school level, apart from formal schooling system, the National Institute of Open Schooling (NIOS) was established to provide opportunities for continuing education to those who missed completing school education. Within the category of open and distance learning system, nearly 1.4 million students are enrolled at the secondary and higher secondary levels.

It is quite visible that India owns a vast education system, therefore, studying each and every level of Indian education sector in depth is prolonged and a very complex task. This book will particularly look at the emerging quality issues in school-level education rather than higher education. There were strong reasons behind this decision. *Firstly,* school education provides inputs for higher education system which further generates skilled labour force and motivates research and development, fostering higher growth rates and enabling people to compete in a globalized labour market. Basic education confers several social and private benefits which include higher returns in the form of higher wages in the labour market. *Secondly*, estimates show that of the total educational institutes in India, nearly 97% constitutes schools, while less than 3% accounts for higher education. Moreover, schools in India are estimated to grow by a compound annual growth rate (CAGR) of 5.6% from 2006 to 2014. Although school resources are not the only factors responsible for the quality of education, it plays a great role in improving educational outcomes. This book, as mentioned earlier, has focussed on secondary education. The pattern of trends, growth, and key challenges of secondary education in India have been discussed below.

7.2   Secondary Level of School Education

Secondary education is a crucial stage in the educational hierarchy as it prepares youngsters (between age group 14 and 18 years) for higher education and their career. In secondary education, governmental intervention is observed at two levels —(a) Through apex national level bodies like National Council of Educational Research and Training (NCERT), Central Board of Secondary Education (CBSE),

National Institute of Open Schooling (NIOS), Navodaya Vidyalaya Samiti (NVS), Kendriya Vidyalaya Sangathan (KVS), and Central Tibetian School Administration (CTSA); and (b) Through its various schemes like boarding and hostel facilities for girl students of secondary and higher education, integrated education for disabled, ICT in schools, etc.

Government allocations in the education sector through its budgetary provision as per the Eleventh Five Year Plan period can be disaggregated into five broad components—elementary; secondary; university, higher and distance learning; technical education; and others, which includes adult education, promotion of language, etc. Budgetary allocation and expenditure by the Central Government has increased significantly between 2007–08 and 2012–13 from 3.4% of GDP to 4.1% in 2012–13. Despite the fact that the rate of growth in budget allocations on secondary education has increased more than elementary education, the overall share of budgetary allocation on secondary education is still the smallest as compared to elementary and higher education.

A major initiative for expanding secondary education was initiated in the Eleventh Five Year Plan. The target during the Eleventh Five Year Plan was to make lower secondary and senior secondary school within reach of every habitation and to ensure reducing the dropout rate and 100% retention up to the higher secondary stage. At present, various schemes have been implemented in the form of centrally sponsored schemes to make secondary education of good quality available, accessible and affordable to all young persons in the age group of 14–18 years. But the bitter fact is that despite putting in so much efforts and investments in secondary education during the Tenth and Eleventh Five Year Plan, not much has been achieved till now. Among all these schemes, there are only few that focus purely on quality issues of secondary education, trying to enhance learning and achievement level. Remaining schemes mainly aim at increasing accessibility and coverage area. There are problems of high dropout rates, low learning levels, inadequate school infrastructure, poor functioning schools, high teacher absenteeism, poor quality of education and above all inadequate funds (Lall 2005). It further adds that there is no common school system; instead children are channeled into private, government and aided schools on the basis of ability to pay and social class. Moreover, the most worrisome and problematic trend is that the quality of education that children receives in India varies widely according to their means and background. While universalization of education at secondary level is important, maintaining minimum quality standards of new projects and improving the quality of existing ones is equally important at the same time. Progress reports suggest that most of these schemes, as launched by the government, are still stuck at the level of budget sanctioning or attaining approvals. Those schemes that have been implemented so far have been handicapped by various limitations imposed on their coverage by factors like age, gender, caste, etc. On the whole, it is not wrong to mention here that few of such schemes need revisions in order to achieve the target of quality improvement at more broader and universal level. A study by Biswal (2011) argues that 'there is a large deficit in policy planning for secondary education development, which not only goes against the principle of inclusive development and the service-led growth strategy but also affects India's capacity to connect effectively to globalisation. It further concludes that India needs to step up investment in pre-reform activities for creating a sustainable environment for initiating change; improving political will; introducing strategic management models ensuring continuity in change at the school level; and increasing budgetary allocation to make more inclusive quality secondary education a reality'.

As per Educational Statistics at a Glance 2014–15, the population of children in the age group of 14–18 years is estimated at 107 million in 2001, 119.7 million in 2006, and 121.1 million in 2011. The current enrolment in lower secondary and senior secondary is 61.8 million only (2014–15) which is quite low. In comparison, the enrolment in primary level is 130 million in 2014–15, while it is 67 million in the upper primary level. During the period 2000–01 to 2014–15, the number of lower secondary and senior secondary schools increased from 1.2 lakh to 2.4 lakh, that is, it had almost doubled. Nearly 61% secondary schools are privately managed where the share of private unaided schools is higher; 31% secondary schools are government aided and less than 5.7% is run by local bodies. The combined gross enrolment ratio (GER) for both lower secondary and senior secondary is only 68% in 2014–15, while dropout rate is very high at 47%. The total number of teachers has increased from 1.3 million in 1990–91 to 1.76 million in 2001–02, and 3.2 million in 2014–15 for lower secondary and senior secondary levels. The state data show that the public spending on education in the country is the highest in Maharashtra for both secondary and technical education, while Uttar Pradesh spends the most on elementary education.

7.3   Key Challenges in Secondary Education System

India has the third largest higher education system in the world after China and US. Despite this fact, India also had the highest illiterate adult population in the world, three times that of China, and was ranked 58 out of 70 countries on e-readiness scales in 2009 (*NCAER's latest E-Readiness Report 2009*). India's pupil–teacher ratio is far below world standards for secondary schools at 38 compared to 16.5 in China and 14.8 in USA in 2014. Although through SSA, we are running the world's largest universalization of education programme, due to shortage of resources and lack of political will, this system suffers from massive gaps including high pupil–teacher ratio, shortage of infrastructure, and poor level of teachers training, pushing quality to lower levels, despite higher enrolment ratio. Linden (2012) in one of his study has highlighted three major challenges in secondary education in India that need to be addressed: Access, quality and Equity.

The latest trend shows that despite growing investment in education, 30% of India's adult population (15+ age group) is still illiterate; only 15% Indian students reach high school, and just 7% to the level of graduation. The quality of education at primary, secondary, or tertiary level is significantly poor as compared to major developing nations. Figures released by the Indian government in 2014–15 shows that there were 5.2 million elementary schools teachers in India, while 3.3 million teachers in secondary schools in India.

Education is a fundamental right of every citizen of our country (Right to Education Bill 2005). Unfortunately, despite several programmes to improve the state of education in our country since independence, not much progress has been made towards making it relevant to the needs of the time. Rote learning and reproducing half-baked ideas in the examination halls has been the yardstick of assessing the quality of school goers at all levels whether it is primary, secondary or higher education.

One of the greatest task before the nation is to expand and extend the outreach of good education to its younger generations, first at the elementary level and then emphasizing on secondary education (Anand 2011). The impact of the recent initiatives undertaken for the universalization of elementary education is resulting in increased demand for expansion of secondary education. Unless steps are taken to expand the secondary education system, it would be difficult to accommodate the increasing number of upper primary pass outs. There have been an increasing trend towards the number of secondary schools, the spread is uneven. Further, the significant gender gap also has to be narrowed down. In today's fast-changing world, education needs to respond to the change. In fact, education needs to react to everything that is happening in the environment external to the process of teaching and learning and the system that is responsible for it. With the unprecedented advent of ICT, a global perspective has to be developed and one has to perforce respond to the implication of globalization. Literature shows various initiatives that have successfully addressed the challenges of quality education, through provision of resources, professional development for teachers and the use of ICTs and further strengthening the argument that the three-way relationship between learner, teacher and materials lies at the heart of the education quality (Angeline 2007).

Education, even at this stage, is confined to the four walls of the classroom where teachers lecture on their specified subjects and students do not listen actively to the lectures. The profession of teaching has just been reduced to passing on some information to the students so that the latter in turn reproduce it at the time of examination. This fails to involve students in the learning process and their critical faculties remain untouched. The courses of study and patterns of education only bring uncertain future staring in the face of aspiring students. The uncertainty about their future provides potential fodder for the phenomenon known as 'students' unrest'. This is the real challenge that lies ahead for secondary education in India. Hence, responding to global and local socio-economic changes, decision makers need to know clearly what the changes and challenges are, why are these going to happen, and how will it be tackled.

7.4 India in International Perspective

Today, secondary education is back on the agenda for most of the countries all around the globe, considering its vast importance. In fact, it is now emerging as the cornerstone of the transformational process of education. This section throws light on some of the indicators related to secondary education at the international level and will also showcase Indian performance compared with the rest of the world. Globally, as more children enter and progress through primary school, the demand for secondary education has been expanding, and views about its role are changing. After universalization of primary education, many countries are now moving to make the lower secondary level mandatory as well. Not only this, but demand for upper secondary education has also increased with the need for more sophisticated workers with relevant competencies, knowledge and skills, acquired after the primary level of education. While ensuring equitable access to secondary education is a challenge particularly in developing countries, the completion of secondary school remains an important test for the world's richest countries as well. Maclean (2001) clearly argues that, "As countries make strenuous efforts to achieve universal literacy and primary education for all, while at the same time expanding and improving the quality of their system of tertiary education, for many nations secondary education has become the weakest link in the education chain". But secondary education is very important for increasing demand for highly skilled labour force in the global economy.

India's educational achievements have been of mixed success. On the positive side, it has made encouraging progress in raising schooling participation and has also emerged as an important player in the worldwide information technology revolution with the support of substantial number of well-educated computing and other graduates. On the negative side, India has 22% of the world's population but 46% of the world's illiterates, and is home to a high proportion of the world's out-of-school children and youth. The UNDP data (2015) on human development reveals that India still performed weak on human development indicators and gender equality front. Figure 7.2 reflects a comparative portrayal of the Indian position vis-à-vis major groups of countries with regard to human development index (HDI) and gender equality index (GEI).

In 2014, India scored 130th rank for both Human development index and gender inequality index. In absolute terms, in 2014, the HDI in India is 0.609 points compared with 0.660 points for developing countries and 0.711 points for overall world. Among the five major groups of countries based on the level of development, India's position is only better than the least developed and low developed nations, whereas medium, high and very high developed groups of countries are quite ahead of India in terms of human development. As far as gender inequality index is considered, the situation is vice versa. This clearly indicates that although we are not very good in formulating the developmental strategies for our human resources issues like gender inequality makes the situation even worst.

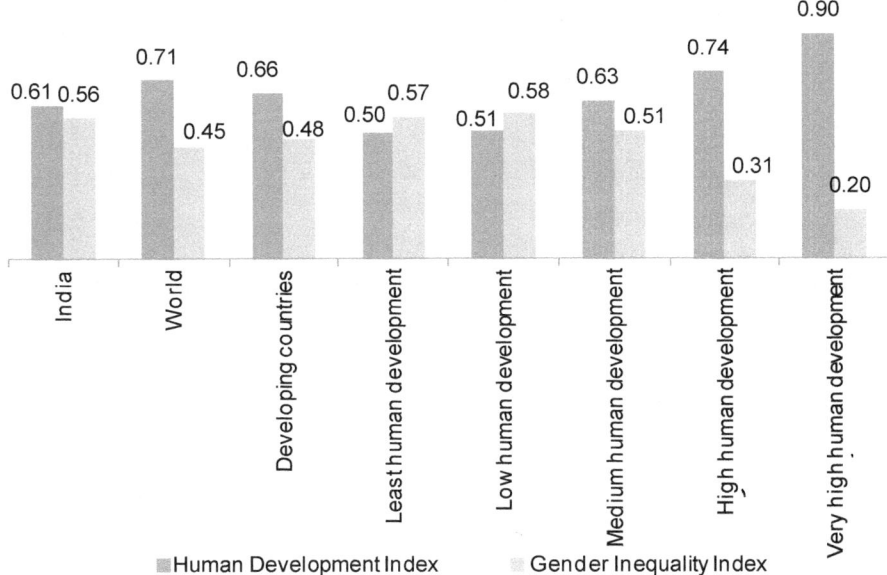

Fig. 7.2 Global human development and gender inequality index. *Source* Human development index trends 2015, UNDP

Most developing countries have attained near universal primary education, but secondary education and high-quality education are essential foundations for an employable workforce for the future. Currently, lower secondary education is compulsory in approximately 80% countries in the world, and the transition to secondary education needs to be ensured in those countries. In order to better understand the implications of these international commitments for the education sector, Table 7.1 provides a global overview of the current situation of secondary education.

Table 7.1 shows that around 81.2% of the adults in the age group of 15 years and above are literate at world level in 2013. India's adult literacy rate is 63%, lower than almost all developed and most of the developing countries. However, it is at par when compared with the literacy rate measured in other South Asian countries. However, in terms of public expenditure on education as percentage of GDP, India is still at a better position. India's gross enrolment ratio (GER) for secondary education is 69% which is lower than the world estimate of 74%; India is ahead of a few backward nations like Nepal, Bangladesh, and Pakistan. In countries like Brazil, France, Japan, and Singapore, the GER exceeds 100% which indicates that the national system can accommodate all its school-age population at a given education level, whereas, in case of India, the low GER reflects shortage of supply and impact of other factors, such as the indirect and direct costs of attending school, which may limit enrolment.

Table 7.1 International comparison on secondary education indicators

Countries	Adult literacy (15 yrs and above %)	GER—secondary	Secondary education, pupils (% female)	PTR in secondary education	% population with at least secondary education	Transition rate from primary to secondary education (%)	Govt. expenditure on education as % of GDP
	1	2	3	4	5	6	8
	2013	2013	2014	2014	2013	2012	2014
Bangladesh	58.8	54.0	50.9	35.2	37.8	94.5	87
Brazil	91.3	105.0	50.5	16.7	53.6	99.2	46
China	95.1	89.0	47.4	14.3	72.3	–	64
France	–	109.7	49.2	12.9	80.5	100	66
India	62.8	69.0	48.0	38.0	42.1	920	69
Indonesia	92.8	83.0	48.6	15.5	44.5	96.4	78
Japan	–	101.8	48.9	11.7	86.0	–	60
Nepal	57.5	67.0	50.4	28.8	28.3	87.9	83
Pakistan	54.7	38.0	42.3	21.4	33.2	80.1	53
Philippines	95.4	84.6	50.6	27.0	64.8	98.9	83
Korea	–	97.2	49.1	17.5	85.4	100.0	49
Singapore	96.4	106.9	48.2	14.9	77.4	90.8	87
Sri Lanka	91.2	99.3	50.9	17.3	74.0	98.5	83
UAE	90.0	92.0	–	13.3	64.3	99.4	70
UK	–	95.4	49.8	15.8	99.9	–	65
US	–	93.7	49.1	4.8	95.0	–	68
World	81.2	74.0	48.0	7.7	59.7	91.5	63

Note (–) data not available

Sources (1) human development report 2015 (UNDP), (2) Education dataset from UIS 2012–2014, UNESCO and (3) world development indicators 2015 (World Bank)

Owing to improvement in transition rates from primary to secondary over the years, which is 91.5% for world in 2012, there has been greater participation in secondary education. In developed countries like Korea it is 100% and near to 100% in case of UK and US, while for India it is 92% in 2012. Globally, the participation of young women in secondary education has increased. Around 48% of female all over the world are enrolled in secondary education in 2014 similar to 48% in case of India. Countries like Brazil, France, Philippines, and few neighbouring countries like Nepal, Sri Lanka have higher female participation in secondary education.

Globally, there exists a huge gap between participation in lower and upper secondary education levels. This gap is mainly due to developing nations where GER for lower secondary levels are 82.1%, whereas in case of upper secondary it is merely 59.6% (as in 2014), showing a difference of around 25% points. In developed countries, the difference between these two levels of secondary enrolments is quite low. India has also contributed significantly in widening this gap with 78.5 and 54.2% of enrolments in lower and upper levels of secondary education, respectively. However, when compared with the last ten years, the participation in upper secondary is on an increasing trend across the globe. The greatest progress in upper secondary GER was made in East Asia and the Pacific, followed by Latin America and the Caribbean and Central Asia.

As far as completion rates for secondary education are concerned, the world has made significant progress. In 2013, the world has 59.7% of population with secondary education. This proportion was 42% in India and 42% for Southern Asia. For medium developed nations, the proportion of population with secondary education was 45%, while for low and high developed nation it was 21.6% and more than 65% of the population respectively in 2013. The gender distribution of the data till 2014 shows about 54.5% of the female population in the world had completed secondary education, while this proportion was 65.4% in case of males. In case of India, these estimates were quite low at 27% females and 56.6% males during the same period. These figures were quite high above 90% in case of developed countries like UK and US. In case of medium-developed nations, this proportion was 35% for females and nearly 55.3% for males.

Worldwide, the level of growth among total number of teachers was generally linked to the demand for education at these levels. The pupil–teacher ratio (PTR) is an important indicator which measures the overall level of teacher deployment. High PTRs may signify an overstretched teaching staff, while low ratios may indicate additional capacity. PTRs are lower at the secondary than the primary level in all regions. In 2014, the global PTR for secondary education was 17.7 compared with 38 in India. For developing nations, PTR is higher than that of developed nations.

On the whole, in the past 10 years countries have made vast strides towards increasing attendance in secondary education, but 65 million lower secondary school-age children still remain out of school in 2013, 26 million live in South and West Asia, and 23 million in sub-Saharan Africa. These children face complex, compounding disadvantages that prevent their full participation in education. Even in the case of India, progress has been made over last few years in terms of secondary level participation, female participation, PTR, etc. though a long way needs to be still travelled to achieve a better place at the global level. The data clearly indicates that we are still lagging behind at global level. To achieve the targets, greater access to secondary education should be planned while ensuring its quality and relevance. Along with this, the key challenge for policymakers is to identify the children who are out of school and the barriers that prevent their participation in education.

References

Anand, O. (2011). *Challenges for secondary education in India.* Article webcasted on February 5, 2007.http://www.e-pao.net/epSubPageExtractor.asp?src=leisure.El.OinamAnand.

Angeline, B. (2007). *Initiatives to improve the quality of teaching and learning a review of recent literature.* Background paper prepared for the global monitoring report 2008, UNESCO 2008/ED/EFA/MRT/PI/12.

Biswal, K. (2011). *Secondary education in India: Development, Policies: Programs and challenges.* Create pathways to access, research monograph series No. 63.

Lall, M. (2005). *The challenges for India's education system.* Asia program, briefing paper ASP BP 05/03, Chatham House.

Linden, T. (2012). *Chapter 12: Secondary education.* India infrastructure report: Private sector in education, IDFC Foundation, Taylor and Francis Group, London.

Maclean, R. (2001). Overview: Secondary education at the cross roads. *Prospects, 31*(1), 39–45.

Right to Education Bill. (2005). http://www.education.nic.in/htmlweb/RighttoEducationBill2005.pdf.

UNDP. (2015). *Human development reports.* Oxford: Oxford University Press

UNESCO (UIS) (2012 and 2014). *Education statistics.*

World Development Indicators. (2015). *World bank.*

Chapter 8
Secondary Education in India: Growth, Performance, and Linkages

Abstract The recent initiatives undertaken for the universalization of elementary education has led to a dramatic growth in enrolments and improvements in retention and transition rates for elementary education, thereby resulting in an increased demand for the expansion of secondary education. Meeting this demand is essential firstly because secondary education forms the bridge between elementary and higher education, and secondly, the required input fulfils large manpower needs of the semi-organized and organized sectors of the economy. Also, investment in secondary education yields considerable social and private returns, offering young people the chance to acquire attitudes and skills that are unlikely to be developed in the primary grades. However, it is seen that as access to secondary education has expanded, its overall quality has often been on the decline as overstretched resources has combined with less efficient systems. Low participation rates and poor quality at the secondary stage are a bottleneck in improving both higher education participation and schooling at the elementary stage. In the light of the foregoing discussion, the present chapter aims to provide an in-depth review of trends in growth and performance of secondary education at the national level, covering various aspects such as expansion or access in terms of student enrolments, number of institutions, teachers, gender parity indicators, dropouts, transitions, etc. Along with these, the chapter also throws light on the management and financing issues of secondary education in India. Further, it evaluates the relationship between secondary education at the national level and socio-economic outcomes such as economic growth, health, demographic transition, employment, and income level. This is followed by the last section that summarizes major findings of the chapter.

Keywords Educational growth · Performance · Expenditure on education · Gross enrolment · Gender parity · School management

© Springer Nature Singapore Pte Ltd. 2018
C. Jain and N. Prasad, *Quality of Secondary Education in India*,
https://doi.org/10.1007/978-981-10-4929-3_8

8.1   Growth Trends

Achievement in basic education is the pre-requisite for the growth of secondary education besides other factors like accessibility, availability, and affordability. The data available for the last six decades clearly indicates that the achievement in basic education in terms of expansion of educational institutions, enrolment of students, and teachers is quite commendable mainly due to the success of Sarva Shiksha Abhiyan (SSA). The achievement of elementary education has thrown open the challenge of expanding access to secondary education. Rapid change in technology and demand of skilled labour also make it necessary for people to acquire more than eight years of education to compete in labour markets.

8.1.1   Institutions, Student Enrolments, and Teachers

In independent India, the network of educational institutions has expanded remarkably during the past six decades. The growth rate of secondary level schools during the period has increased from 7.4 thousand in 1950–51 to 79.7 thousand till 1990–91. The annual average growth rate of secondary schools during 1990–01 was 4.7% which remained almost stagnant or marginally higher at 4.8% during 2001–15 (that is, within a time period of 15 years). This raises the question whether the government had made ample investments towards the expansion of the infrastructure of secondary education. Within secondary educational institutions, 55.3% schools were lower secondary and the remaining 44.7% were senior secondary schools as reported in 2014–15. This is an improvement in case of senior secondary schools whose share was just 30.5% in 2001 amongst the secondary schools' category. Senior secondary schools have increased at a much faster rate than lower secondary schools in the last two decades. With regard to enrolment, nearly two-thirds of the students are enrolled with lower secondary level education, while about one-third remained with the senior secondary levels in 2014–15.

Apart from physical expansion of institutions, there has also been an improvement in the spatial distribution of schools at the secondary level of education. In 2007–08, 82.9% of rural and 99% of urban households had access to secondary schools within a distance of 5 km (GOI 2007–08). In comparison, more than 90% students in both rural and urban areas had accessibility to primary and middle schools within a distance of 1 and 3 km, respectively. According to the NSSO 71st Round (2014), there is a significant difference not only between rural and urban India, but also between primary and secondary schools in terms of physical access to schools. More than 12% of rural households in India have access to secondary schools at a distance of more than 5 km, while those households with secondary schools up to the distance of 5 km constitutes 27% of the rural households. Only 37% of rural households had secondary schools within a distance of 1 km. This proportion is 73% in case of urban India. In case of primary schools, 93–94%

rural–urban households had access to primary schools within 1 km. This indicates that although accessibility of secondary schools has improved over the years, we have to go a long way to make it accessible to all within a reach of 1 km in both urban and rural areas.

The population of children in the age group of (14–17) years has increased from 85.5 million in 2001 to 94.5 million in 2014, whereas the current enrolment in lower secondary and senior secondary education together have increased from 30.5 million in 2001–02 to nearly 61.8 million by 2014–15 (Table 8.1). This means that one-third of the eligible population remains out of the secondary school system which is not a good sign. However, the participation of girls at the secondary level of education has increased steadily over the years. In 2000–01, 32.7% of the total enrolments in secondary schools were for girls that reached 38.6% in 2010–11 and 47.3% in 2014–15.

Teachers form a vital input in the education process. The number of teachers has registered a substantial increase since 1990–91. The strength of teachers in secondary schools has increased from 1.3 million in 1990–91 to 1.76 million in 2000–01 and further to 3.3 million in 2014–15. The number of female teachers per hundred male teachers has improved over the years from 46 in 1990–91 to 49 in 2000–01 and to 66 in 2011–12. This is mainly due to more recruitment of female teachers after 2001.

Table 8.1 Number of institutions, enrolment and teachers by levels of school education in India

Years	Institutions (in '000s)			Enrolment (in millions)			Teachers (in '000s)		
	P	M	S	P	M	S	P	M	S
1950–51	209.7	13.6	7.4	19.3	3.1	1.5	538	86	127
1960–61	330.4	49.7	17.3	34.9	6.7	3.4	742	345	296
1970–71	408.4	90.6	37.1	57.1	13.3	7.6	1,060	638	629
1980–81	494.5	118.6	51.5	73.8	20.7	11	1,363	851	926
1990–91	560.9	151.5	79.8	97.4	34	19.1	1,616	1,073	1,334
2000–01	638.7	206.3	126.0	113.8	42.8	27.6	1,896	1,326	1,761
2004–05	767.5	274.7	152.0	130.8	51.2	37.1	2,161	1,589	2,083
2005–06	772.6	288.5	159.7	132.1	52.2	38.4	2,184	1,671	2,154
2006–07	784.9	305.6	169.6	133.7	54.5	39.9	2,323	1,717	2,248
2007–08	787.8	325.2	173.0	135.5	57.3	44.5	2,315	1,780	2,127
2008–09	778.8	365.6	186.3	135.3	58.4	46.4	2,229	1,899	2,218
2009–10	819.9	394.1	193.8	133.6	59.5	48.5	2,217	1,778	2,330
2010–11	748.5	447.6	203.2	134.7	61.9	51.3	2,099	1,887	2,508
2011–12	714.3	478.8	212.5	139.8	63.0	55.1	2,254	2,057	2,466
2012–13	853.9	577.8	341.3	134.8	65.0	54.6	2,656	2,427	2,742
2013–14	858.9	421.5	237.1	132.4	66.4	59.6	2,684	2,513	3,071
2014–15	847.1	425.1	244.9	130.5	67.4	61.8	2,670	2,560	3,332

Source Based on Selected Educational Statistics, various years
Note P primary, *M* middle and *S* secondary

Despite the fact that the network of schools, enrolments, and teachers has expanded over the years for all levels of school education, there exists huge differences between various levels of school education. The number of secondary level institutions remains much lower even today compared to that of the middle and primary level institutions and so is the case of student enrolments. However, in case of number of teachers, the situation of secondary schools is better than middle and primary level now. The growth of the system in terms of institutions, enrolment, and teachers could be on account of a multiple set of inter-related factors: an increased demand for secondary education because of the rise in the enrolment at elementary levels of education; increase in the social demand for education; and finally, public policies plays a vital role in the development of nation. Despite the long implementation lag, there has been improvement in the access and continuity in schooling. The rise in the share of the population shift to the service sector leading to overall higher per capita income in the country is being reflected in the growth and demand for secondary education.

8.1.2 Gross Enrolment Ratios

Gross enrolment ratio (GER) estimates the number of children enrolled in a particular level of education among the child population of that age group. The data shows that the participation in secondary education has improved over the years. GER at secondary stage has increased from 33.3% in 2001 to 52.2% in 2010–11 and further to 65% in 2014–15. For the other two levels of school education, that is, primary and middle level, GER is comparatively much higher at 100.1 and 91.2% (as in 2014–15). At the secondary level, the increase in gross enrolment ratios had been modest (Fig. 8.1). Over more than two decades (1990–91 to 2010–11), the GER has nearly touched 50% enrolment ratios in the country. This shows that the progress seems to have been very low. Despite this, the good point is that GER for secondary education is increasing at a steady rate from 2000–01 onwards.

It may be noted here that the bifurcation of GER figures for the lower secondary stage (Ninth–Tenth standards) and senior secondary (Eleventh–Twelfth standards) were not available separately until 2004–05, making it difficult to study their growth trends before this period. In 2004–05, the GER at the lower secondary stage (Ninth–Tenth standards) was 51.7%, which increased to 78.5% in 2014–15; hence only around 4.3% improvement is evident during this period. Similarly, the GER at the senior secondary stage (Eleventh–Twelfth standards) was 27.8% in 2004–05 in India, which increased to 54.2% in 2014–15, only around 7% improvement in its size. The rate of growth in GER is higher in senior secondary levels as compared to lower secondary level. However, improvement in GERs at both lower secondary and senior secondary levels for all categories is driven by a number of factors including general lack of access, paucity of public schools, high cost of private senior secondary education, and poor quality of education, along with high opportunity cost of deferred entry into the workforce. India's GER at the secondary

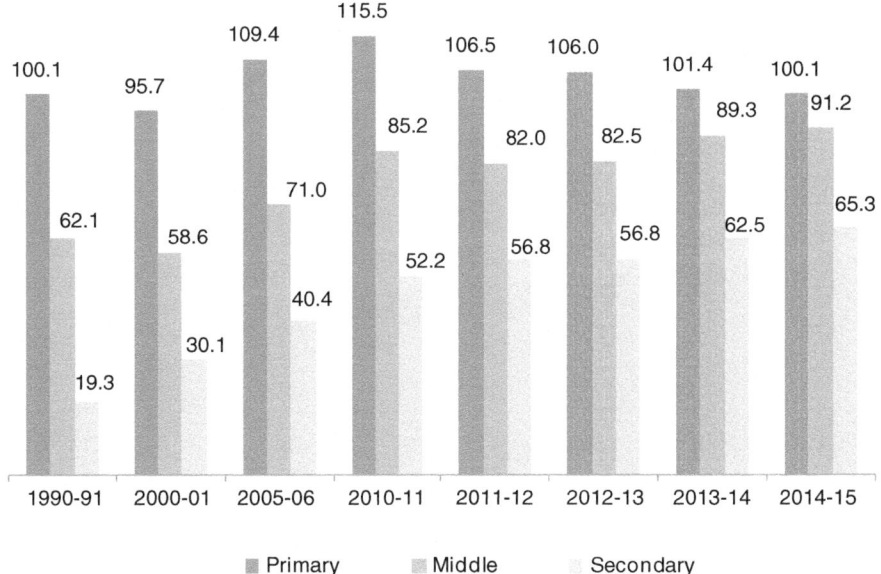

Fig. 8.1 Trends in gross enrolment ratios by level of school education. *Source* Based on Selected Educational Statistics, various years

level is close to that of the average for all developing countries (65%), but substantially lower than that of emerging economies like China, Indonesia, Thailand, and Brazil.

8.1.3 Gender Parity Index

Even after visible progress in secondary education, regional, gender, and social disparities in access and participation continue to be a major concern. Although the share of girls in the total enrolment at the secondary stages (Ninth–Twelfth standards) has increased substantially from 27% in 2000–01 to 47.3% in 2014–15, the wide gap in the participation of boys and girls still exists. Girls' GER for secondary level of education together from 1990–91 to 2010–11 has increased by the annual growth rate of 1.8% only, while in case of boys, it is much higher at 8.8%. It is only after 2000–01 that the growth rate in the enrolment of girls has increased sharply. The available data shows that between 2000–01 and 2014–15, the GER of girls, on an average, has increased by 7% annually, higher than that of 4.4%, as recorded in case of enrolment of boys. Within lower secondary level of education, the GER for boys and girls is 78.1 and 78.9% in 2014–15, while at the senior secondary level, this proportion is 54.6 and 53.8% for boys and girls, respectively. Till 2010–11, the gap in GER between boys and girls was higher at both levels of secondary education particularly at lower secondary level of education but since then it has

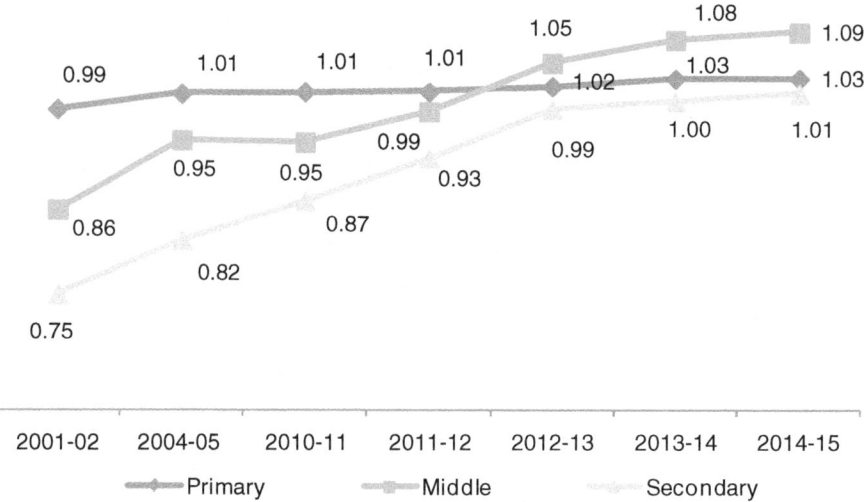

Fig. 8.2 Gender parity index. *Source* Statistics of School Education 2014–15, Educational Statistics at Glance, MHRD (2016)

declined gradually and now has reached to the point where both boys and girls at the secondary level reflects equal participation in terms of GER.

The gap between male and female enrolments is given here by gender parity index (GPI). GPI is defined as a socioeconomic index usually designed to measure the relative access to education of males and females. In its simplest form, it is calculated as the quotient of the number of females by the number of males enrolled in a given stage of education (primary, secondary etc.). Among all levels of school education, GPI is lowest for secondary education. Gender Parity Index for secondary education has improved from 0.80 points in 2005–06 to 0.87 points in 2010–11 and 1.01 in 2014–15. In comparison, GPI is 1.09 points in case of middle-level schooling and 1.03 in case of primary education in 2014–15 (Fig. 8.2).

In 2011–12, the GPI for secondary education has improved tremendously to 0.93 as a result of new schemes launched for girls' enrolment in senior secondary level during the Twelfth Five Year Plan. Within secondary education, the GPI is higher for lower secondary level than senior secondary level of education in 2014–15.

8.2   The Performance of Secondary Education

It is generally seen that the expansion of secondary education is simply looked at in terms of institutions, enrolment, teachers, or GERs, but besides these growth indicators, it is equally important to measure the performance of the sector. Simply measuring the expansion of inputs would not reflect the accurate picture of overall growth of the education system unless the growth in inputs is linked with the final outcomes. The outcome indicators in the development of secondary education have been discussed here in terms of examining the transition rates, dropout rates and completion rates in secondary education.

8.2.1 Transition Rates and Promotion Rates

Although in recent years there has been an increase in the participation in secondary education, there still exists a large gap between movements of students from the Eighth to Ninth grade. This is well captured here by the trends in transition rates over the years. Transition rate refers to percentage of students joining from one level to the next level of education (Varghese and Mehta 1998). Figure 8.3 shows that at the all-India level, there has always been substantial transition loss between elementary and secondary stages, although this gap is now reducing but at a very slow rate. The transition of students from the elementary to secondary level has increased from 86.9% in 1980–81 to 89% after two decades in 2010–11 and further to 90.6% in 2014–15. Even though secondary enrolment had increased much more during the same period, but no such improvement is visible at the transition rates. Moreover, transition from secondary to higher secondary is just 69% in 2014–15.

Another measure is promotion rates which indicate the transfer/promotion of students between various levels of education. Since data on the number of repeaters

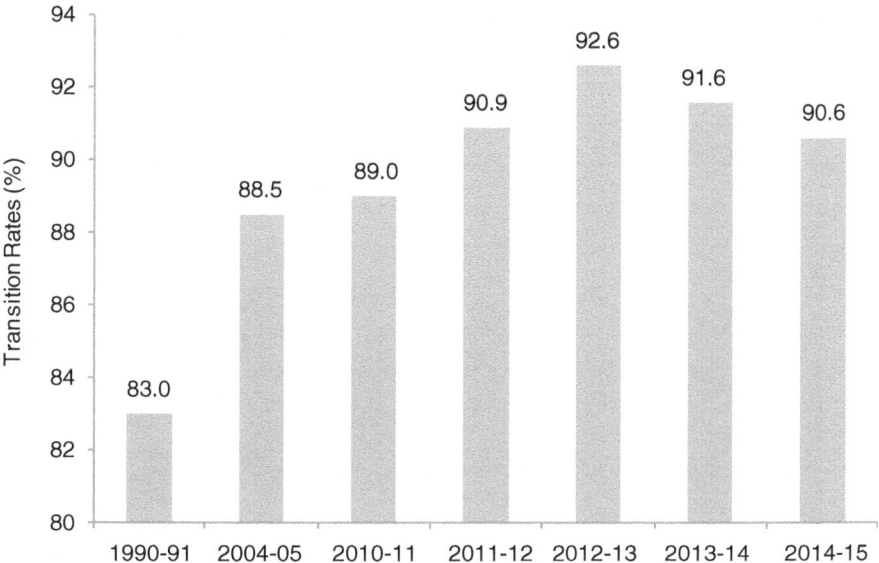

Fig. 8.3 Transition rates from middle to lower secondary education in India. *Source* Paper by Varghese and Mehta, NUEPA and 2010–11 figures taken from UNESCO Institute of Statistics (UIS Statistics in Brief-Education all levels profile-India)

was not available year-wise, hence, ratios of enrolments at various levels were considered. The promotion rate for Eighth–Ninth standards in this study indicates the ratio of enrolments of students in the Ninth Standard in a particular year to that of students' enrolment in the Eighth Standard in the previous year. While the promotion rate from the Ninth to Tenth Standard seems to be very low, it is higher in case of Eighth to Ninth Standard. The promotion rate from Eighth to Ninth Standard is 95.4% in 2014–15 which indicates that out of every 100 students enrolled in the Eighth Standard only 95 students are able to enroll themselves in the Ninth Standard. In the case of those moving from the Ninth to Tenth Standard, it is 79.9%, while it has increased to 98.8% for those shifting from Eleventh to Twelfth Standard (as in 2014–15). This clearly reveals that although the gap between upper middle and lower secondary level is declining over the years, the pace of movement from lower secondary to higher secondary is slow. Hence, it would take a long way for universalization of secondary education unless some strong and effective policy measures are taken.

8.2.2   Dropout Rates

Dropout rates is a major problem in secondary education as compared to other levels of school education (Fig. 8.4). How well an education system has performed

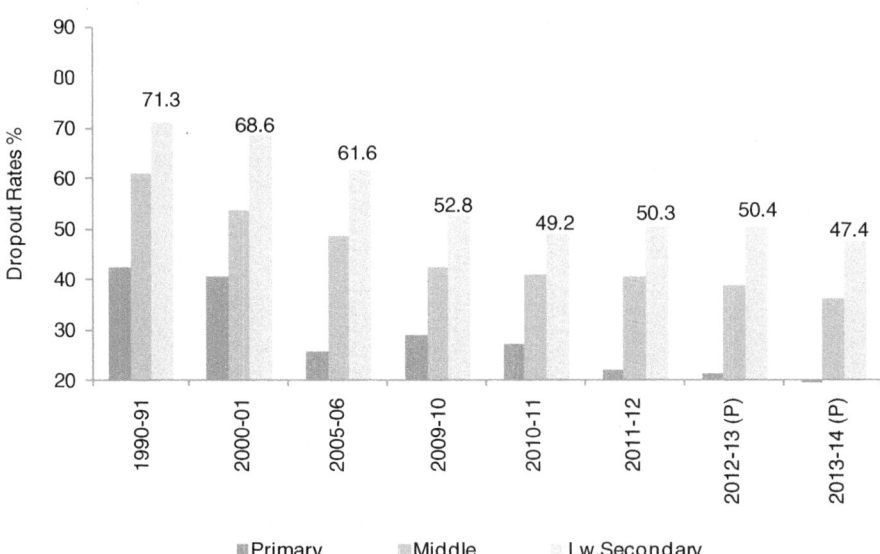

Fig. 8.4 Trends in drop-out rates in school education in India. *Source* Ministry of Human Resource Development Govt. of India. (13456) and Rajya Sabha Unstarred Question No. 867, dated on 30.11.2012 and Statistics of School Education 2014–15, Educational Statistics at Glance, MHRD (2016)

can be measured by its ability to minimize the dropout rates. The reduced level of dropout rates gives a strong indication of its development and growth. Although the dropout rates have declined over the years, they are much higher compared to other levels of education. Moreover, the rate of decline in dropout rates has been quite slow as seen in the last three decades. From 2000–01 to 2013–14, the dropout rates declined with growth rate of 2.8% in secondary education; however, it dropped to the level of 47.4% in 2013–14. It is important to note that from 2005–06, the dropout rate in secondary education declined by higher growth rate of 3.2% till 2013–14. As compared to secondary education, the dropout rates in primary and middle level was much lower at 19.8 and 36.3%, respectively, in 2013–14.

The new estimates of dropout rates show that the average annual dropout rate among school education levels is highest in case of secondary education (at 17.8%), in comparison to primary and middle education (3.7 and 4.1%, respectively, in 2013–14). Gender bifurcation reveals that till 2008–09, the dropout rates in secondary education was higher for girls compared to that of boys; however thereafter, the dropout rates for boys was higher than girls. In 2013, the average annual dropout rate for girls was at 17.7%, while for boys it was 17.9% (from First–Tenth standards). The same is in case of middle-level education, while at the primary level, girls' dropout rates are lower than that of boys. On an average, almost 17.8% of the pupils reflect dropouts on an annual basis, which indicate huge wastage in school education in India. This is an important proxy indicator of low efficiency of the school system in the country.

Few studies have been conducted to understand the reasons behind these huge dropout rates. The results reveal that both school and family factors were responsible for this. It was found that adolescents dropout not merely due to poverty or financial constraints but also because schools did not respond to their special education needs. Further, the students may also dropout due to factors such as uncongenial atmosphere, poor comprehensions, absenteeism, attitude and behavior of teachers, failures or repetition of the same grades. In some cases, students dropout due to family pressures, financial constraints, or get engaged in work to earn for the family. It is really important to carefully design the preventive measures and intervention strategies that could be adopted in order to help the dropout students.

8.2.3 Completion Rates

Completion rates in secondary education are an important indication of successful education. Completion of secondary education is considered the minimum requirement for taking part in a global knowledge economy. Completion rates in high schools are analysed by looking at the proportion of successful students who has appeared among those enrolled. Along with the low transition rates and high dropout rates, another major problem raising the question on quality and

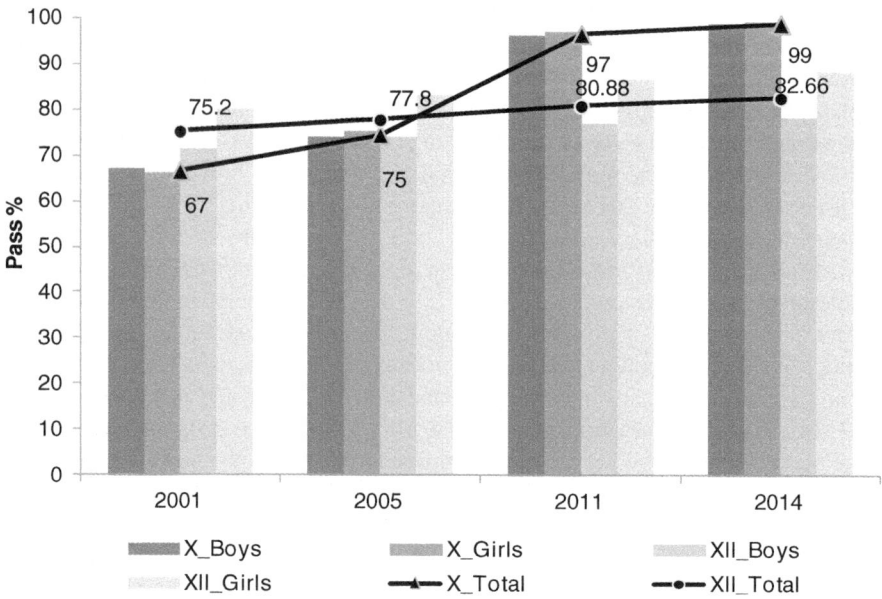

Fig. 8.5 Passed percentage in secondary level of education in India. *Source* Taken from paper by Rani (NUEPA) till 2000; from 2006 onwards Educational Statistics at Glance, MHRD (2016), CBSE data

performance of secondary level education is low completion rates at both lower secondary and senior secondary level of education

Figure 8.5 reveals the fact that the percentage of passed students in lower secondary level is better compared to the percentage of successful students in higher secondary schools. In 2005, among the total students who appeared for the Twelfth Standard examination, 76.8% passed out at all-India level, while for the Tenth Standard, lower proportion of students, that is, 75% cleared the exam. At this stage, about 25% of the students were not able to reach higher secondary level of education. Not only the proportion of students passing these examinations are low, but as pointed out by one study (Rani 2007), for every ten students enrolled in high schools only six students appeared for the board examination. This indicates that even within the system of secondary education, that is, within the Tenth–Twelfth standards, a high proportion of students move out of the chain. It may be due to the fact that the system of board examination at lower secondary school level had already filtered the students with low levels of competencies. Hence, only the better performing students enter the higher secondary schools.

After introducing grading system in 2009–10, a significant jump in passing percentage at this level has been observed. As a result, the proportion of students passing from the Twelfth Standard increased to 81% in 2011 and reached 83% in 2014, whereas from the Tenth Standard, it increased to 97% in 2011 and further to 99% in 2014 (CBSE Result 2011, 2014 GOI). It may also be noted that although

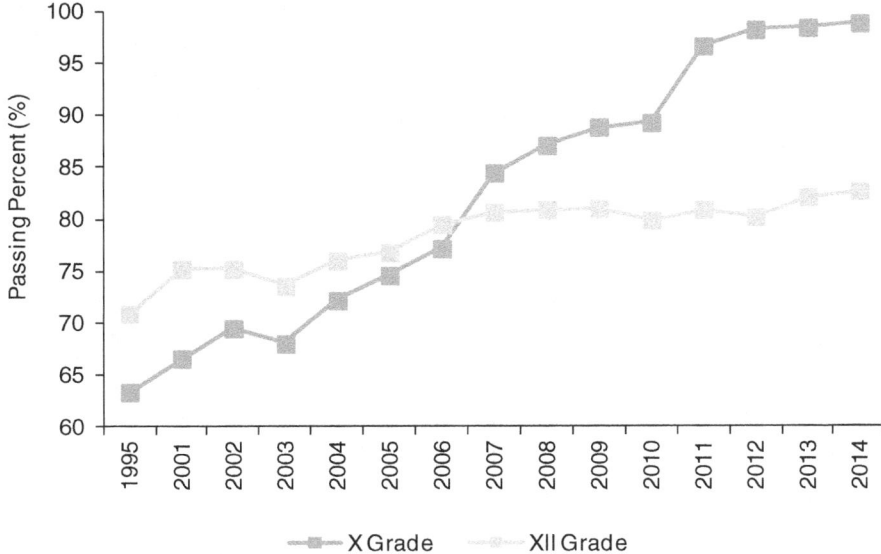

Fig. 8.6 Percentage of students passing from CBSE board examinations. *Source* CBSE Board Result 2014

enrolment rates and the proportion of girls appeared for secondary exams are lower than that of boys, however, the passing percentage is higher in case of girls at both lower secondary and senior secondary levels. In 2014, nearly 89% girls passed out Twelfth Standard examinations, while this proportion was 78% in the case of boys. Similarly, for the Tenth Standard, 99% of both girls and boys passed out the examination. The performance of girls has always outshined boys and a similar trend has been seen during the last two decades as well. This indicates that if given a chance, girls can perform better than boys.

It is interesting to note that till 2006, the performance of Twelfth Standard was better than Tenth Standard; however, from 2007 onwards the performance rate of Tenth Standard outshined the passing percentage of Twelfth Standard (Fig. 8.6). From 2010 onwards, the passing percentage for Tenth Standard increased significantly compared to the previous few years. It has almost reached near to 100% in 2014. The main reason behind such a remarkable improvement has been the introduction of grading system (made effective from 2009–10 by CBSE).[1] According to this new system, those awarded qualifying grades (D and above) in all the subjects excluding additional subject are eligible for admission in the Eleventh Standard and the practice of declaring compartment/fail was discontinued. While

---

[1]CBSE was established in 1929 and has about 15,000 affiliated schools in India and across four countries across the world. The Board conducts final examinations every spring for All India Senior School Certificate Examination (AISSCE) for the Tenth and Twelfth standards. The Board has eight regional offices in different parts of the country.

this system, on one hand, has improved the passing percentage in recent years and has given chance to more number students to enter into senior level of education, it has also adversely affected the overall quality of learning outcomes and teaching atmosphere in schools.

Overall, at the all-India level, the extent of ineffectiveness of secondary education in the country can be well understood by the steepness of the pyramid that reflects the skewed slope with relatively broad base of GER and a narrow top of passed out students successfully completing secondary education cycle. The challenges in secondary education system are rather multiple, that is, expanding accessibility and simultaneously improving effectiveness in terms of arresting dropout rates and improving completion rates. Moreover, it should be seen that the strategies developed in order to increase the passing percentage of students so that more students can enter the next level of education, should not affect the overall quality of learning and teaching.

8.3 Management of Schools by Level of Education

India has a long tradition of partnership between public and private sectors in secondary education. There are four types of schools: (a) government—established by state governments (as well as some centrally established institutions); (b) local body—established by elected local government bodies; (c) aided schools—private schools that receive state government grants-in-aid; and (d) private unaided schools. Government and local bodies are entirely managed and financed by public sector. These types of schools are known as government schools and accounts for approximately 40% of the total secondary schools.

Private schools that receive grants-in-aid are financed by the states and not by central government. Aided schools receive regular public funding to pay salaries to teachers and administrative staff but they remain under private management and finance their own capital expenditures. These types of schools are allowed to collect voluntary contributions from parents, but their fee is subject to government regulations. Private unaided schools, on the other hand, are entirely financed by school fees and funds raised by themselves. They have more autonomy regarding their curriculum, medium of instruction, student type, pupil–teacher ratio, and fee structure. However, for teachers' administration like their qualifications and condition of services, they have to follow state legislations. As per the latest available estimates, the share of such schools in India is 36% (as in 2011–12).

Overall, about 60% of the lower and senior secondary schools in India are privately managed (both aided and unaided). It is essential, therefore, that the private sector's capabilities and potential are tapped through innovative public–private partnerships, while concurrently stepping up public investment by the central and state governments at the secondary level. Considering the increasing demand for private-owned schools, the Twelfth Five Year Plan has made various interventions, setting up 6,000 high quality secondary model schools at the block level, 3,500 schools in partnership with state, 2,500 model schools in public–private partnership (PPP) mode, and upgradation of 11,200 upper primary schools to secondary schools to meet the increased demand by 2017. However, how far these targets have been achieved is visible only after the completion of the Twelfth Five Year Plan.

The available data shows that the share of local body and government schools is declining over the years with private unaided schools showing an increase from 24% in 2001–02 to 60% in 2011–12. Most of the growth of secondary schools in the private sector in the last two decades has occurred among unaided schools which indicate that parents are willing to pay for education that is perceived to be of good quality. A growing dissatisfaction with the quality of public education has led to an increased focus on private education. Even few studies have been carried out in different parts of India (Tamil Nadu, Madhya Pradesh and Uttar Pradesh respectively) concluding that private school students generally outperform their public school counterparts in learning achievement even after controlling for schools student intakes (Govinda and Varghese 1993; Kingdon 1996).

Figure 8.7 clearly depicts that the percentage share of government and local body schools is lower in case of secondary education during 2011–12, while it was quite high in case of primary and middle-level schools. In case of lower secondary and senior secondary levels, the share of private unaided schools is highest at 37.6 and 40.3%, whereas for private aided schools the share is 22% for lower secondary and 26% for senior secondary. This shows that contribution of the private sector is higher in case of secondary levels of education, while for those below this level, the government plays a major role.

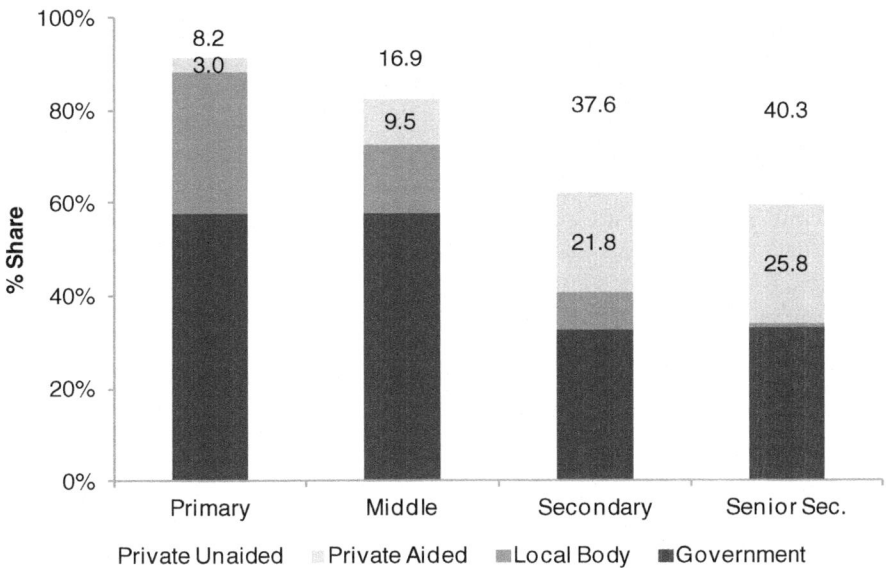

Fig. 8.7 Number of institutions by management (% share). *Source* Statistics of School Education 2014–15, Educational Statistics at Glance, MHRD (2016)

8.4   Financing of Secondary Education

The basic purpose of planning in India is to widen people's choices and improve their well-being. In this context, promoting human development is the key issue so that people could lead a long and healthy life, acquire knowledge and a decent standard of living. Education is an important and basic input required to improve the quality of human resources. For overall expansion of secondary education in India, huge investments are required from both public and private sources. It is evidenced that early expansion of public investment in secondary education paid rich dividends in East Asia (Tilak 2001). Therefore, one of the necessary conditions for the overall development of a nation is improvement in the quality of human resources through proper investment in education. The financing of education sector includes both public and private sources which are discussed in detail in this section.

8.4.1   Public Expenditure on Education

Recognizing the importance of education in national development, various Five Year Plans have placed an unprecedented focus on the expansion of education, improvement of its quality, and assurance that educational opportunities are available to all segments of the society through its budgetary allocations. The budgets of the central government as well as the state governments are classified into Plan (broadly development) and Non-Plan (broadly maintenance) outlays. Moreover, expenditure on revenue accounts constitutes the bulk of the budget expenditure on education in India. The data for 2013–14 shows that that the states are contributing about 73.3% of the total revenue expenditure on education in the country, while the centre contributes about 26.7% to the education sector as a whole (GOI 2013–14). The total revenue account of Rs. 465,142 crore constitutes 15.7% of the total budget of the centre and the states for 2013–14. About 82.7% of the central expenditure on education is under plan, whereas in the case of states/union territories, it is only 21.03% in the year 2013–14. Table 8.2 gives the contribution of government at both state and central levels together as per the Five Year Plans.

The data clearly reveals that although the pattern of spending in education has increased, it has not changed much over the Five Year Plans. The total expenditure on education as percentage of total outlay was 7.6% in the First Five Year Plan, which thereafter declined and even touched 2.7% during the Sixth Five Year Plan (Document of Tenth Five year plan 2002–07). This proportion has reached just at 9.5% in the Eleventh Five Year Plan, even after a span of 60 years. The more discouraging fact has been the expenditure on education as a percentage of total social sector expenditure which is 31.5% in the Eleventh Five Year Plan (2007–12), while it remained above 32% throughout till the Fourth Five Year Plan.

Coming to the expenditure on education as percent of GDP plan-wise, the data shows that the percentage share increased gradually till the Seventh Five Year Plan. However, since the Eighth Five Year Plan, it started reporting fluctuations. During

Table 8.2 Education expenditure outlay by five year plans

Five year plans	Total outlay (in crores)	Exp. on social sector as % of total exp.	Exp. on educ. as % of total exp.	Exp. on education as % of social sector exp.	Exp. on primary education as % of total plan exp.	Exp. on secondary education as % of total plan exp.	Exp. on higher education as % of total plan exp.	Exp. on education as % of GDP
I	1,960	20.2	7.6	36.5	56	13	31	0.76
II	4,672	16.5	5.9	35.5	35	19	46	1.29
III	8,577	14.5	6.9	47.2	34	18	48	1.56
IV	15,779	15.1	4.9	32.6	30	18	52	2.16
V	39,426	17.3	4.3	25.0	35	17	48	2.63
VI	110,467	14.4	2.7	18.7	30	25	45	3.14
VII	221,435	15.8	3.5	22.0	34	22	44	3.69
VIII	485,457	18.3	4.5	24.3	47	18	35	3.58
IX	813,998	23.5	6.1	26.0	66	11	23	3.95
X	1,618,460	27.0	6.3	23.2	66	10	24	3.45
XI	3,644,718	30.2	9.5	31.5	50	20	30	3.92

Source Analysis of budgeted expenditure on education, various years, MHRD, GOI

the Eighth Five Year Plan (1992–97), the education expenditure as percentage of GDP was 3.58% which has reached to 3.92% during the Eleventh Five Year Plan.

It is important to mention here that the Central Advisory Board of Education (CABE) committee on financing higher and technical education 2005 suggested that of the agreed 6% of GDP to education, 3% (50%) is to be allocated to elementary education, 1.5% (25%) to secondary education, 1% (16.7%) to higher general education, and 0.5% (8.3%) to higher technical education (NCERT 2005). In the Eleventh Five Year Plan, out of the total plan outlay for education, around 50% for elementary education and literacy, 20% for secondary education and 30% for higher education, including technical education was allocated. On the other hand, in the First Five Year Plan, out of the total Plan expenditure for education, there was 56% for the elementary level, 13% for secondary level, and 31% for the development of higher education. Hence, in the last 60 years, the share of Plan expenditure on secondary education has increased from 13% to mere 20%, which is quite low. In this sense, it is not wrong to mention that so far the government has not been able to contribute as much as desired, especially for secondary level of education. Although, in absolute terms the outlays might have increased over the Five Year Plans, but in terms of percentage shares of public expenditure and GDPs there are huge fluctuations in the pattern of spending in education over the years.

How much the Government of India is interested in developing education facilities in the country can be understood, among other things, from the trends in public expenditure on education. Public expenditure on education as a percentage of GDP is considered as an indicator of state policy towards promoting education. How much a country should invest in education as a proportion of their GDP depends on many factors and the level of economic growth. Normally, expenditure on education should grow at double the rate of economic growth in the early stages of educational development (Tilak 2006). In India, in 1966, D.S. Kothari Commission on education had recommended that we should allocate 6% of GDP to education and the same was accepted by the Government of India which is reflected in the National Policy on Education 1986. The pattern of public expenditure on education as a percentage of GDP not only shows an irregular rise and fall but also reflects that the goal of 6% investment in education sector still remains unfulfilled.

The decadal public expenditure on education as percentage of GDP is calculated taking the averages for each decade starting from 1950 till 2011. The analysis shows that the public expenditure on education was 1.1% of GDP during 1950–61 which gradually increased to 3.6% of GDP in 1980–91. Thereafter, it increased but at a very slow rate during 1990–2001, but in the last decade, that is, from 2000 to 2011 it dropped again. Overall, the public expenditure on education as percent of GDP stood at 3.7% for the decade 2000–2011, down from 3.8% during 1990–2001. This decline during 2000–2011 indicates that the growth in educational spending by the government has not been in pace with the economic growth.

The annual share of educational expenditures as percent of GDP and percent of public expenditure indicates that the education sector has always received low priority in comparison to other sectors in the economy (Fig. 8.8). Although in absolute terms, the public expenditure on education has increased from

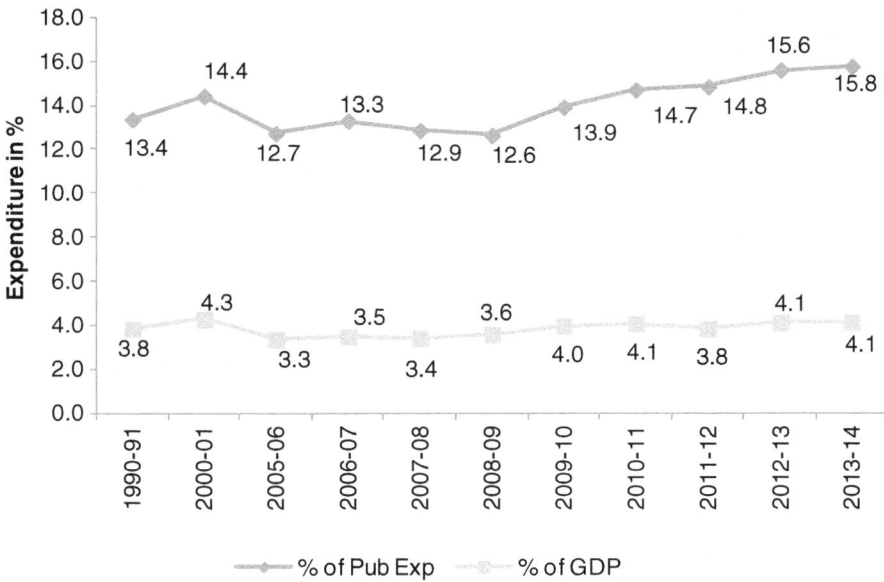

Fig. 8.8 Annual education expenditure as percent of GDP and percent of public expenditure. *Source* Calculation based on data from CSO and budgeted expenditure on education, MHRD, GOI, various years

Rs. 64.46 crore in 1950–51 to Rs. 365,963 crore in 2013–14 (Kumar 2011 and Analysis of Budgeted expenditure, GOI). In relative terms, public expenditure on education has never crossed 15% in the last six decades, until recently in 2011–12 when the share of public expenditure on education stood at 15.6%. As a percentage of GDP, the public expenditure on education has crossed 4% only for five times in the following six decades: 2000–01, 2009–10, 2000–10, 2012–13, and 2013–14. The latest available data shows that public expenditure on education as percent of GDP is 4.13% in 2013–14.

Unlike up to the Tenth Five Year Plans, the Eleventh Five Year Plan has recognized the importance of education and has increased the public spending on education. During the Eleventh Plan, the share of spending in secondary education increased by less than 2% between 2007–08 and 2011–12, while in case of university education it increased by nearly one percent only. During the Eleventh Five Year Plan, education expenditure as percentage of GDP rose from 3.4% in 2007–08 to over 3.8% in 2011–12. The bulk of public spending on education is incurred by the state governments and their spending grew at a robust rate of 19.6% per year during the Eleventh Plan, whereas central spending on education increased even faster at 25% per year during the same period. Aggregate public spending on education during the Eleventh Plan period is estimated at Rs. 1,244,797 crore for both the centre and states taken together. Of this, about 43% of the public expenditure on education was incurred for elementary education, 25% for secondary education, and the balance 32% for higher education. In the state sector,

44% of the expenditure is on elementary education and 30% on secondary education, while in the case of central government's expenditure, secondary education constitutes 12% share only. Public expenditure on secondary education has increased from Rs. 35,806 crore in 2007–08 to Rs. 94,183 crore in 2011–12, leading to an increase in its share as a percentage of GDP from 0.78 to 1.05% in 2011–12, but in 2013–14 it declined to 1.03% of GDP. In 2013–14, major share of 52.4% goes to elementary education; the second priority goes to university and higher education with 20.19% share, followed by secondary education at third place with 11.9% of share.

On the whole, the imbalance in the pattern of public expenditure within school education system in India is quite visible. While India spends around 60.6% of plan education budget on elementary education, secondary education receives only about 19.6% of the budget (2013–14). The major area of concern is that over the years there has been increase in private expenditures on post compulsory levels of education, while the public subsidy has remained more or less stagnant.

8.4.2 Private Expenditure on Education

Private expenditure on education incurs expenditure in the form of payment of fees of different kinds, purchase of books, stationery and uniforms, expenses on conveyance, private coaching, etc., by the households. The available estimates as released by the National Sample Survey (NSSO) reveal that Indian households are increasingly spending more and more on education. The share of households' expenditure on education has increased from 2% in 1993–94 to 7% in 2011–12. Education has witnessed one of the fastest growth rates among different expenditures heads of household expenditure. The NSSO survey in 2011–12 shows that nearly 65.8% of rural families and 75.6% of the urban families are spending on education. Educational expenditure per person per month in 2011–12 was about Rs. 50 (3.5% of monthly per capita expenditure, i.e., MPCE) in rural India and Rs. 181.50 (about 7% of MPCE) in urban India. During 2007–08 to 2014, the private spending on education has increased by 18.4% per annum (MOSPI 2015). Average per student educational expenditure was, however, as much as 2.3 times higher in the urban sector than in the rural in 2014. Among major components of private expenditure on general education about 46% of the share of household annual expenditures goes for tuition fees followed by stationery, books, uniform each of which constitute 22% (as in 2014). This private coaching accounting for 15% of total spending and transportation cost constituting 11% share. In rural India, course fee, which includes tuition fee, examination fee, and other compulsory payments, contributed 41% of the total expenditure while another 27% was spent on books and stationery. In urban areas, more than 50% of the educational expenditure was spent on course fee.

Table 8.3 gives a comparative view of average annual private expenditure on education by various levels in 1995–96 to 2014. It shows that the average annual expenditure on general education increased from Rs. 904 in 1995–96 to Rs. 2,461

Table 8.3 Average annual private expenditure per student by level of education

Level of education	1995–96			2007–08			2014		
	Total	Rural	Urban	Total	Rural	Urban	Total	Rural	Urban
Primary	501	297	1,149	1,413	826	3,266	4,610	2,811	10,083
Middle	915	640	1,529	2,088	1,370	4,264	5,386	3,242	11,446
Secondary	1,577	1,180	2,219	4,351	3,019	7,212	7,459[a]	5,100[a]	13,547[a]
Overall	904	570	1,686	2,461	1,551	5,128	6,788	4,487	12,904

Note [a]Excludes higher secondary expenditure
Source NSSO 71st, 64th and 52nd round

in 2007–08. In rural India, the average annual expenditure on education per student has gone up from Rs. 570 in 1995–96 to Rs. 1,551 in 2007–08, while in the urban sector it has increased from Rs. 1,618 to Rs. 5,122 in 2007–08. As per latest NSS estimates 2014, average annual expenditure on general education increased to Rs. 6,788 with Rs. 4,487 average spending in rural and Rs. 12,904 in urban areas (MOSPI 2014). The 2014 NSS data shows that on secondary education, on an average, Rs. 7,459 per student was spent, while this was Rs. 12,619 in the senior secondary level. In comparison, the expenditure per student was lower in the primary and middle-level education, clearly indicating that secondary education is the most costly among school education. The household annual share on secondary education has increased by nearly 2.5 times in 2014 over 2007–08.

Private expenditure by types of institutions shows that the average annual household expenditure has increased maximum in case of private unaided institutions followed by private aided ones. The latest NSS data 2014 shows that at the secondary level, average expenditure in government institutions was Rs. 3,724 against Rs. 15,785 in private unaided institutions (4.2 times higher), whereas for higher secondary level expenditure at private unaided institutions was nearly three times of that in government institutions (Fig. 8.9). Even within government institutions, the average expenditure incurred on secondary education is more than three times higher than primary education and at the higher secondary level it is six times higher. The average expenditure incurred at private unaided institutions for higher secondary level is double than that of primary education. A huge difference is found in the average educational expenditure between schools run by government and the private ones. At the secondary level, average expenditure varied between three–four times for urban and rural sectors between government- and private-aided schools.

On the whole, it is quite clear that the private share of education expenditure is significant in India and has increased manifold over the years. In spite of that huge inequalities exist at various levels of education, between rural and urban sectors and in various economic sections of society. The main reason behind the increase in private share of expenditure on education has been the growing demand for private schools that comes at a higher price. Among all types of institutions, the demand is reflected the highest in case of private unaided institutions followed by the private aided ones. The striking fact is that compared to university-level education, school-level education seems to be more expensive in India.

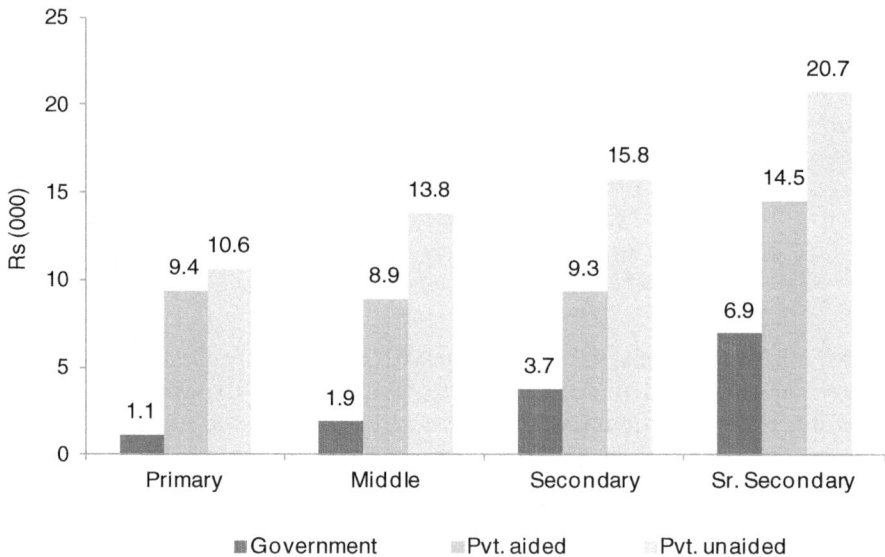

Fig. 8.9 Average annual private expenditure per student on education by school type and level of education. *Source* Education in India, NSS Report 575 (2014)

8.5　Secondary Education and Socio-economic Benefits[2]

That expenditure incurred on education is an investment is now a well-established and widely-accepted idea. Like other investments, it is natural to ask whether or not the benefits from education are worth the costs. A vast literature has emerged over the years documenting the magnitude of the returns. Microeconomic evidences suggest that private returns to education are substantial and its impacts on social outcomes are significant (Psacharopolous and Patrinos 2004). Different methods have been used by different researchers in finding statistically significant and economically plausible impacts of education on growth regressions. Few studies shows that investment in secondary education yields considerable social and private returns, offering young people the chance to acquire attitudes and skills that are unlikely to be developed in the primary grades. This in turn enables youth to develop job-oriented skills, participate fully in society, take control of their own lives, and continue learning (Mingat and Tan 1996; Lewin and Caillods 2001). Now it is well accepted that the benefits of education extend to economic factors as it also affects health, employment patterns, and productivity of individuals, reinforcing

---

[2]The analysis presented in this section is part of the paper entitled 'Evidences of Linkage between Secondary Education and Socio-Economic Outcomes in India' by Jain and Prasad published in the Journal of Educational Planning and Administration (JEPA), NUEPA, Jan 2016 issue.

economic growth and human welfare. This section will review the importance and contribution of secondary education in terms of its linkages with economic, health, demographic performances and income levels all over India.

8.5.1   Economic Linkages

Education is a force that develops well-rounded and engaged citizens, and builds more cohesive and participatory societies. Access to and completion of education is a key determinant in the accumulation of human capital and economic growth. For faster economic growth, it is not sufficient to exclusively concentrate on primary education. It is evidenced that early expansion of public investment in secondary education paid rich dividends in East Asia (Tilak 2001). To measure the impact of school education on economic performance of the country, three indexes have been developed: Elementary Education Development Index, Secondary Education Development Index, and Economic Performance Index through Principal Component analysis (*for details about development of national level indexes refer* Chap. 6). Simple linear regressions were run to estimate the relationship of elementary and secondary level education (independent variables) on economic performances (dependent variable). The results of regression are presented in Table 8.4.

The regression shows that other things being constant, about 80% of the variation in Economic Performance Index is due to school-level educational development which is a good fit model. The result suggests that secondary education development index has a positive impact on Economic Performance Index, while elementary education development index shows insignificant results. It also shows that an additional unit of improvement in the secondary education development index can increase the Economic Performance Index by 0.6 units. Even a small unit, in this case, can bring huge change in economic growth and development. In addition to this, separate regressions were also estimated taking gross enrolments in various education levels as independent variables to see its impact on GDP at factor cost and per capita national income (Jain and Prasad 2016). The results were positive and significant at 1%. The regressions reveals that there are chances that by one unit increase in gross enrolment ratio for secondary education, both GDP at

Table 8.4   Regression results for education indices and economic performance index

	Coefficients	Standard error	t stat	P-value
Intercept	0.0512	0.0582	0.8796	0.0514
EEDI	0.3017	0.1909	1.5809	0.1323
SEDI	0.6077	0.1927	3.1536	0.0058*

Notes *Significant at 1% level, R square = 0.8085, F statistic = 35.9 significant at 1% level
EEDI Elementary education development index, *SEDI* secondary education development index
Source Authors calculations

factor cost and per capita national income can increase by 0.65 units. In comparison, for other levels of educational enrolments, the results were insignificant except for primary enrolments which have positive and significant impact on per capita national income; although its impact is lower than secondary education. Hence, it has become clear that educational attainment, particularly secondary education, compared to that of elementary is more vital to the economic well-being of the nation.

8.5.2   Education and Health Performance

Although, the impact of primary education on health and fertility levels are well established (World Bank 1993), in most countries it is also found that these outcomes have improved further with secondary level of education. Just in an attempt to test this relationship, simple linear regressions were run to measure the impacts of enrolments in different levels of school education on Health Performance Index. Here, gross enrolments at various levels of education are taken as independent variables, while Health Performance Index is taken as dependent variable. The result shows positive relation between enrolments in various levels of education and health performances (Table 8.5).

The findings suggest that other things being constant, 65% of the variation in health performances is explained by education levels. The result reveals that gross enrolment ratios in primary, middle, and secondary levels of education do have an impact on health performance. The results for primary and middle enrolments were significant at 5%, while for secondary enrolments, the results were significant at 1%. Moreover, for primary and secondary enrolments, the relation is positive with health performance, while for middle-level enrolments, it is negative. The result indicates that with one unit increase in GER for secondary education, the improvement in health performance can be up to 0.25 units. In case of primary education, the impact on health performance is lesser than secondary enrolments. Overall, it is worth mentioning that with an increase in the level of educational attainments, especially secondary education, the health of an individual improves.

Table 8.5 Regression for health performance index and education level

	Coefficients	Standard error	t stat	P-value
Intercept	0.588143	0.037931	15.5056	0.000
ZPGER	0.195109	0.091988	2.12103	0.050
ZMGER	−0.25228	0.104071	−2.42407	0.028
ZSGER	0.253067	0.061014	4.14771	0.001*

Notes *Significant at 1% level, R square = 0.6578, F statistic = 10.25 significant at 1% level
ZPGER Primary level GER, *ZMGER* middle level GER, *ZSGER* secondary level GER
Source Authors calculations

It is also seen that female education plays an important role in improving overall health performances. The (World Bank Document 2009) on 'Secondary Education in India: Universalizing Opportunity' (2009) clearly provides the evidences on the positive effects of upper primary and secondary education on reduced fertility rates, increasing the mean age of marriage for women and mothers' age at birth, improving birth practices and child rearing and higher proportion of women with HIV/Aids awareness. Hence, secondary education in its expanded form and involving more females contributes significantly to slower population growth, all of which are important goals for the government.

8.5.3 Demographic Transition and Social Benefits

The social outcomes of secondary education is not just limited to the improvement in health performance of society as a whole but can also be seen in terms of demographic transitions. Secondary education also puts great impact on young people's age at marriage, their propensity to reduce fertility and improves birth practices and child rearing. Further, with the expansion of secondary education to girls, maternal and child mortality was reduced significantly and population growth slowed down, all of which are important goals for the government. Secondary education also helps in bringing the demographic transition for the well-being of the society. To reflect this, an index on Demographic Performance Index was developed on the basis of key indicators like birth rates, death rates, infant mortality rates, maternal mortality rates, sex ratio (males per 1,000 females), total fertility rates, and natural growth rates. The simple regressions were run to see the relation. The result shows that 91% of variation in demographic indicators is due to education of individuals, other things being constant (Table 8.6).

The results reveal insignificant impacts for elementary education, while secondary education shows significant result. Findings further suggest that by one unit improvement in secondary education performance index, demographic index can decline by up to 0.88 units. The relation between demographic index and secondary performance index is negative; as people attain more of secondary education compared to elementary education, indicators like maternal mortality rates, infant mortality rates, fertility rates, death rates, etc., tend to decline which is a very good sign for an economy. Since there is a negative relation between sex ratio and

Table 8.6 Regression for demographic index and education indexes

	Coefficients	Standard error	t stat	P-value
Intercept	0.9710	0.0448	21.6660	0.0000
EEDI	−0.1966	0.1470	−1.3372	0.1988
SEDI	−0.8888	0.1484	−5.9881	0.0000*

Notes *Significant at 1% level, R square = 0.9120, F statistic = 88.0 significant at 1% level
EEDI Elementary education development index, *SEDI* Secondary education development index

secondary education development index, overall development in secondary education plays an important role in reducing the gap between male and female birth rates which further promotes gender equality. In addition to this, separate regressions were also run taking gross enrolments at various levels of school education as independent variables and demographic and health indicators as dependent variable, where it is found that there is significant relation between secondary education enrolments on various health and demographic indicators (Jain and Prasad 2016).

The positive externalities of education are also reflected in poverty reduction. The latest available data by Indian Human Development Survey (IHDS) shows that poverty diminishes substantially with household education as only 15% of the households in which an adult has completed secondary education are in poverty range, compared to 30% for those with education up to Ninth Standard (Desai 2008). Hence, education, including secondary education, decreases the likelihood that people will be poor. Overall, this section highlighted that the positive externalities of secondary education on health, demographic changes, poverty reduction, and gender equality are huge but cannot be quantified in economic terms. Female education has rather greater impact on social outcomes as they can go far in reversing the spread of HIV by contributing to poverty reduction, gender equality, female empowerment, and awareness of human rights GOI 2011.

8.5.4 Private Returns: Household Earnings

Data from middle-income countries show that higher wage premiums for secondary school completers can be observed for both women and men. Workers with upper secondary education earn higher salaries than those with a lower level of education (UIS and OECD 2003). Some similar evidences have been found which shows that secondary schooling has greater impacts on improving earnings in India. One study shows that secondary education has more significant effect on the redistribution of income, growth and reducing poverty than primary education (Tilak 1989). Jain and Prasad (2016) clearly show the relationship between GER at various levels of school education and income behaviors. They reveal the positive and significant impacts of secondary education enrolments on personal disposable income and female participation rate. The primary GER also shows positive and significant impact on personal disposable income and female participation; however, the impacts were lower than that of secondary education. In addition to the above regression results, literature shows that there are few studies conducted at the national level which reflect that households with higher secondary qualification are better off than those with up to elementary education (Tilak 1989; Rani 2007).

The NSS 68th round gives data on average daily wage/salary earnings per day of the regular wage/salaried employees. The difference in the wage rates across education levels of the regular wage earners is clearly visible. Figure 8.10 clearly shows that wage increases sharply with an increase in the level of education which also indicates that individuals with secondary education tend to have higher income

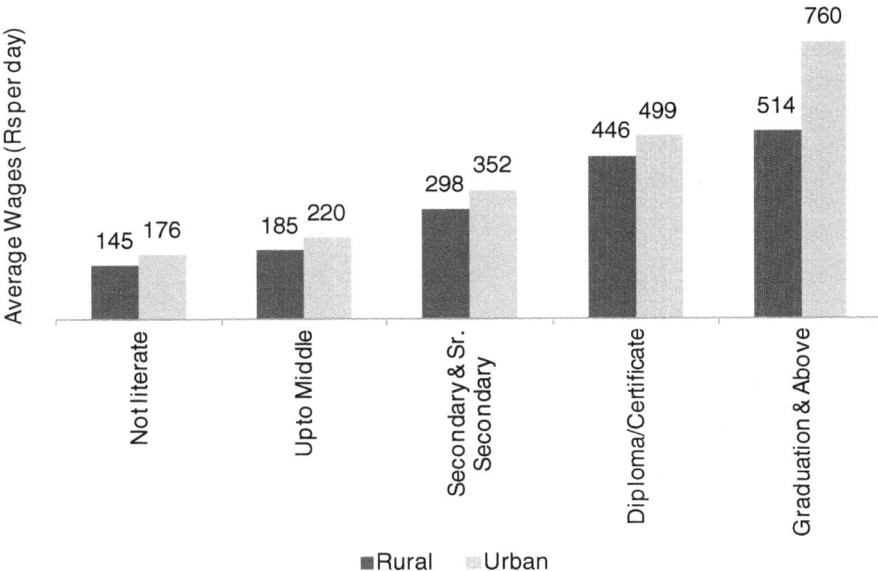

Fig. 8.10 Average wage/salary earnings (Rs.) per day received by regular wage/salaried employees of age 15–59 years by education (2011–12). *Source* NSS Report No. 554: Employment and Unemployment Situation in India, 2011–12

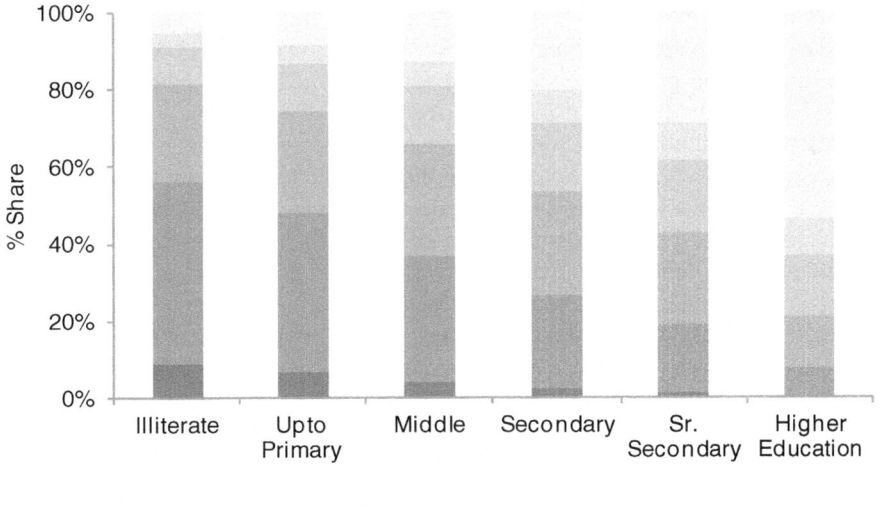

Fig. 8.11 Percentage share of MPCE by education level (2011–12). *Source* Employment and Unemployment: NSS 68th round: July 2011–June 2012

levels as compared to those with primary/middle level of school education. In addition to this, the NSS data on MPCE for the 68th round reveals that larger proportion of households with higher education comes in the category of higher expenditure band, whereas majority of the households with below secondary education comes in the lower three MPCE categories of up to Rs. 1,500 per month (Fig. 8.11). MPCE has been considered here as a proxy indicator for household income which clearly reflects the monthly expenditure pattern of household by different education levels.

8.6 Summary

The main objective of this chapter was to enhance the overall understanding about the present situation of secondary education at the national level and discuss how this level of education has grown over the years while highlighting various imbalances. It not only presented the growth and expansion of secondary education in India but also discussed the performance side to measure its effectiveness. The findings revealed that while on the expansion side, there has been huge growth in the number of institutions, teachers and enrolments over the years; the performance side on the other hand still poses great challenges in terms of slow growth rates in improving transition rates and promotion rates and reducing dropout rates. The findings further reveals that despite huge expansion, the number of secondary schools available per lakh population is still quite low which indicates that the goal of achieving universalization of secondary education in India is still distant. Another major point that has come out is that while most of the institutions at the secondary level of education are privately managed, institutions below this level, that is, middle and primary schools are mainly managed by government and local bodies. Even on the financing side, the private share of educational expenditure for secondary education is significant in India and has increased largely over the years. Public expenditure towards education, on the other hand, has always received low priority in comparison to other social sectors in the economy. This is well reflected by the fact that the public expenditure on education as percentage of GDP has not yet achieved the target of 6%. The analysis in this chapter further provides evidences that secondary education has strong correlations with economic performances, individual incomes, social outcomes in the form of health and demographic benefits. Considering its huge implications at the socio-economic levels, the findings emphasized the need for more investments and quality improvement in this sector of education in India. Although, in the last six decades the progress has been made in the secondary sector of education, the rate of progress does not correspond with the pace of requirement. Even the global comparison gives indication that despite positive growths over the last few years in terms of secondary level participation, female participation, pupil–teacher ratio, India still needs to go a long way in achieving a better place at the global level.

On the whole, it is quite clear from a discussion in the chapter that mere quantitative expansion in secondary level of education is not enough unless quality improvement is also taken care of simultaneously. To conclude, reforming secondary education in India from an elite system to an inclusive one is a huge challenge. Needless to mention, the context of schooling is changing; so does the framework for bringing about sustainable educational change. Increased investment in pre-reform activities, improved political will, strategic thinking and management ensuring continuity in change at the school level, and an increased budgetary allocation seem to be the necessary conditions for undertaking an inclusive quality secondary education process in the country.

References

Desai, S., Dubey, A., Vanneman, R., & Banerji, R. (2008). *Private schooling in India: A new educational landscape*. India Human Development Survey, Working Paper No. 11.

Document on Tenth Five Year Plan. (2002–07). *On secondary education*, India.

Government of India. (2007–08). Press note on '*education in India: Participation and expenditure*. National Sample Survey Office, Ministry of Statistics and Program Implementation.

Government of India. (2011). *Selected socio-economic statistics India*. Ministry of Statistics and Program Implementation, Central Statistics Office, Social Statistics Division, GOI. www.mospi.gov.in.

Government of India. (2011–2014). CBSE Annual Report.

Government of India. (2013–2014). *Indian public finance statistics*. Ministry of Finance, Department of Economic Affairs Economic Division.

Government of India. (Various Years). *Analysis of budgeted expenditure on education*. Ministry of Human Resource Development, Department of Higher Education, Planning & Monitoring Unit.

Government of India. (Various Years). *Educational statistics at a glance*. Ministry of Human Resource Development, Bureau of Planning, Monitoring and Statistics.

Govinda, R., & Varghese, N. V. (1993). *Quality of primary schooling in India: A case study of Madhya Pradesh*. Paris: International Institute for Educational Planning and New Delhi: National Institute of Educational Planning and Administration (NIEPA).

Jain, C., & Prasad, N. (2016). Evidences of linkage between secondary education and socio-economic outcomes in India. *Journal of Educational Planning and Administration, NUEPA, XXX*(1), 25–43.

Kingdon, G. G. (1996). The quality and efficiency of public and private schools: A case study of urban India. *Oxford Bulletin of Economics and Statistics, 58*(1), 55–80.

Kumar, G. (2011). *Growth and development of education in India since 1951–52*. Centre for Indian Development Studies.

Lewin, K. M., & Caillods, F. (2001). *Financing secondary education in developing countries; strategies for sustainable growth* (p. 370). Paris: International Institute for Educational Planning.

MHRD. (Various Years). *Budgetary resources for education*. Ministry for Human Resources Development (MHRD), Annual Publication, New Delhi.

Mingat, A., & Tan, J. P. (1996). *Full social returns to education: Estimates based on countries economic growth performance*. Working paper, World Bank, Washington, D.C.

MOSPI. (2014). *Education in India, Report no. 575*, NSS Round 71, January–June 2014, NSS (GOI).

MOSPI. (2015). *Key indicators of social consumption in India education*, NSS Report, GOI.

National Sample Survey Organisation (Various Years). Highlights from Report: Household Consumer Expenditure Surveys in India.

NCERT. (2005). *Universalization of secondary education in India—Vision*. Chapter 1 drawn from the report of the sub-committee of CABE (2005), constituted for Universalization of Secondary Education by CABE (MHRD).

NUEPA. (various years). Flash Statistics on Secondary education in India: Progress towards universalization.

Planning Commission Report of the Steering Committee on Secondary, Higher & Technical Education for the Eleventh Five Year Plan (2007–2012). New Delhi, GOI.

Planning Commission, Report of the Working Group on Secondary and Vocational Education for 11th Five Year Plan (2007–2012). Government of India, New Delhi.

Psacharopoulos, G., & Patrinos, H. (2004). Returns to investment in education: A further update. *Education Economics, 12*(2), 111–134.

Rani, G. (2003). Education in India across households by income groups. *Indian Journal of Social Development, 3*(2), 201–227.

Rani, G. (2007). *Secondary education in India: Determinants of development and performance*. Working Paper ID 907, E-Social Sciences.

Tilak, J. B. G. (1989). *Education and its relation to economic growth, poverty and income distribution*. Discussion Paper no. 46, World Bank, Washington D.C.

Tilak, J. B. G. (2001). *Building human capital: What others can learn*. World Bank Institute Working Paper, World Bank, Washington, D.C.

Tilak, J. B. G. (2006). *Education: A saga of spectacular achievements and conspicuous failures' in India*. Social Development Report, Oxford University Press, Council for Social Development, New Delhi.

UIS (UNESCO Institute for Statistics) and OECD. (2003). *Literacy skills for the world of tomorrow: Further results from PISA 2000*. Paris: OECD.

UNDP. (Various Years). *Human development reports*. Oxford University Press.

Varghese, N. V., & Mehta, A. C. (1998). *Universalization of elementary education—A study of upper primary education in India*. NIEPA.

World Bank. (1993), *The East Asian miracle*. New York: Oxford University Press.

World Bank Document. (2009). *Report on 'secondary education in India: Universalizing opportunity*. Human Development Unit South Asia Region.

Chapter 9
Identifying Inter-state Disparities and Socio-economic Linkages

Abstract India aspires to become a knowledge hub, transforming millions across the world into educated global citizens. For this transformation, the entire education system in the country needs to be sound and robust. To achieve this goal at the national level, it is desirable to first strengthen the education system at state level. Education in India is in the concurrent list; the union government has some responsibilities while the states have autonomy. Therefore, the responsibility for financing secondary education is a shared responsibility between the union and state governments. The patterns of school management of secondary education are complex and vary considerably not only across states but even within states, between lower and higher secondary levels of education. Given the well-known regional disparities in India in various fields—social, economic, health, education, science, and technology—the comparative performance of individual states has become an important area of research. Despite the fact that secondary education forms an integral part of the development of the entire education system, very few studies have been conducted so far that have taken up the issues on the growth of secondary education particularly at the state level and in identifying the inter-state disparities in India. To fill up the gap, this chapter discusses the issues related to access, participation, and quality of lower and higher secondary education (Ninth–Twelfth standards) in 20 major states in India and examines the existing level of inter-state disparities. State-level analysis of secondary education is required especially if states need to progress in a balanced way. Moreover, the results from state comparisons can throw up successful experiments and examples which can be replicated or adapted by other states. While, the first section of this chapter discusses the state profile in terms of economic, social well-being, health, education, income and employment, and demographic performances, the next section presents facts on the status of secondary education in states. The third section discusses state financing patterns and the fourth section deals with disparities existing among and within states. This part of the chapter highlights various capabilities and inefficiencies of states in terms of socio-economic and demographic profiles and has tried to relate these with educational attainments in selected states. The fifth section tries to evaluate the inter-relationship between attainment of school education attainment and socio-economic outcomes at both macro and micro levels. The major findings are summarized in the last section of the chapter.

Keywords Educational outcomes · Socio-economic linkages · Inter-state disparity · Gender disparity · Linear regression

9.1 States' Profile

Considering the fact that the development of any nation is a multi-dimensional phenomenon, this section provides profile of 20 major states in India in terms of its various demographics, economic growth, health facilities, quality education, social well-being, and income and employment levels.

9.1.1 Demographic Profile

With remarkably diverse demographics, India is the second most populous country in the world constituting more than one-sixth of the world's population. As per the latest Census data, the stock of population in India has changed from 102.8 crore in 2001 to 121.01 crore in 2011, recording an exponential rate of growth of population at 1.64 during 2001–11 (Fig. 9.1). Although, decadal growth rate of population came down during 1991–01 to 2001–11 from 2.15 to 1.76%, the congestion of population in India is still increasing as shown by the population density which is increasing from 325 in 2001 to 382 in 2011. India occupies only 2.2% of the world's land area but supports over 15% of the world's population. Almost 35% Indians are younger than 15 years of age. The Census 2011 data shows that among 20 major states, Uttar Pradesh is the most populous one, followed by Maharashtra and Bihar, whereas Himachal Pradesh is the least populated. Bihar has the highest decadal (2001–11) growth rate of population (25.1%), while Kerala has the lowest rate (4.9%). Some larger states like Gujarat, Haryana, Madhya Pradesh, Rajasthan, and Uttar Pradesh also have a high decadal growth of population. Kerala has the highest sex ratio with 1084 females per 1000 males followed by Tamil Nadu (995), while Haryana is at the bottom (877). Interestingly, the sex ratios in some of the developed states like Gujarat and Maharashtra are also low at 918 and 925, respectively (Table 9.1).

India is on the brink of a demographic revolution with the proportion of working-age population between 15 and 59 years likely to increase from approximately 58% in 2001 to more than 64% by 2021, adding approximately 63.5 million new entrants to the working-age group between 2011 and 2016, the bulk of whom will be in the relatively younger age group of 20–35 years. Given that it is one of the youngest large nations in the world, a great demographic

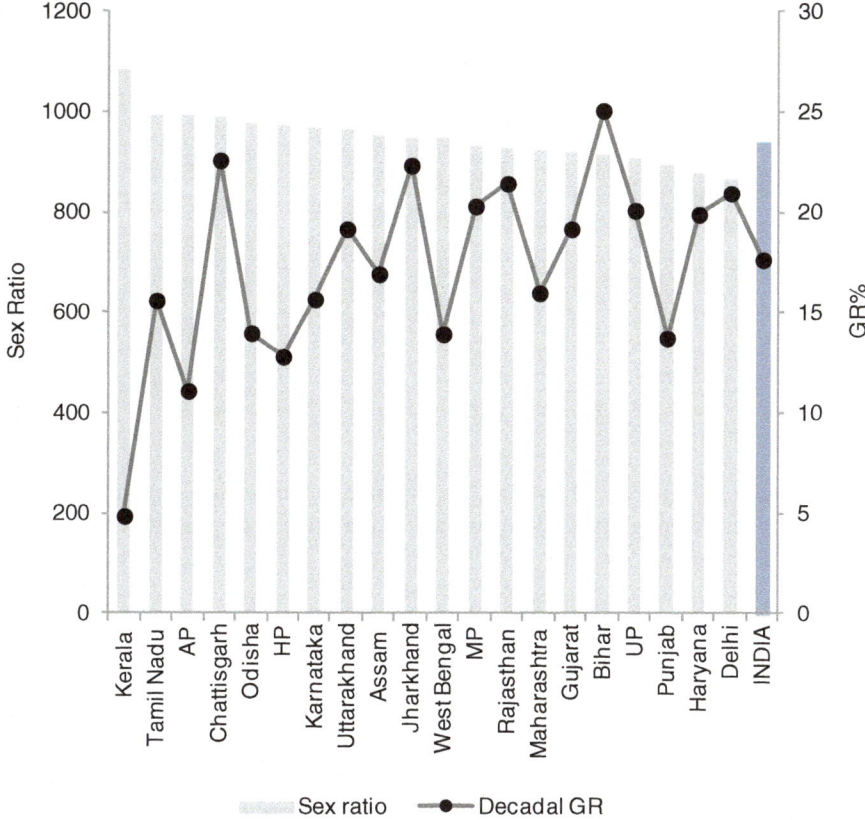

Fig. 9.1 Demographic indicators by States. *Source* Census of India 2011

Table 9.1 Demographic profile of Indian States

States	Population (in 000's)	% Urban population	Life expectancy at birth
AP	84665.5	33.5	63.5
Assam	31169.3	14.1	61.0
Bihar	103804.6	11.3	65.5
Chhattisgarh	25540.2	23.2	…
Delhi	16753.2	97.5	…
Gujarat	60383.6	42.6	64.9
Haryana	25353.1	34.8	67.0
HP	6856.5	10.0	…
Jharkhand	32966.2	24.1	…
Karnataka	61130.7	38.6	64.9
Kerala	33387.7	47.7	71.5

(continued)

Table 9.1 (continued)

States	Population (in 000's)	% Urban population	Life expectancy at birth
MP	72597.6	27.6	61.1
Maharashtra	112373.0	45.2	67.9
Odisha	41947.4	16.7	62.2
Punjab	27704.2	37.5	67.4
Rajasthan	68621.0	24.9	64.7
Tamil Nadu	72139.0	48.5	67.1
UP	199581.5	22.3	61.8
West Bengal	91347.7	31.9	67.4
Uttarakhand	10116.8	30.6	…
India	1210193.4	31.2	64.6

Source Census of India 2011, Planning commission 2011, DCH data book

dividend can be reaped only if this young population is healthy, and skilled. Moreover, these demographic dividends can bring huge economic significances in the long run.

9.1.2   Economic Profile

The best performing states in terms of Gross State Domestic Product (GSDP) during 2014–15 are Maharashtra, followed by Tamil Nadu and Uttar Pradesh However, in terms of growth rate in GSDP the best performers in 2014–15 over the corresponding period previous year are Bihar (13%), Jharkhand (12.5%), Andhra Pradesh (8.5%), and Delhi (8%). The worst performers are Punjab (4.9%), followed by Uttarakhand and Haryana. In terms of growth in per capita income, the best performer is Bihar followed by Jharkhand, Andhra Pradesh, and Kerala due to high growth GSDP in 2014–15 despite the high decadal growth in population particularly in states like Bihar, Jharkhand, and Delhi. Per-capita income growth is the lowest in Uttarakhand (3.0%), followed by Punjab and Madhya Pradesh which are below the all-India per-capita income growth. The poverty estimates (Tendulkar methodology) indicate that the highest percent of population below poverty line exists in Chhattisgarh at 39.9% as against the national average of 21.9%, while lowest poverty is in Kerala (7.1%), followed by Himachal Pradesh (8.1%) in 2011–12 (Fig. 9.2). As per usual status (adjusted) NSS 68th round 2011–12, the unemployment rate (per 1000) among the major states is highest in Delhi (78%), Kerala (68%) and Assam (45%) in rural areas (Government of India 2011-12). In urban areas, the unemployment rate is highest in Kerala (61%) followed by Assam and Bihar (56% each). Kerala, which has performed well in most of socio-economic and educational indicators, performs less in terms of employment. This may be due to the higher level of education in Kerala resulting in people not opting for manual

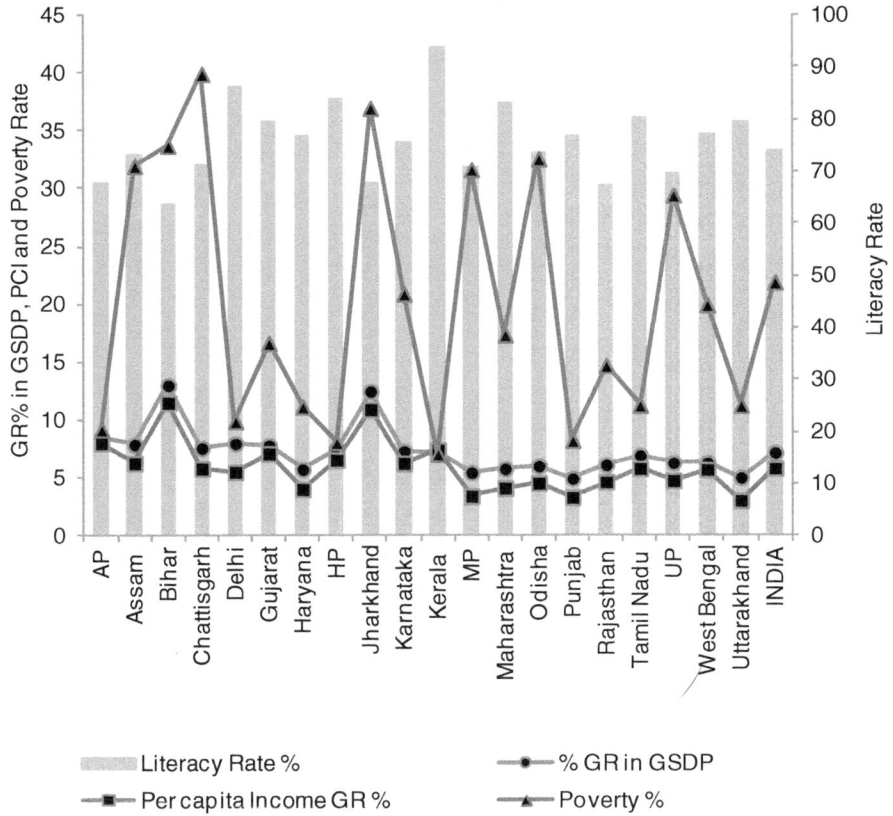

Fig. 9.2 Socio-economic indicators by States. *Source* Census of India 2011, Economic Survey 2014–15, CSO 2014-15, Planning commission 2011, DCH data book

jobs as observed by some studies (Shiva Kumar 1991). The employment in organized sector, on the other hand, shows the highest levels in Maharashtra, followed by Tamil Nadu and Karnataka. These levels are found lowest in case of Uttarakhand, Chhattisgarh, Himachal Pradesh, and Bihar (Table 9.2).

According to Census 2011, the all-India literacy rates stand at 74%, while for males and females it is about 82 and 64.4%, respectively. Among the major states considered here for analysis, the highest number of literates resides in Kerala (94%), followed by Delhi (86.3%), Himachal Pradesh (83.8%), and Maharashtra in 2011. Consequently, these states performed well in terms of socio-economic and demographic indicators as seen above.

Table 9.2 Socio-economic profile of Indian States: 2014–15

	GSDP at FC constant prices for 2014–15 (Rs. Cr)	Per capita income GR %	Poverty %	Literacy rate %	Employment in organized sector (lakh)
Andhra Pradesh	4,41,741	8.0	9.2	67.7	20.3
Assam	1,66,709	6.3	32.0	73.2	11.2
Bihar	3,04,766	11.5	33.7	63.8	4.3
Chhattisgarh	1,96,023	5.8	39.9	71.0	2.9
Delhi	4,22,920	5.5	9.9	86.3	8.8
Gujarat	7,91,569	7.1	16.6	79.3	22.0
Haryana	3,66,636	4.0	11.2	76.6	7.5
Himachal Pradesh	89,032	6.5	8.1	83.8	3.9
Jharkhand	1,86,491	10.9	37.0	67.6	15.8
Karnataka	7,60,282	6.2	20.9	75.6	23.0
Kerala	4,32,237	7.4	7.1	93.9	10.9
Madhya Pradesh	3,83,994	3.4	31.7	70.6	9.9
Maharashtra	15,24,846	4.1	17.4	82.9	49.5
Odisha	2,74,721	4.5	32.6	73.5	7.1
Punjab	3,13,276	3.3	8.3	76.7	8.3
Rajasthan	5,12,095	4.6	14.7	67.1	12.9
Tamil Nadu	9,00,628	5.8	11.3	80.3	23.4
Uttar Pradesh	8,53,872	4.7	29.4	69.7	22.1
West Bengal	NA	5.7	20.0	77.1	19.2
Uttarakhand	1,40,791	3.0	11.3	79.6	3.2
India	105,22,686	5.8	21.9	74.0	295.8

Note Figures for poverty are for 2011–12 and literacy rate 2.11
Source Economic Survey 2014–15, Census 2011, NSS, Ministry of Labour and Employment (GOI)

9.1.3   Health Profile

Analysis shows that the state of Kerala is the best performer in terms of life expectancy at birth for both males (71.5 years) and females (76.9 years), whereas Assam is the worst performer for both males (61 years) and females (63.2 years) during 2006–10. The infant mortality rates (IMR) are found highest in Madhya Pradesh, Assam, Orissa, and Uttar Pradesh in 2013, whereas the southern states of Karnataka, Kerala, Tamil Nadu, and Andhra Pradesh have IMR well below the national average of 40. Birth rates are lowest in Kerala (14.7) and highest in Bihar

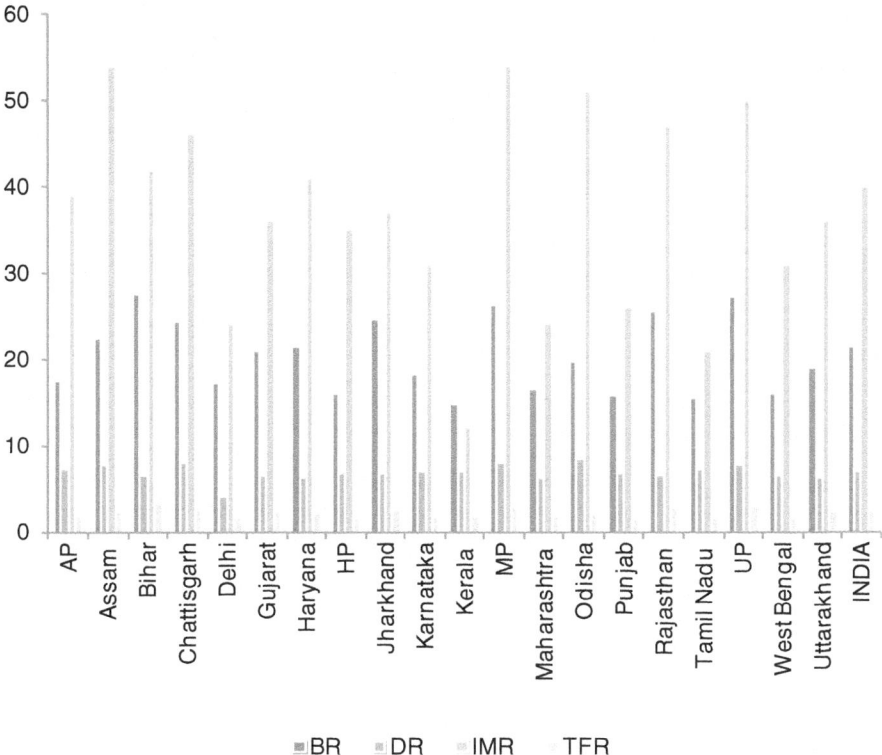

Fig. 9.3 Distribution of States by health indicators. *Source* SRS 2013, Census of India, MHFW 2013

(27.6) and Uttar Pradesh (27.2) against the national average of 21.4 as per 2013 estimates. Death rate is lowest in Delhi (4.1) and highest in Odisha (8.4) against the national average of 7 in 2013 (Fig. 9.3).

Few studies have shown that education as an input can lead to better health and nutritional status of an individual, which feeds back into improved learning ability and better attendance at school (Malhotra and Singh 2006). Improvement in the standard of living and health status of the population has remained one of the important objectives for policymakers in India. The health indicators in India like crude death rate (CDR), crude birth rate (CBR), infant mortality rate (IMR), and total fertility rate (TFR) show an improvement over the decade. However, in absolute terms, the overall situation continues to be worrisome due to inter-state disparities. It is seen that certain states like Kerala, Tamil Nadu, Himachal Pradesh, Delhi, and the smaller north-eastern states consistently perform well in terms of various health indicators. This is primarily due to state government interventions in the health system; while on the other end of the spectrum are the relatively poorer states like Bihar, Chhattisgarh, Jharkhand, Madhya Pradesh, and Uttar Pradesh, which perform

Table 9.3 Health profile of Indian States

States	Mean age at effective marriage (females)	Ayush hospitals and dispensaries	Ayush registered practitioners per crore population	Contraceptive use by any methods (%) 2012–13	Effective couple protection rates all methods % 2011
AP	20.7	609	1183	69.9	61.5
Assam	21.4	460	417	67.2	13.1
Bihar	21.1	2183	11,943	41.2	16.5
Chhattisgarh	20.3	1109	1756	60.7	–
Delhi	22.8	162	5278	55.5	18.3
Gujarat	21.6	854	6681	54.3	47.9
Haryana	21.1	535	5004	51.6	36.9
HP	22.5	1165	8308	58.8	41.8
Jharkhand	20.5	371	97	57.5	–
Karnataka	21.3	889	6573	63	49.6
Kerala	23.1	1742	10,379	60	31.8
MP	20.6	1796	8208	63.2	46.4
Maharashtra	21.1	607	11,785	66.9	41.8
Odisha	21.4	1350	3193	62.4	25.9
Punjab	22.7	645	3396	64.6	46.2
Rajasthan	20.7	4021	2410	70.2	45.7
Tamil Nadu	22.4	1418	4351	53.3	41.5
UP	21.6	3947	4192	59.9	27.7
West Bengal	20.7	2543	4883	71.8	27.9
Uttarakhand	–	613	2756	62.7	29.9
India	21.3	29,321	5778	47.1	40.4

Source MHFW, GOI 2011, National Health Profile 2012, Census Data 2011, SRS

well below the national average in terms of health indicators. Fertility rates in Kerala and Tamil Nadu suggest that their Reproductive and Child Healthcare (RCH) Programs have been successful. The demographic transition of Kerala is widely acclaimed because its mortality and fertility levels have reached those of the developed countries. This can largely be attributed to the high literacy rates among men and women in the state. Moreover, the improvement in MMR, TFR, and IMR over the years can also be attributed to the increase in the mean age of marriage for females in which education has actually contributed to a great extent (Table 9.3).

In addition to this, there has also been increase in the percentage of children immunized against various diseases like DPT, BCG, DT, and Polio over the years. In fact, there is also an increase in tetanus immunization for expectant mothers

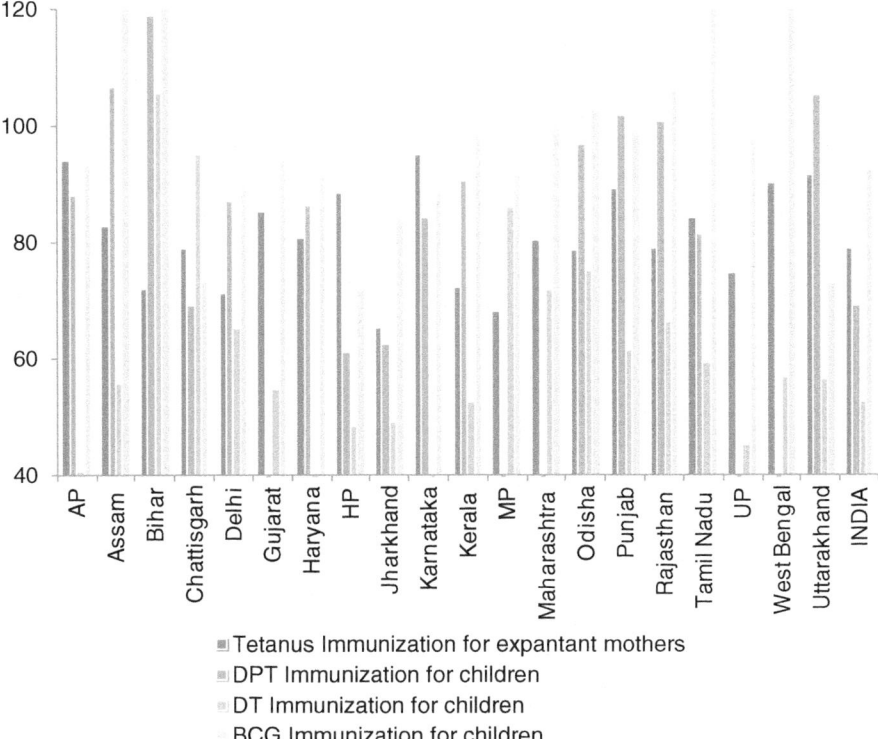

Fig. 9.4 State profile for immunization against chronic diseases. *Source* SRS 2013

which has reached to 78% in 2011 and further 79% in 2013. The highest immunization levels are recorded in Bihar, Tamil Nadu, Assam, Odisha, and Rajasthan, while Uttar Pradesh, Gujarat, and Madhya Pradesh lack in immunization facilities against chronic diseases (Fig. 9.4).

Another important health indicator to look at is HIV prevalence among Indian states. The latest available NACO data shows HIV prevalence among adults in Andhra Pradesh, Gujarat, and Maharashtra. Ironically, these are the states where percentage of contraception use and even couple protection rates are also very high compared to other states. In contrast, Assam, Madhya Pradesh, Kerala, Uttarakhand, and Uttar Pradesh have much lower HIV prevalence (Fig. 9.5).

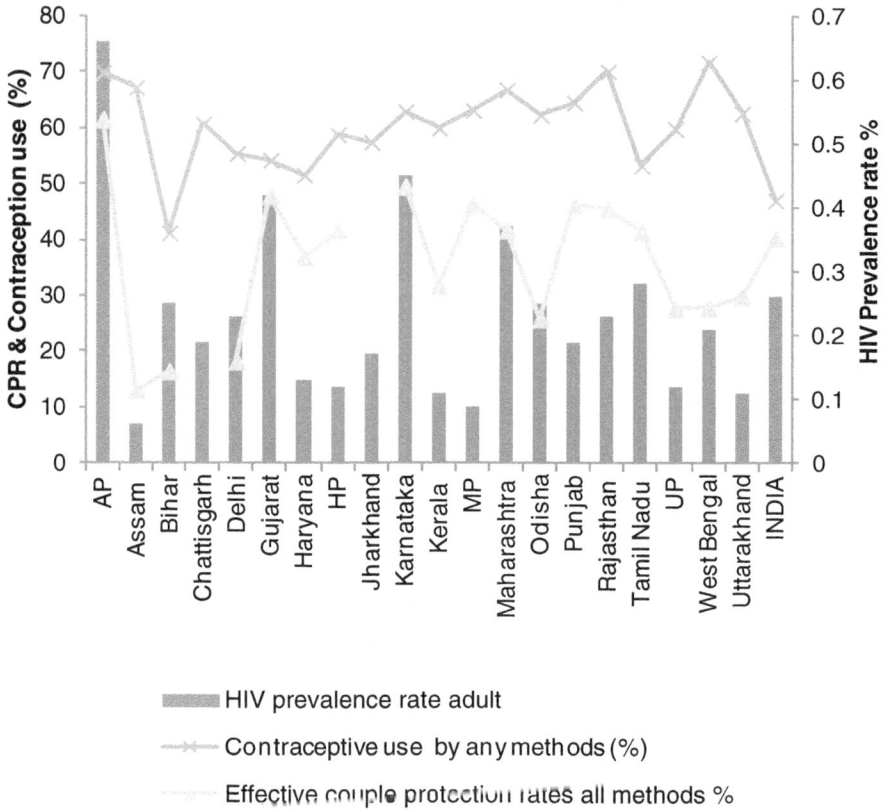

Fig. 9.5 State-wise prevalence of HIV and couple protection methods. *Source* National Health Profile, Census Data 2011 and NIRD

9.1.4 Educational Profile

Education is an important input as well as an outcome indicator, influencing health, nutritional status, income and family planning. In fact, unlike any of the other social service inputs, it impacts all types of human development outcomes not only knowledge, but also family size, health status, nutritional status, and healthy living conditions. The benefits of education, particularly girls' education, accrue from one generation to another.

The available data shows that the number of schools and share of public expenditure has improved over the years. However, if we look at the number of schools serving per thousand population in respective states or the share of expenditure on education as percent of state revenue budget, then the figures are really low which clearly suggests that quality issues remain a serious area of concerns in the school education system.

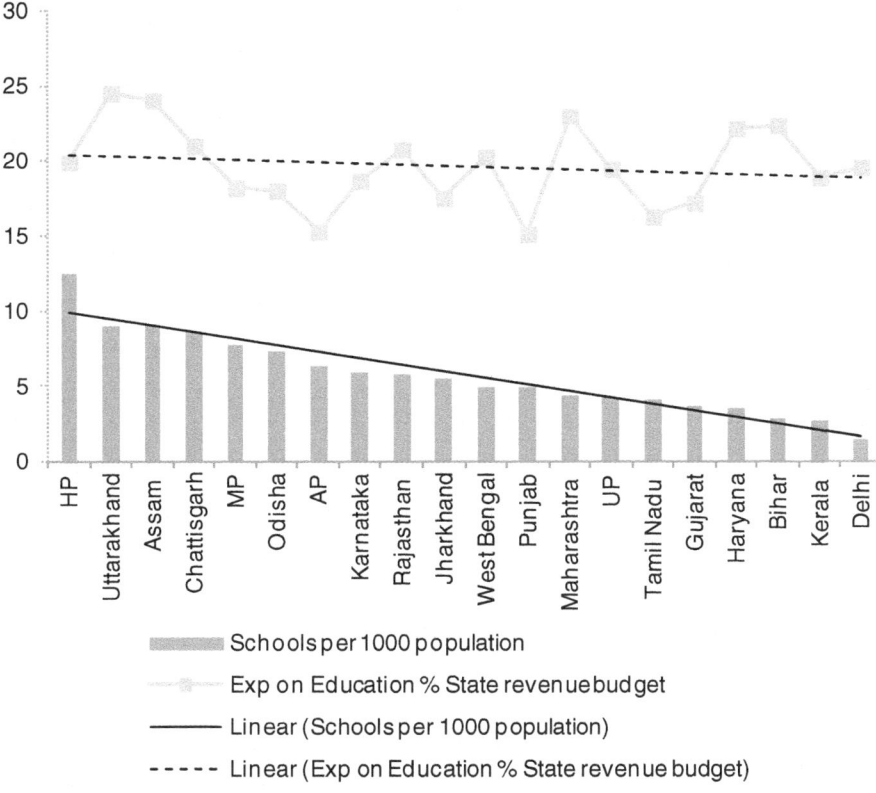

Fig. 9.6 Number of schools per 1000 population and expenditure on education as percent of State Revenue Budget. *Source* Census 2011, Annual Budgeted Expenditure 2011–14 and U-Dise School Education in India 2014–15

The number of schools serving per 1,000 population across various major states in India and the expenditure incurred by states on education as percentage of state revenue budget are given in Fig. 9.6. It shows that states which have incurred high expenditure on education in proportion to their state revenue budget do not necessarily have the highest number of schools per 1,000 population. For example, although states like Maharashtra, Bihar, Haryana, Kerala, Uttar Pradesh, and Delhi have incurred higher percentage of state revenue budget on education, the number of schools per thousand population among these states is the lowest. On the other hand, there are states like Andhra Pradesh, Odisha, MP, and Karnataka where although the expenditure shares are lower comparatively, the number of schools per thousand population in these states is high. Overall, the top five states with highest number of schools per 1,000 population are Himachal Pradesh, Uttarakhand, Assam, Chhattisgarh, and Madhya Pradesh; while Uttarakhand, Assam, Maharashtra, Bihar, and Haryana are the largest spending states all over India.

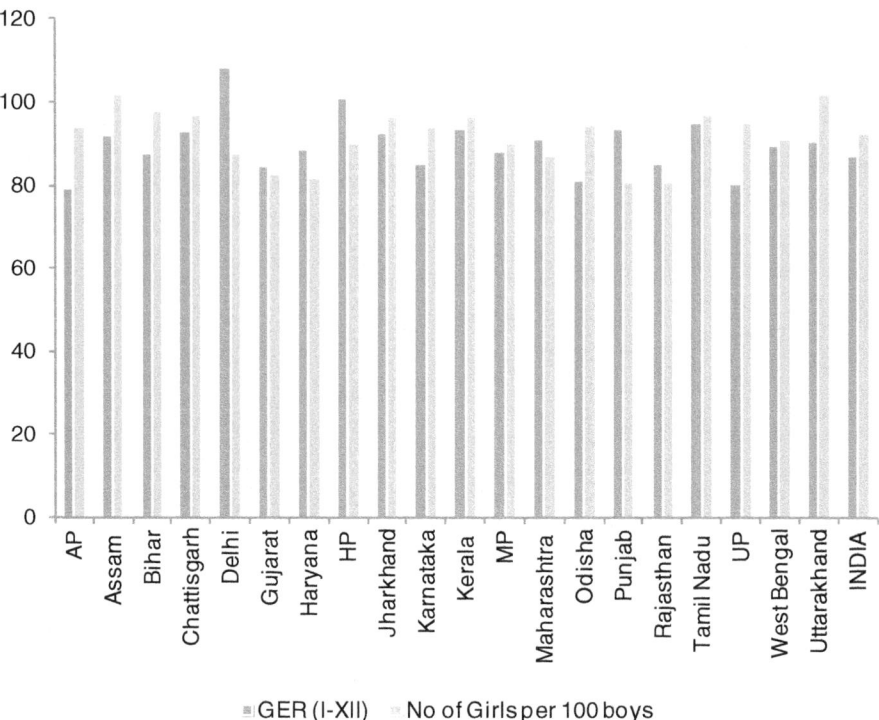

Fig. 9.7 State-wise school GER (I–XII) and female participation. *Source* U-Dise School Education in India 2014–15

Apart from indicators like literacy rates, funding, and accessibility of schools, another most important indicator to measure educational achievements among states is participation rates. Participation rates can be well measured by gross enrolment ratios (GERs). Figure 9.7 shows that GERs at school level are the highest in Delhi, Himachal Pradesh, and Tamil Nadu in 2014–15, while Andhra Pradesh and Uttar Pradesh have the lowest of all. Female participation is equally important and has huge demographic and health implications. At the all-India level, 93 girls were enrolled per 100 boys in 2014–15, reflecting an improvement over 89 girls per 100 boys as recorded in 2011–12. At the state level, Uttarakhand has the highest female participation followed by Assam, Bihar, and Tamil Nadu. The lowest female participation at school level is recorded in Rajasthan, Punjab, Haryana, and Gujarat. Although, Gujarat is a developed state and performed well on economic indicators, in education its performance is not at par as compared to the best performing states.

Thus, the inter-state comparison of performance of states based on different indicators shows that while some states have performed well in terms of economic growth rates, they have performed poorly in terms of other indicators like poverty, rural–urban disparity, unemployment, education, and health. This calls for rethinking on the criteria used for devolution of funds to states. On the whole, at the macro-economic level, there exists a two-way relationship between various interventions. For instance, investment in health and education can enhance human functioning which can eventually reduce income poverty by generating employment opportunities and further economic growth. Similarly, resources generated through income–poverty reduction and economic growth can be used to enhance human functioning. Faster and more sustainable economic growth can be attained if, among other policy-determined interventions, poverty is reduced and health and educational status of the population is enhanced.

9.2 Status of Secondary Education: Inter-state Analysis

To reap full benefits of the demographic dividend, India has to provide education to its population and that too of good quality. After universalization of elementary education now it is essential to focus on secondary education, not just expanding its accessibility but also its quality. This is well reflected in the Twelfth Five Year Plan that emphasize on the need to build up capacity in secondary schools to absorb the pass-outs from increased primary enrolments. To see the accessibility of secondary schools, Fig. 9.8 presents the state-wise distribution of schools per 1,000 population at both lower secondary and senior secondary level of education.

Figure 9.8 shows that except for Tamil Nadu, almost all major states in India have more number of lower secondary schools per thousand population compared to senior secondary schools. Among all, the number of lower secondary schools per thousand population are highest in case of HP, followed by Rajasthan, Punjab, and Uttarakhand, whereas in case of senior secondary schools per 1,000 population HP, Tamil Nadu, Uttarakhand, and Rajasthan tops the list in 2014–15. While looking at distribution of schools at both the levels of secondary education within states, it is found that in 2011, the states of HP, Uttarakhand, Chhattisgarh, Tamil Nadu, Kerala, Delhi and few others have higher senior secondary schools per thousand population compared to lower secondary schools. However, in 2014–15, Tamil Nadu is the only state where senior secondary schools are higher than lower secondary schools per 1,000 population. In addition to this, data also reflects wide disparity between both the types of schools in few states. The gap between lower and senior secondary schools per 1,000 population is the highest in Himachal Pradesh, Odisha, Andhra Pradesh, Karnataka, and Assam. This clearly indicates about the existing disparities between states in terms of provision and schools and accessibility to the majority of population. Moreover, within many states, the share of types of schools between government, local, private- aided, and unaided schools varies between lower secondary and senior secondary levels.

The Indian states have mixed pattern on the types of secondary schools managed by different authorities like private, local, or government. However, the share of local secondary schools are quite less prominent as these types of schools are limited to few states only like Andhra Pradesh, Maharashtra, Tamil Nadu, Delhi,

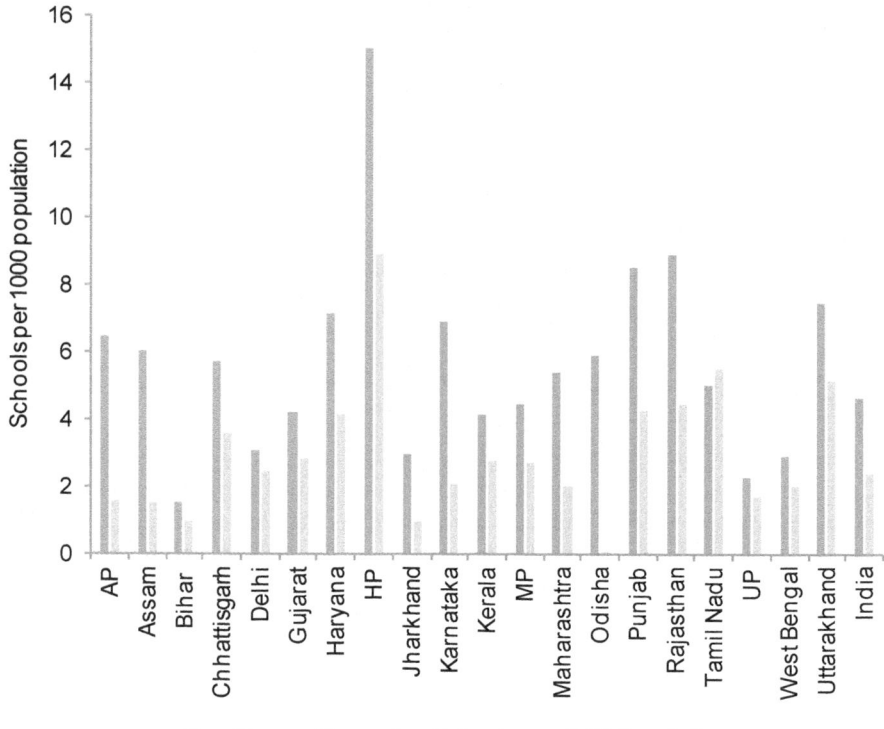

Fig. 9.8 State-wise secondary schools per 1000 population: by level of education. *Source* Calculations based on data from Secondary Education in India NUEPA 2014–15

and Gujarat and that too with very low shares except for Andhra Pradesh where these schools have a significant share of 35% in 2014–15. Figure 9.9 shows that at both the levels of secondary education i.e. lower and senior secondary, the share of private schooling is much higher compared to government schools. At all India level, 55.5% of the schools re privately owned at lower secondary level, while this proportion is 58.8% in case of senior secondary education. Among various states, the share of private schools (including aided and unaided) for both lower and senior secondary level of education is the highest in Maharashtra, Uttar Pradesh, Gujarat, Kerala, and Karnataka. On the other hand, the share of government secondary schools is the highest in states like West Bengal, Bihar, Uttarakhand, Chhattisgarh, Himachal Pradesh, and Jharkhand. Between both the levels of secondary schools, the proportion of private schooling in majority of the states is higher in case of senior secondary education than that of lower secondary. Moreover, gap between government and private schooling together in lower and senior secondary level of school education is the highest in Maharashtra followed by Uttar Pradesh, West

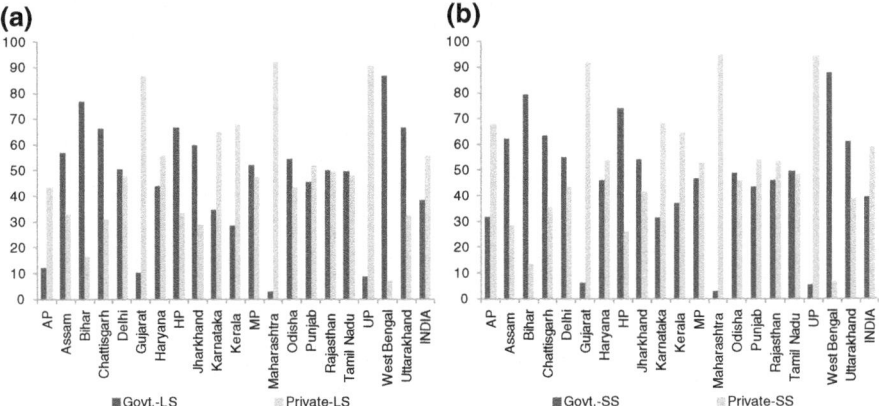

Fig. 9.9 a State-wise percentage share of secondary schools by management type: lower secondary (LS). *Source* Calculations based on data from Secondary Education in India NUEPA 2014–15, **b** state-wise percentage share of secondary schools by management type: senior secondary (SS). *Source* Calculations based on data from Secondary Education in India NUEPA 2014–15

Bengal, Gujarat, and Bihar. Overall, comparison between government-owned and private-owned schools reflects that the majority of states have high percentage of private schooling at the secondary level except for some states where the government still plays a major role. Within private schooling as well, there are disparities between aided and unaided schools. Majority of secondary schools in Uttar Pradesh, Haryana, and Rajasthan are private-aided schools having shares of more than 51%, whereas Maharashtra and Gujarat have high shares of private unaided schools. The differentiation between states with respect to school management further creates differences in school enrolment ratios, overall learning quality, and performance of students.

The other key indicators at the state level for both lower and senior secondary levels are discussed in Table 9.4. Table 9.4 shows that Himachal Pradesh, Delhi, and Kerala are the top-ranking states for gross enrolment ratios at both lower and senior secondary levels, while Bihar, Uttar Pradesh, Assam, Jharkhand are the lowest ranking states among all. As far as female participation rates are concerned, Rajasthan and Gujarat show lowest female participation per 100 males in 2014–15, followed by other states like Haryana and Punjab. In case of senior secondary level, female participation is higher than males in South Indian states: Tamil Nadu (113 girls per 100 males), Kerala (108 girls per 100 males), and Karnataka (105 girls per 100 boys). However, at the lower secondary level, the highest female participation per 100 males is reported in West Bengal (116), followed by Assam (109) and Chhattisgarh (102). However, there are a few states like West Bengal, Odisha, Bihar, and Assam where although female participation per 100 males is above the national average for lower secondary levels, as they move up the ladder towards senior secondary levels, female participation declines. This clearly indicates that

Table 9.4 Key indicators of secondary education by levels and states 2014–15

States	Lower secondary (IX–X)			Senior secondary (XI–XII)		
	PTR	GER	Girls per 100 boys	PTR	GER	Girls per 100 boys
AP	19	72.4	96	35	51.6	93
Assam	13	74.8	109	20	34.0	95
Bihar	59	69.1	96	61	31.8	82
Chhattisgarh	33	101.8	102	26	63.3	95
Delhi	30	103.6	86	25	91.6	91
Gujarat	34	74.3	70	31	44.9	77
Haryana	14	84.3	78	18	65.8	77
HP	19	115.9	86	15	100.6	90
Jharkhand	61	71.9	97	68	48.7	88
Karnataka	16	81.8	92	28	33.0	105
Kerala	17	103.2	94	20	76.9	108
MP	40	80.2	87	40	45.5	80
Maharashtra	23	89.3	84	43	62.2	85
Odisha	20	77.1	98	20	–	86
Punjab	17	85.6	77	28	69.4	80
Rajasthan	23	76.2	72	39	56.5	66
Tamil Nadu	21	91.9	95	26	77.5	113
UP	57	67.8	89	106	63.8	90
West Bengal	37	90.4	116	56	80.4	97
Uttarakhand	18	78.2	92	32	50.0	95
India	27	78.5	90	38	54.2	89

Source Statistics of School Education 2014–15

these states seriously need to improve on the school quality issues and should focus on providing more facilities in order to encourage greater participation from females.

Teachers play an important role in creating quality learning environment in schools. Qualified and trained teachers can not only affect the school quality but students' performance level as well. Thus, it is utmost important to consider pupil–teacher ratio (PTR) as another important indicator that reveals the level of quality at secondary education in Indian schools. High PTR reveals higher number of students per teacher that points towards poor quality levels and reduces performances and development of students. Moreover, it also reflects lack of qualified and trained faculty available in schools. Few studies have shown that PTR rates of around 31 should be fine. Even, all-India PTR at the lower secondary level is 27 and at the senior secondary level of schooling is 38. Table 9.4 shows that in terms of PTR rates, there are disparities between states at both levels of secondary schooling. According to Table 9.4, states which performed worst at lower secondary level in terms of PTR are Jharkhand (61), Bihar (59), and Uttar Pradesh (57), whereas the best performers constitute Assam, Haryana, Karnataka, and Kerala. At the senior secondary level, Uttar Pradesh, along with Jharkhand and Bihar, recorded the highest PTR. Even states like West Bengal, Madhya Pradesh and Maharashtra have PTR rates much higher than national averages. Hence, states with high PTR rates need to focus on channelizing their funds towards recruiting more trained teachers at secondary schools so as to improve the overall quality of education.

9.3   Pattern of States Financing on Secondary Education

Since the early 1990s, public spending on education has expanded strongly, though not faster than GDP. The expansion in funding has helped to underpin significant growth in the supply of education services. In most states, elementary education takes relatively larger share of public spending. Figure 9.10 shows state-wise distribution pattern of spending on education by sectors. The states which are spending

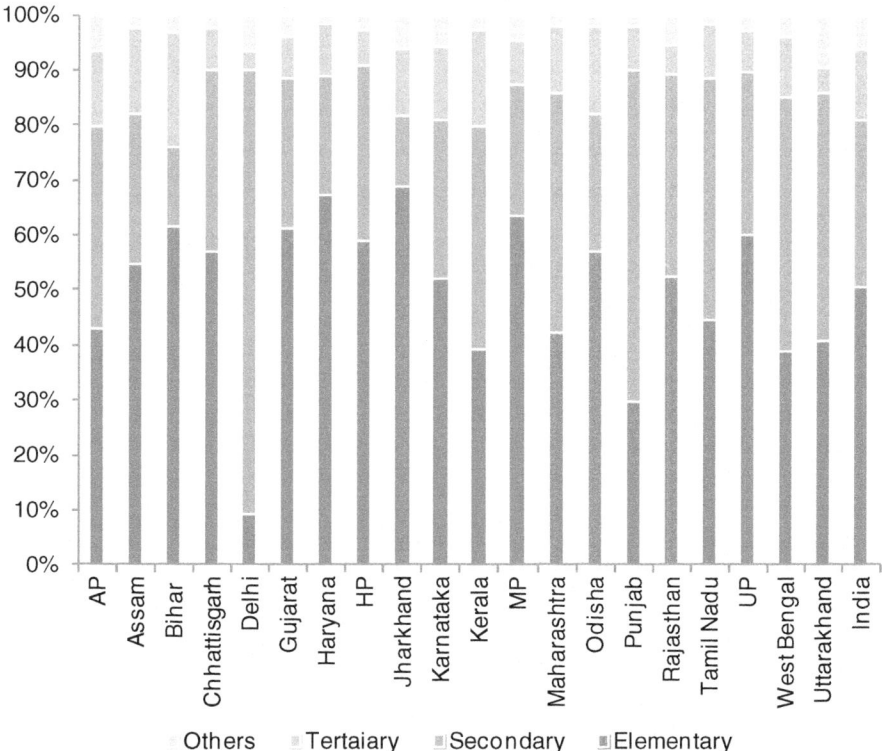

Fig. 9.10 State-wise percentage share of education expenditure by education department: by education level. *Source* Author's calculations based on data from Analysis of Budgeted Expenditure 2011–14 (MHRD)

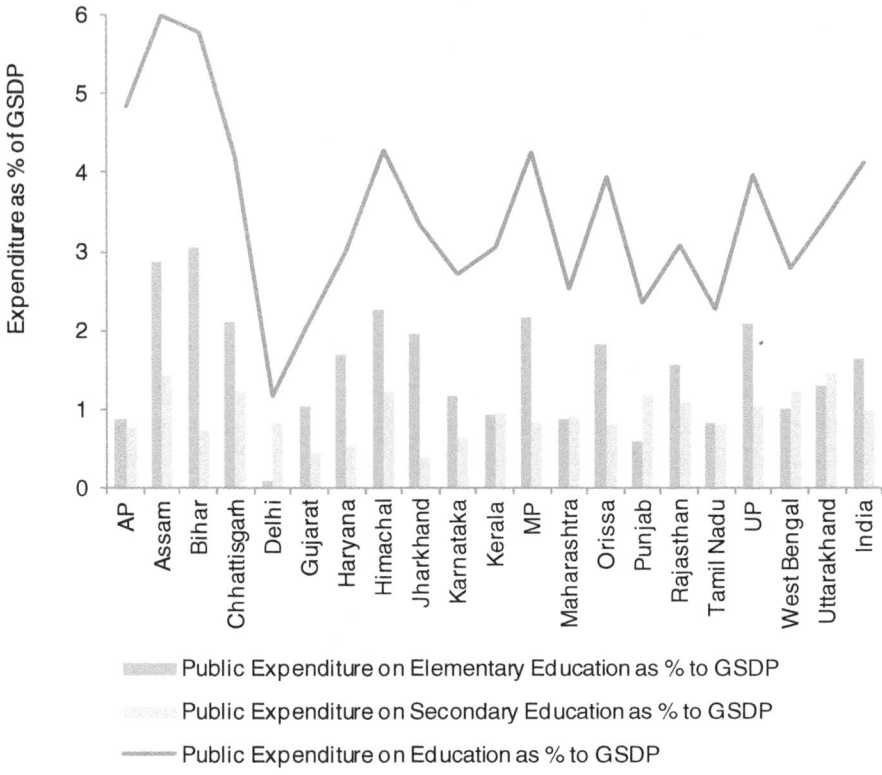

Fig. 9.11 State-wise public expenditure on education as % of GSDP. *Source* Analysis of Budgeted Expenditure 2011–14 (MHRD)

the highest on secondary education out of the total expenditure on education from state revenue budget are rich states like Delhi (77%), followed by Punjab (60%), Uttarakhand (48.6%), and West Bengal (46%). All these states including Maharashtra and Kerala, are spending more on secondary education compared to other levels of school or higher education. In contrast, Bihar and Jharkhand are among the least spending states on secondary education in India.

In addition, over the past decade, most states increased their spending per student in secondary education in real terms partly due to the fact that economic growth in those states made higher spending possible and also because the private unaided sector absorbed much of the expansion in number of students. Despite the fact that almost all states have increased their spending on secondary education, both in real terms and as a share of GSDP, most states still spend less than 1% of GSDP which is quite less. Figure 9.11 shows the variations in the pattern of public spending on education as percentage of GSDP by states at both elementary and secondary levels. The latest available data for 2013–14 shows that majority of the states in India spends higher share of educational expenditure as percentage of

GSDP on elementary education as compared to that of secondary education, with a few exceptions like Delhi, Odisha, West Bengal, and Uttarakhand. At the all-India level, about 1% of the educational expenditure as percentage of GSDP goes for secondary education, while for elementary education it is 1.6% (as in 2013–14). Among all major states in India, seven states have recorded the share of spending on secondary education as percentage of GSDP higher above national average of one. Although share of expenditure for secondary education (0.8%) in Delhi is higher than the expenditure incurred for elementary level (0.1%), Delhi's spending on secondary education is lower than the national average. Among the lowest spending states, Jharkhand, Gujarat, and Haryana tops the list. Gujarat is not only developed but is also one among the richer states; however, its share on education expenditure particularly secondary education is low.

It is generally seen that lower-income states have lower attendance ratios. Therefore, if secondary education is to expand proportionately among states, the Centre needs to provide more funds to lower-income states for investments and recurrent financing. This sub-section highlights huge disparities existing between states in terms of their spending patterns on various levels of education both in real terms and as shares of GSDP. The spending pattern across states not only varies by levels of education but also differs widely across different types of schools from the national averages. Hence, these established patterns between states' spending indicates a need for differentiated financing polices, with more or less emphasis on government or private-aided schools, in the drive to expand both access and quality of secondary education India.

9.4 Inter-states Disparities at Secondary Level Education

As seen above, the progress of socio-economic development is not uniform across states; so is the case of quality education dissemination. Factors such as literacy rates, female education, secondary enrolments, public expenditures, access to secondary schools, teacher's quality, income and employment levels, etc., and their interactions contribute to striking variations across states. It is evident from literature as well that the states in India are marked with wide disparities in socio economic development and these disparities mainly emanates from quality and scope of education, healthcare and PDS Abhiman Das (1999). This study further worked out that economic growth in the sense of expanding GDP and other related variables is one of the most fundamental input to the overall development. However, faster development may require government actions to improve education particularly for younger generation. Hence, it is really important to examine the variability in inter-state development of quality indicators for secondary education development. However, it is equally important to mention here that even broad-state level comparisons may not be able to capture the extent of diversity among the indicators due to several facets of development. Nevertheless, studying

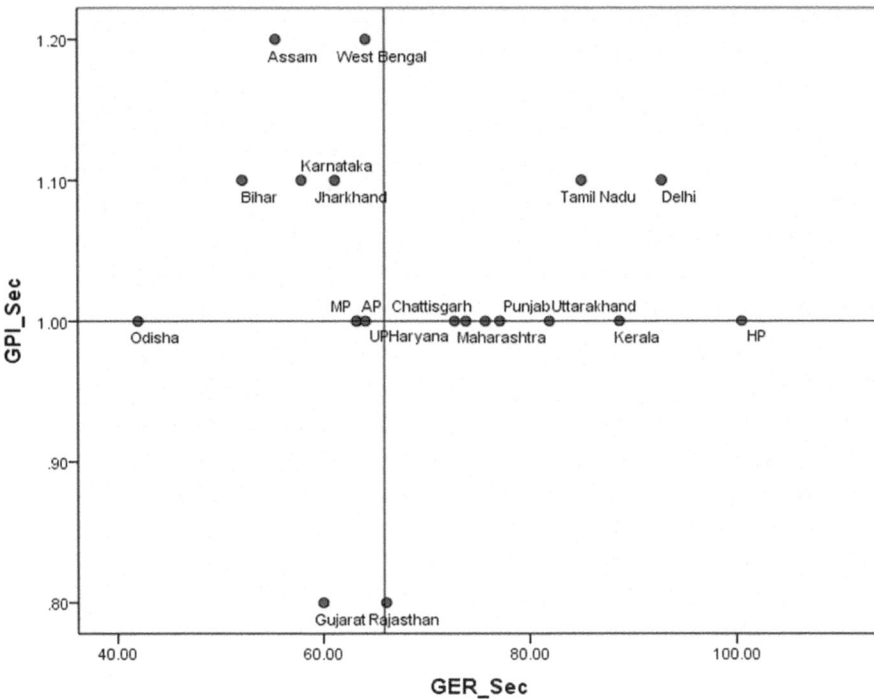

Fig. 9.12 GER versus gender parity index in secondary education. *Source* Calculations based on data from Secondary Education in India NUEPA 2014–15

state-level indicators are of prime importance as far as states are crucial and political units.

The strong supply-side expansion, together with rising household incomes and falling poverty has ensured that good progress continues to lift up enrolment at all levels of education. The GER at the lower secondary level has risen from 58.2% in 2007–08 to 65.2% in 2011 and further to 78.5% in 2014–15; for senior secondary levels it has gone up from 33.5% in 2007–08 to 39.2% in 2011 and to 54.2% in 2014–15, which is a great achievement, although at international levels these are still quite low. One of the reasons behind lower GER at the secondary level is the wide disparities existing at various levels across and within states. Efforts are made at the national level to reduce gender disparities in GER in secondary education, however, they are not significant. Moreover, the progress has been very uneven across states. Figure 9.12 shows inter-state variations in gender disparity in secondary school enrolment rates. The gender parity index reflects the male to female secondary school enrolment ratio. A ratio of '1' represents gender equality.

States such as Gujarat, Rajasthan, and Haryana have grotesque gender inequality; less than three-fourth girls are likely to enroll in secondary school than boys. In addition to this, states like Punjab and Haryana also have appalling gender

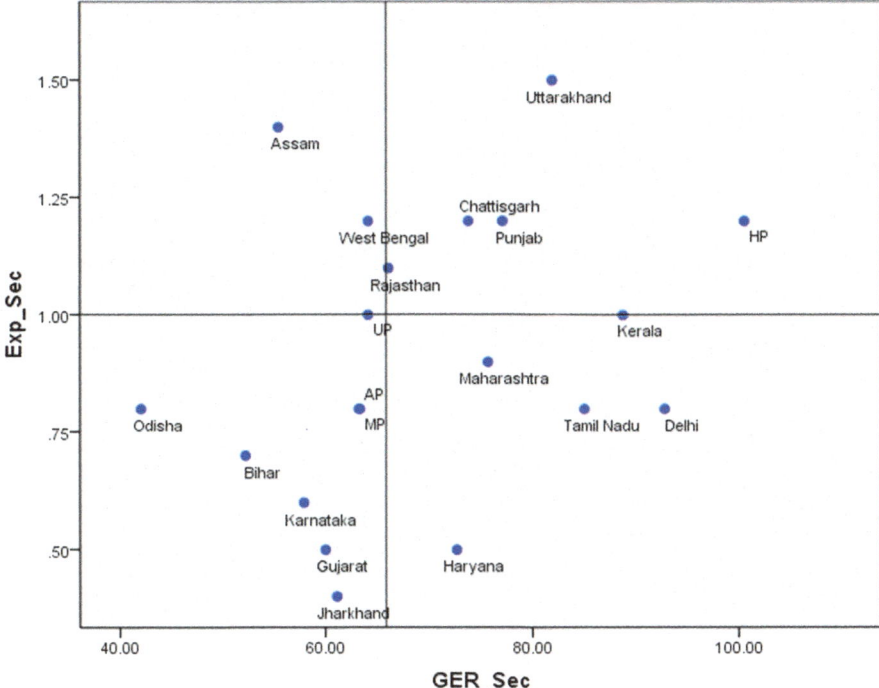

Fig. 9.13 GER secondary versus expenditure on secondary education as % of GSDP. *Source* Calculations based on data from Secondary Education in India NUEPA 2014–15 and ABE 2011–14

inequality rates. However, on the brighter side, many states have gender parity or even slightly pro-female secondary enrolment rates, for example, Tamil Nadu, Kerala, West Bengal and Assam. Kingdon (2005) finds that an important part of the reason for gender inequality is to be found within the household, as opposed to institutional explanations. Kingdon explains that within the household a strong bias prevails against daughters' enrolment in educational institutions and educational expenditure.

Figure 9.12 clearly depicts that states with higher GER at the secondary level also reflects higher gender equality. Tamil Nadu, Delhi, Kerala, Himachal Pradesh, Haryana, Uttarakhand, and Chhattisgarh are performing really well on GER due to higher female participation rates as shown by higher GPI. But then, there are even those states where GPI is although higher but still not performing that well on GER. However, the positive point to note here is that these states with higher GPI and lower GER are still improving and are moving towards achieving higher GER at the secondary level. Among these states, West Bengal and Jharkhand are ahead in the race. Public expenditure on secondary education as percentage of GSDP is also affecting the GER either directly or indirectly depending upon the education system in states (Fig. 9.13).

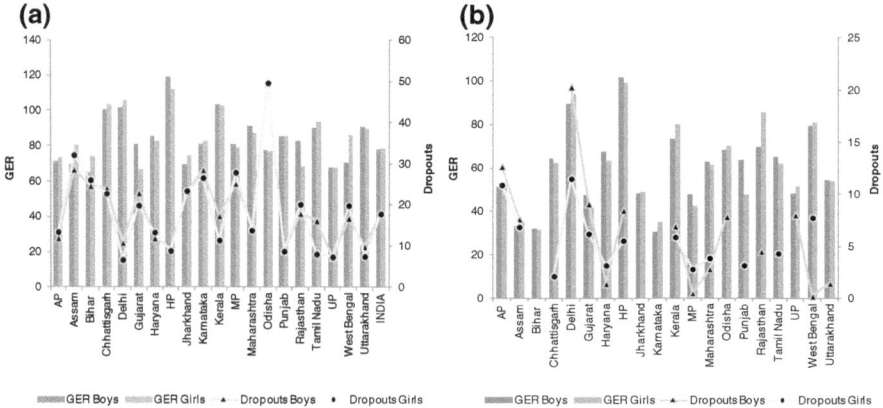

Fig. 9.14 **a** Gender disparity in secondary GER and average annual dropouts: lower secondary. *Source* Secondary Education in India NUEPA 2014–15, **b** gender disparity in secondary GER and average annual dropout: senior secondary. *Source* Secondary Education in India NUEPA 2014–15

The percentage of passed students in higher secondary level is better compared to the percentage of successful students in lower secondary schools. In 2013–14, 84% students from senior secondary level and 81.4% from lower secondary level cleared the exam. This clearly indicates that nearly 20% students were not eligible to enter senior secondary levels of education.

Although public expenditure is solely not responsible for raising up the bar of GER, the amount of private investment in secondary school education also matters a lot which varies widely across states. For instance, public expenditures on secondary education is 0.8% of GSDP in Delhi which is lower than the few best performing states and even below the national level of 1% expenditure of GSDP; however, in Delhi, there is huge private investment in education at the secondary level which has actually played an important role in raising up the enrolment rates (Fig. 9.13). Hence, both public and private investment are equally important in raising up the bar of secondary education in India.

The high instances of gender disparity across states is one of the major cause which is hindering the growth of secondary enrolments and overall education quality in India. Figure 9.14 depicts the level of variations between various states in GER and dropouts rates for both boys and girls at the secondary level.

It is seen that at the lower secondary level of education, states with higher dropout rates for both girls and boys are actually the states with lower GER (Odisha, Assam, Karnataka, Madhya Pradesh, Bihar, Jharkhand, Gujarat and Rajasthan) (Fig. 9.14a). It further shows that the highest enrolments for both boys and girls are observed in Himachal Pradesh, followed by Kerala, Delhi, Chhattisgarh, Maharashtra, and Tamil Nadu, and in these states except for Chhattisgarh, the average annual dropout for both girls and boys are found to be the lowest in 2014–15. However, at the senior secondary level of education, the highest dropouts for boys and girls is in Delhi followed by Andhra Pradesh (Fig. 9.14b). While, GER for boys and girls is higher in

Delhi, in case of Andhra Pradesh, male–female GER is quite low. In Delhi, the probable reason behind higher dropouts at senior secondary levels may be due to of the availability of several options for vocational education.

Generally, we have preconceptions in our minds that girl dropouts is higher in India compared to boys but actually this is not the case. The situation is the other way round as far as dropout rates are concerned in India; boys shows higher average annual dropouts at lower secondary level (17.9%) compared to girls (17.8%) at the all-India level. In fact, in majority of the states, this is what the situation is except for eastern and north-eastern states where dropout of girls is higher than boys. Moreover, amongst these states where girls show higher dropouts than boys at the lower secondary level, the gap between them is highest in case of Assam followed by West Bengal, Madhya Pradesh, and Rajasthan. There are even states where dropout of boys is much higher than that of girls and this gap is highest in case of Tamil Nadu, Kerala, and Delhi. Not surprisingly, these gaps also exist at regional levels for several sub-populations. For example, in lower secondary education, nearly 78% children aged between 14 and 15 years attend school in urban areas, while less than 55% children of the same age in rural areas attend school (as in 2014–15). Thus, it is utmost important to understand the gender and regional patterns of dropouts and enrolments and in identifying the reasons behind them at the state level before developing policies state-wise in order to minimize overall dropout rates and increase retention rates, thus enrolments for boys and girls in both rural and urban India.

Gender disparities in secondary education is not just limited to the students' level but also at the teaching level. Few studies indicate the positive impact of employment of female teachers in schools with improved learning quality in schools and in some cases even on increased female participation rates in India (Ammermueller and Dolton 2007; Dee 2007; Kingdon 2007). Hence, the number of females per 100 male teachers is also one of the important quality indicators which need to be studied here.

Figure 9.15 reflects the variations across states between male and female teachers in secondary schools at both lower and secondary schooling in 2014–15. It shows that the number of female teachers are higher at the senior secondary level than at the lower secondary one. At the national level, there are 72 females per 100 male teachers in lower secondary schools, while it is 71 females per 100 male teachers in senior secondary schools. There are a few states like Kerala, Punjab, Delhi, Tamil Nadu, Haryana, and Chhattisgarh where this proportion is much higher than the national averages at both lower and senior secondary levels of education. The proportion of female teachers per 100 male teachers is in fact more than double in case of Kerala and Punjab whereas in Delhi and Tamil Nadu it is nearly double at lower secondary level. At senior secondary level of education, only Kerala has more than double female teachers per 100 male teachers. In Punjab, it is near to double for senior secondary education.

The gap between both the levels of secondary education in terms of female teachers per 100 males is the highest in Tamil Nadu, Odisha, Andhra Pradesh, and Punjab. In Odisha, female teachers per 100 male teachers is higher at the senior

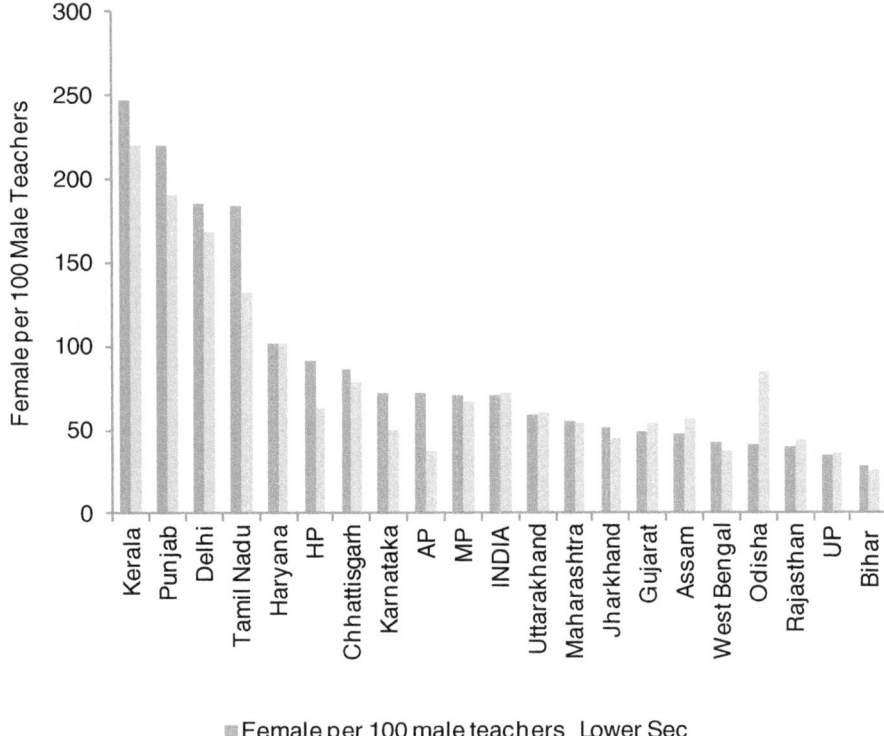

Fig. 9.15 State-wise female per 100 male teachers by level of secondary education. *Source* Secondary Education in India NUEPA 2014–15

secondary level. Another point to note is that at the lower secondary level, comparatively more states have female teachers per 100 male teachers above national averages. The states where this indicator has performed worst among all includes Bihar, Uttar Pradesh, and Rajasthan. At both levels of secondary education, Bihar shows only 26–28 female teachers per 100 male teachers (as in 2014–15). Even Maharashtra which has although performed well in few educational indicators is positioned below national average for this indicator with just 53–54 female teachers per 100 male teachers in secondary education.

Overall, this section presented a wide scenario on disparities existing between different states in India in terms of various quality educational indicators. Bihar, Odisha, Rajasthan, Uttar Pradesh, Gujarat, and Madhya Pradesh are lagging behind in most of the indicators for secondary education. Low gross enrolment ratios among various states is the expected pattern since secondary education is not compulsory and direct and indirect costs of attending schools are significantly greater in secondary education than in elementary education. Hence, these states really need to look into the policies to increase both expenditure and GER at the secondary education level. In addition to this, these states also need to work on improving female enrolments which further have huge implications on health and other social outcomes.

9.5 Secondary Education and Socio-economic Outcomes

The role of education and human capital in promoting the growth of economies and human well-being is well recognized in economic literature. In Chap. 3, we have tried to elaborate the key findings of the studies that have attempted to measure the impact of education on socio-economic outcomes in the literature review section. However, we found that most of these findings lack clarity on the exact relationship between education and the various outcomes. Therefore, in this part of the chapter we have tried to make an attempt to fill up this gap in existing literature and to bring more clarity on relationships between variables. This section will find answers to questions on how educational indicators perform at the state level, how these indices varies between states, and how at an aggregate state level it links with various socio-economic outcomes of the society as a whole. It will present a comparative view of educational performance by level of education, that is, elementary versus secondary. The model will also study the social, economic, demographic, and health profiles of states by the level of their advancement in secondary education and will try to understand the impact on various socio-economic outcomes. It is quite possible that infrastructural development could be the contributing factor for improvements in quality of educational services in some states, while in other states; it could be factors like economic factors, governmental policy efficiencies, or quality of human capital. Hence, it is really important to understand the efficiencies and capabilities of each state, analysing how they affect the quality of education. The section also looks at the profiles of households at the micro level in various states by studying employment, income, and well-being patterns of youths who have already attained secondary level education. While the first part of this section will show the impacts and importance of secondary education over elementary education at the macro level, the latter part of the section will show the benefits of secondary education at the household level. Hence, the model will proceed in two stages: macro-level and micro-level approach. We believe that the findings will help policymakers in formulating policy state-wise, in achieving best quality of education in India, while considering the social, economic, and demographic factors of each state separately.

9.5.1 Macro Model at Aggregate State Level[1]

The macro model has been constructed using latest data available for 19 major states in India from various renowned secondary sources on seven broad dimensions: elementary education development, secondary education development, economic performance, social performance, demographic performance, demographic-health performance, and health performance based on data obtained till 2011–12. For each of these dimensions a separate composite index was developed using principal component analysis (PCA) approach. Before developing this index at state-level, lot of literature was reviewed and was found that there have been very few efforts in educational development literature to show secondary educational development in the country and interstate comparison. In Indian context, Tilak (1979) has developed educational development index (EDI) for primary and upper primary level of education using enrolments and institutional cost indicators. Therefore, an attempt has been made through this study to develop separate indices for both elementary and secondary level of education. This model will study the educational perspectives at the macro level, that is, at the state's aggregate level. The value of index for each dimension is between 0 and 1. It shows that higher the score value of index and is near to 1, better is the performance of that particular dimension, except in case of Demographic-Health Index where impact is negative in relation to educational attainment and value near 0 denotes better performance and the higher score values of this index near 1 reflects weak performance (*The methodology for development of various indices is discussed in Part II of this book and Indicators list is given in Box A3 in Appendix*)

The educational development index at both the levels of education, that is, elementary and secondary, includes indicators which project the development of education in that sector. Economic index reflects the prosperity of states in economic terms. While demographic index considers variables related to population growth in respective states and other population-related indicators, demographic-health index, on the other hand, includes variables related to the basic health indicators of population residing in states. This index not only reflects the achievements of states in terms of initiatives taken to improve basic health facilities but also in bringing demographic transition in states. The health index covers indicators related to immunization, contraception's use, female health indicators, and health infrastructure. Finally, social index covers those indicators which have a great influence on society as a whole. All these indicators can bring huge change in society and have linkages with health and economic prospects as well. Moreover, not directly but indirectly education can change the mindsets of people and can bring change in society which does have long-term benefits for the nation as a whole.

---

[1]The results of this model have been presented at Population Association of America (PAA) International conference held in Chicago, Illinois, USA from 27–29 April, 2017.

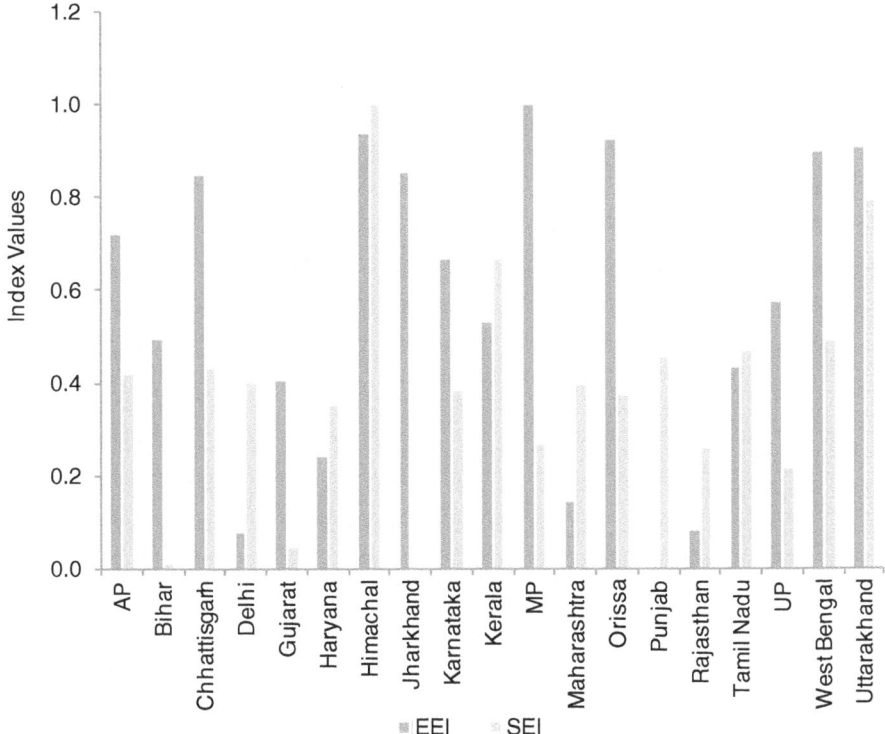

Fig. 9.16 State-wise distribution of elementary and secondary education index. *Source* Author's calculations

On the basis of the above indicators, index scores were calculated for each state and each dimension. The states were ranked on the basis of their index scores for all seven dimensions. The model brings eye-opening results. The result shows that it is not necessary that the states which are performing well at the elementary education level also perform well in secondary education. It shows that there are huge disparities between states and even within states in providing school education at both levels (Fig. 9.16).

Figure 9.16 shows that the best performing state in terms of EEI is Madhya Pradesh while Punjab has the lowest scores. On the other hand, in case of SEI, while Himachal Pradesh performs the best, Bihar demonstrates the worst. In most states, development of secondary education is lesser than elementary education. However, there are a few exceptions where focus is more on development of secondary education than the elementary one like in Delhi, Haryana, Himachal Pradesh, Punjab, Kerala, Rajasthan, Maharashtra, and Tamil Nadu. It is found that there are significant disparities within states in both levels of school education. Only in Himachal Pradesh, Kerala, Tamil Nadu, and Uttarakhand is overall school education been emphasized, since the level of disparities in these states between the elementary and secondary index scores are the lowest. On other fronts as well, the

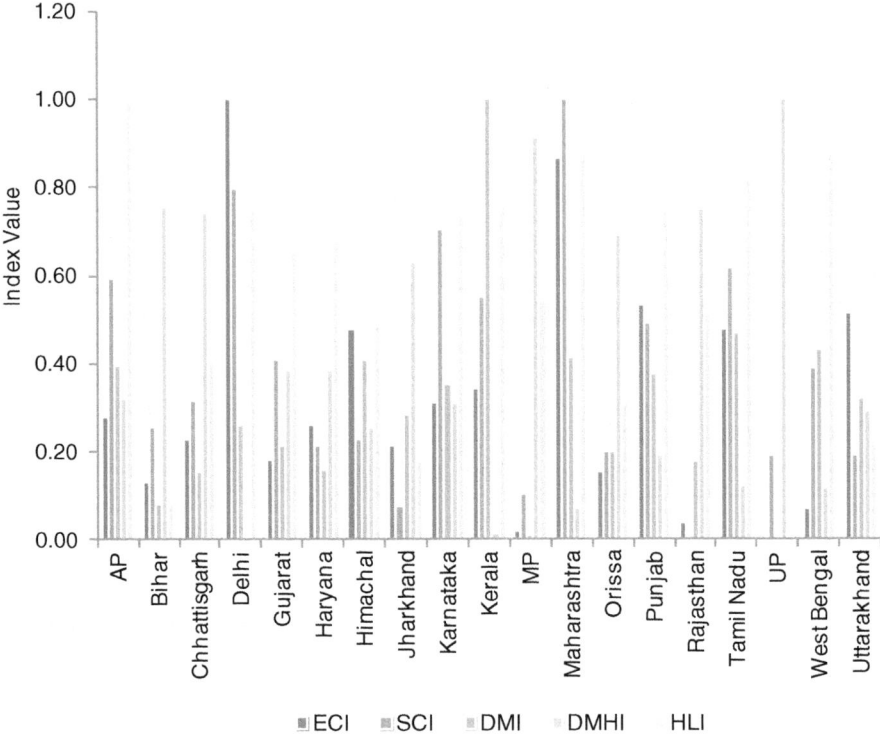

Fig. 9.17 State-wise distribution of various index scores. *Source* Author's calculation

Table 9.5 Regression results for states aggregate level

Indexes	Parameters	Economic index	Social index	Demographic index	Demographic-health index	Health index
EEI	B coeff.	−0.437	−0.380	−0.127	0.430	−0.357
	t-stats	−2.950	−2.114	−0.906	2.430	−1.814
	Significance	1%	5%	NS	5%	1%
SEI	*B* coeff.	0.569	0.292	0.513	−0.785	0.421
	t-stats	2.731	1.207	2.734	−3.303	1.596
	Significance	5%	NS	5%	1%	NS

Source Author's calculations
Note NS—Not significant; EEI—elementary education index; SEI—secondary education index

variation between states are significant. Figure 9.17 shows the level of variations among states with respect to economic, social, demographic, health and demographic-health indices.

Figure 9.17 shows that the performance of Uttar Pradesh is the weakest in four of the five indices discussed here; however, Rajasthan with regard to social index shows the weakest performance amongst all states. Amongst the best performing states, Delhi received the topmost ranking for economic and demographic-health index, whereas Andhra Pradesh scored the highest ranking in health index. Maharashtra has got top ranking for social development index, while Kerala performed best in terms of demographic index.

To have a better clarity on the impacts of elementary and secondary education attainment on various socio-economic outcomes at aggregate state level, simple linear regressions were run taking elementary and secondary education index as independent variables and other indices as dependent variables. The results are presented in Table 9.5. It captures the extent of impact on various socio-economic outcomes by elementary and secondary level of education considering various state-level indicators. The regression results reveal that the impact of secondary education attainment is higher than elementary education attainment on various dimensions at the state level. Secondary education index shows significant and positive impact on economic and demographic index, whereas in case of demographic-health index, the relation is significant but negative. This implies that as the level of secondary education increases, the chances of decline of BR, DR, IMR, MMR, and TFR also rises, which is good for the economy as a whole. In case of social and health index, although the results were not significant, the coefficient beta value were higher in case of secondary education for these two indices which implies that there might be indirect impacts which are surely higher than the attainment of elementary education. In contrast, although elementary educational attainment shows significant impacts on the economic, social, demographic-health, and health index, relations are negative between them which are not good for the growth of society as a whole.

9.5.2 Micro Impacts of Secondary Education

As seen in the previous section, secondary educational attainments have huge implications at the macro level. However, these benefits are not just limited to the macro level, they have huge impacts on individual lives at the household level too. It is equally important to study the implications of secondary education at micro level. The micro perspective will showcase the impact of elementary and secondary education attainments on household earnings, employment patterns, and fringe benefits which defines their status in society. In addition, the micro level analysis will also highlight the level of disparities in accruing these benefits at different stages: by states, location and gender.

To study the benefits at the micro level, information was required at the household level. The idea was to look for such a database which could provide state-wise information on individuals with different education status in order to study their achievements in terms of occupations, earnings, etc. Moreover, to highlight the disparities between the states and various educational attainment levels, the required data should be further bifurcated by rural–urban areas for both males and females. However, it was found that not many such primary data sets are available in India which satisfies the above criterion and in case where such data sets were huge cost factor was also involved. Hence, considering various cost and time limitations and limited availability of such datasets at the state level that fulfils the objectives of this study, it was decided to consider the National Youth Readership Survey (NYRS) data.

NYRS is a primary unit-level data conducted in 2009–10 by National Book Trust (NBT), India, in association with National Council of Applied Economic Research (NCAER) under National Action Plan for Readership Development of the Trust initiative. The NYRS study was conducted with an objective to cover various aspects of reading habits and readership development among youths in India. However, as one of its sub-objective, the survey also prepared the detailed demographic profile of Indian youth according to sex, age, education level, occupation, and other socio-economic characteristics which were required for our study. NYRS data provides responses from about 38,575 youths (13–35 years of age) from 35 states/union territories all over India which is further distributed by rural–urban areas to increase the precision of the estimates.

We have extracted data for 19 major states in India from data of 35 states/union territories, leaving out data on union territories, north-eastern states, and Jammu and Kashmir. For the selected 19 states, information was gathered on important indicators in rural and urban areas. To fulfill the objectives of our study, information was taken on indicators like: individual education attainment pattern, income categories, activity status, and well-being pointers. All these markers were analysed by various levels of education attained and thus an effort was made to locate the disparities at numerous levels.

The data set contains information on more than 35,000 youths (13–59 years) at the all-India level from both rural and urban areas. Of these nearly 52.1% youth had elementary education as their highest level of education while this was 27.5 and 20.4% in the case of secondary and tertiary education, respectively. Data was extracted for those youngsters for whom school education was the highest level of education and had not pursued tertiary level education; this included 27,885 youngsters all over India. Within this sample, the proportion of elementary education as the highest level of education attained was 65.4% compared to 34.6% with secondary level education. To reduce the complexities of data, the comparisons in this section have been done between elementary and secondary education as broad categories. While the elementary level includes below primary, primary, and middle, the secondary includes matric and higher secondary.

Data shows that there exist huge disparities between the states in secondary education attainment by gender and rural/urban. At the all-India level, the share of urban area (68.3%) is higher than rural areas (31.7%) in the attainment of secondary education. Similar disparities are reflected at the state level as well except in the case of Himachal Pradesh where rural sector outshined the urban area. However, as far as gender is concerned, not much disparities are reflected here although males show higher proportion as compared to females with secondary education. Except for Punjab, Bihar, Uttar Pradesh, Tamil Nadu, Karnataka, and Odisha, where

Table 9.6 Percentage distribution of youths by highest education level: by gender and location

States	Elementary				Secondary			
	Rural	Urban	Male	Female	Rural	Urban	Male	Female
Himachal Pradesh	74.1	25.9	48.8	51.2	59.4	40.6	52.2	47.8
Punjab	30.9	69.1	50.7	49.3	29.5	70.5	47.8	52.2
Uttaranchal	56.6	43.4	45.4	54.6	40.7	59.3	56.0	44.0
Haryana	39.5	60.5	51.6	48.4	31.7	68.3	54.1	45.9
Delhi	8.5	91.5	49.6	50.4	5.2	94.8	56.5	43.5
Rajasthan	47.9	52.1	47.7	52.3	37.5	62.5	52.0	48.0
Uttar Pradesh	39.3	60.7	50.4	49.6	30.8	69.2	48.6	51.4
Bihar	54.1	45.9	48.8	51.2	48.3	51.7	47.3	52.7
West Bengal	40.2	59.8	46.1	53.9	27.4	72.6	56.0	44.0
Jharkhand	53.9	46.1	47.8	52.2	40.4	59.6	53.0	47.0
Orissa	57.1	42.9	49.2	50.8	46.9	53.1	49.1	50.9
Chhattisgarh	57.2	42.8	49.2	50.8	34.9	65.1	52.0	48.0
Madhya Pradesh	45.4	54.6	47.8	52.2	36.7	63.3	51.8	48.2
Gujarat	35.5	64.5	48.4	51.6	27.9	72.1	53.2	46.8
Maharashtra	27.5	72.5	48.1	51.9	22.9	77.1	50.9	49.1
Andhra Pradesh	32.8	67.2	47.9	52.1	24.4	75.6	53.2	46.8
Karnataka	36.5	63.5	50.0	50.0	30.5	69.5	47.3	52.7
Kerala	41.9	58.1	52.7	47.3	46.9	53.1	51.2	48.8
Tamil Nadu	27.2	72.8	50.0	50.0	22.0	78.0	49.1	50.9
Total	40.3	59.7	48.9	51.1	31.7	68.3	51.1	48.9

Source Author's calculation based on NBT-NCAER National Youth Readership Survey Data 2009–10

female proportion is higher than males, in the rest of the states, the proportion of males is higher than females. At the elementary level also, there are differences between rural and urban education attainment levels, although the level of disparity is not that high as seen in the case of secondary education. Moreover, in this case, females constitute a higher proportion as compared to males; although with a few exception states (Table 9.6). The disparities in secondary education attainment at various stages are reflected in Fig. 9.18.

Another interesting fact to note is that about 41.4% youngsters who have mentioned elementary education as the highest education level wanted to pursue further education although they could not progress further. Of these, nearly three-fourths wanted to complete secondary level education at least, but could not pursue. The main reason behind the dropouts after middle education was financial problems in most cases (about 60%). The other reasons were family-related problems (nearly 30%) like household responsibilities or parents didn't allow, however, in some cases, the proportion of responsibility of schools for this was about 6% (Table 9.7). Hence, it suggests that majority of students had to discontinue their education after the middle level due to financial problems and family

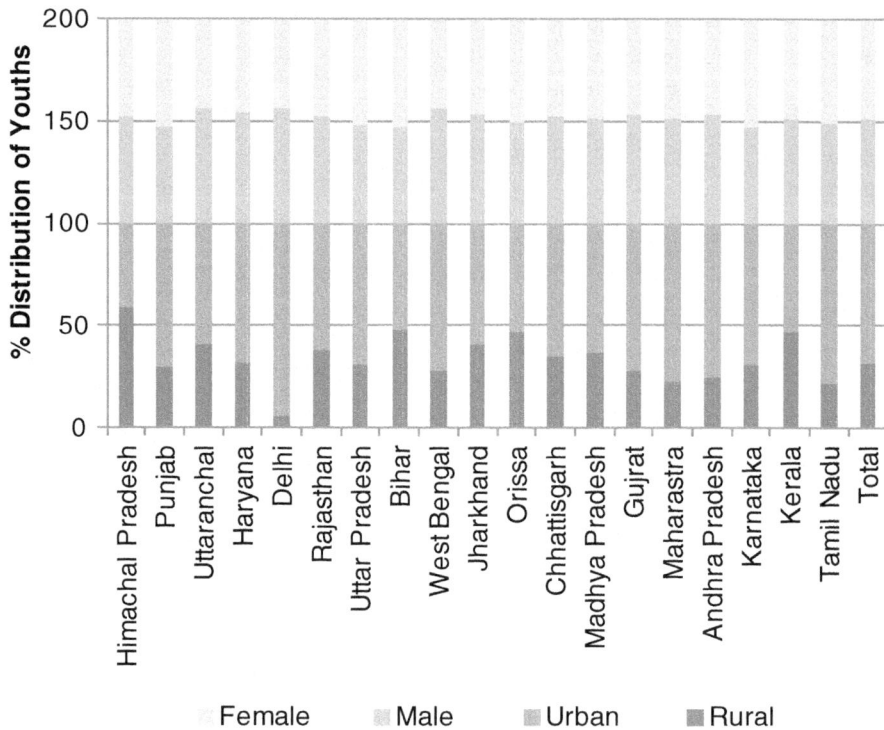

Fig. 9.18 Percentage distribution of secondary educated youths state-wise by: location and gender. *Source* NBT NYRS Survey Data 2009–10

responsibilities. Thus, a small effort by government in making school-level education less expensive can help a long way in opening the doors of education for those who are not able to afford.

The increased participation rates will further have implications on better job opportunities and raising income levels. To study the benefits that accrue to youths with different school education levels at the micro level, liner regression model was developed. In this, elementary education and secondary education were considered as independent variables while chances of being employed, for being into salaried jobs, and other benefits were taken as dependent variables (Table 9.8).

The regression model clearly reveals that the impact on individual-level outcomes is higher in case of secondary school education as compared to the attainment of elementary-level education by youths in India. While attainment of secondary education shows positive and significant impact on all outcomes considered for this model, elementary education on the other hand shows significant results in case of two outcomes only—employment and job stability. The results indicates that at the micro level, youths who have attained secondary schooling as the highest level of education when compared to those who had the elementary one,

Table 9.7 Percentage distribution of youths by dropouts and reasons: by gender and location

States	% Dropouts after middle level		Reasons for dropouts after middle level				
	Who wanted to continue studies	Wanted to complete at least XII	Financial problems	Household responsibilities	Parents didn't allow	Lack of jobs with higher studies	School related issues
Himachal Pradesh	54.4	32.5	44.4	34.2	6.0	13.7	0.0
Punjab	55.5	82.3	75.6	12.1	5.3	3.1	2.2
Uttaranchal	55.0	80.9	60.9	13.9	9.6	0.9	11.3
Haryana	32.2	76.3	68.3	6.5	9.4	7.2	5.0
Delhi	40.1	50.4	49.6	7.9	13.7	12.9	10.8
Rajasthan	42.4	67.4	57.8	13.4	8.5	4.9	8.0
Uttar Pradesh	42.8	66.8	72.5	10.9	10.1	2.6	2.8
Bihar	66.6	76.6	64.7	20.1	3.1	4.1	3.4
West Bengal	54.1	82.6	67.0	7.3	8.8	9.3	1.3
Jharkhand	80.3	84.7	74.1	12.8	6.7	1.3	3.5
Orissa	7.4	56.3	12.5	6.3	20.8	39.6	0.0
Chhattisgarh	53.1	74.7	57.2	13.5	6.7	6.1	4.0
MP	32.9	66.0	65.3	7.4	6.4	7.4	3.4
Gujarat	12.6	63.8	55.9	16.5	7.9	11.0	6.3
Maharashtra	33.6	62.8	71.5	10.1	3.5	6.4	3.5
Andhra Pradesh	68.3	55.2	35.0	7.9	28.8	9.2	18.2
Karnataka	26.0	12.8	54.3	7.3	26.5	2.1	8.1
Kerala	13.9	17.9	17.9	12.8	30.8	20.5	10.3
Tamil Nadu	36.2	29.7	45.6	14.8	20.1	11.7	2.5
Total	41.4	65.0	60.4	11.9	11.2	6.5	5.6

Source Author's calculation based on NBT NYRS Data 2009–10

had better chances of being employed and that too in regular salaried jobs. Moreover, secondary educated youth have higher confidence about their job's stability in comparison with elementary educated youths. While elementary educated youth shows insignificant results for aspired career choices, the secondary educated youth shows positive and significant relation here. Not only this but, in terms of owing security assets like ownership of life insurance and medical insurance policies, secondary education has significant and positive relation while elementary education attainment shows insignificant results.

To study the level of disparities between various outcomes from different education levels, we have to look at these indicators separately (Fig. 9.19a, b). While,

Table 9.8 Regression results for micro model

Indicators	Education level	B	t	Sig.
Employment	Elementary	0.283	4.573	1%
	Secondary	0.587	5.252	1%
Salaried job	Elementary	0.050	0.682	NS
	Secondary	0.268	2.022	10%
Job stability	Elementary	0.184	1.808	10%
	Secondary	1.008	5.490	1%
Life insurance	Elementary	0.101	0.928	NS
	Secondary	0.892	4.543	1%
Medical insurance	Elementary	−0.058	−1.350	NS
	Secondary	0.378	4.905	1%
Aspiring career	Elementary	−0.007	−1.030	NS
	Secondary	0.034	2.584	5%

Source Author's calculations based on NBT NYRS Data 2009–10

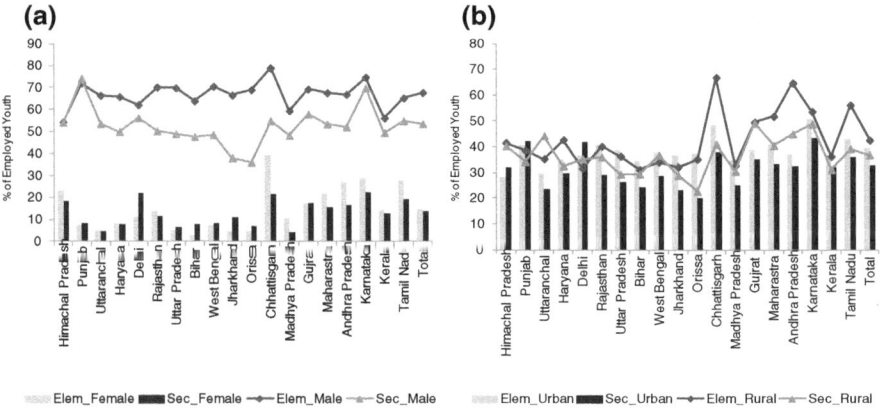

Fig. 9.19 Percent distribution of employed youths by: school education, gender and location. *Source* NBT NYRS Survey Data 2009–10

Fig. 9.19a shows the disparities by gender, Fig. 9.19b highlights the rural–urban inter-state disparities. The figure reveals variations in employment at both levels of education as per gender and rural–urban areas. It shows that males with either elementary or secondary education attainments are more employed as compared to females. Similar trends are noticed at the rural–urban levels as well. It is also seen that with the level of school education, the worker–population ratio tends to decline, though at the tertiary levels it again shows a rising tendency. The declining part at secondary education can be explained by the fact that once a youth pursues education he/she does not participate in the labour market until the desirable level is completed. Moreover, among lower levels of education, the worker–population ratio is high because of low incomes, implying that a greater number of persons were necessary to work to meet their consumption requirements. On the other hand, with increased income, only a few members within a household are required to work as the household can afford a higher dependency ratio. Even data from NSSO 66th round for 2009–10 reflects similar trends of employment in contrast to education attainment levels.

However, the case is not the same if we look at the distribution of salaried class by school education attainment levels. Figure 9.20a, b shows that the proportion of salaried youth are higher in urban than rural areas. Moreover, the proportion of youths employed in regular salaried jobs is higher in case of secondary education compared to the elementary one across all major states in India. Data shows huge disparities within states if we look at the proportion of youth in salaried jobs by gender with different educational attainments. It shows that with elementary education, the proportion of males in salaried jobs is higher than females, whereas, in case of secondary education the trend is opposite. Except for Himachal Pradesh, Gujarat, Tamil Nadu, and Haryana, all the remaining states in India show higher participation of females in regular salaried jobs with secondary education. Thus, it clearly suggests that an increase in the level of education, even if it is at the school level, promotes women empowerment.

The benefits of secondary education are not just limited to employment of youths but also extended to providing better incomes. Figure 9.21 brings out a clear distinction between the income levels of youth with different levels of school education in lowest and next top four quintiles. The reason behind combining top four quintiles is that it is seen that lesser proportion of youths with only school level education as their highest education are available in the top three quintiles. Hence, we have tried to show the difference between secondary and elementary education on the basis of the two lowest quintiles which constitute these youths the most. The figure clearly depicts that youths with secondary education attainments are higher in case of the top four quintiles whereas the youths with elementary education constitutes higher proportion in the lowest quintile. This reflects that with the increase in the level of school education, especially at secondary levels, the incomes of individuals tend to multiply further.

Increase in the level of school education not only increases job prospects and income levels of individual but also provides them greater assurance of job stability which helps the youth in maintaining their lifestyle and social status in a much better way (Fig. 9.22). Figure 9.22 shows that the secondary educated youths are more confident about their job stabilities than elementary educated youths. Not only this but a large proportion of secondary educated youths find their income level adequate enough to meet basic family needs across all states. These proportions are lower in case of elementary educated youths.

In addition to this, youngsters with higher schooling education are also more conscious about the physical and medical protection of their family members which is well reflected in the ownership patterns of life and health insurance polities.

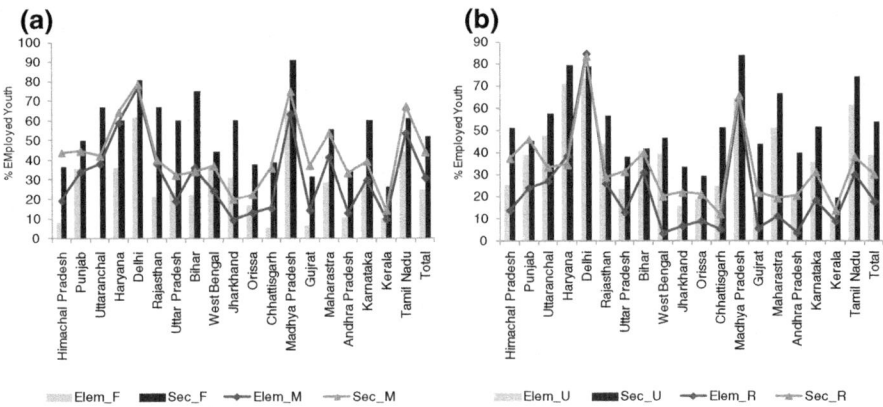

Fig. 9.20 Percent distribution of employed youths as salaried workers by: school education, gender and location. *Source* NBT NYRS Survey Data 2009–10

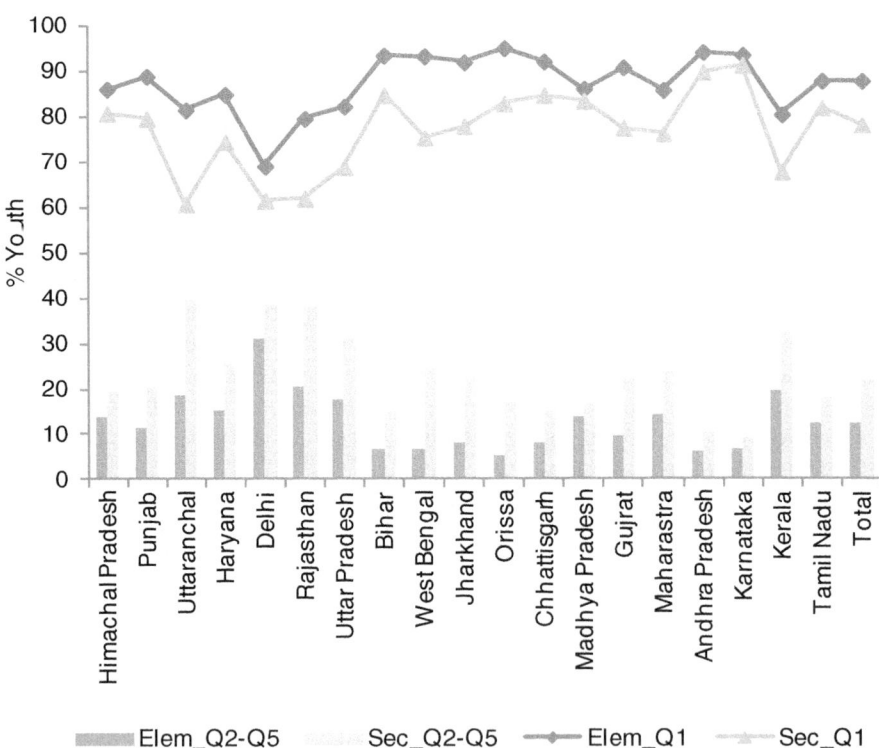

Fig. 9.21 Percent distribution of youths income by school education. *Source* NBT NYRS survey data 2009–10

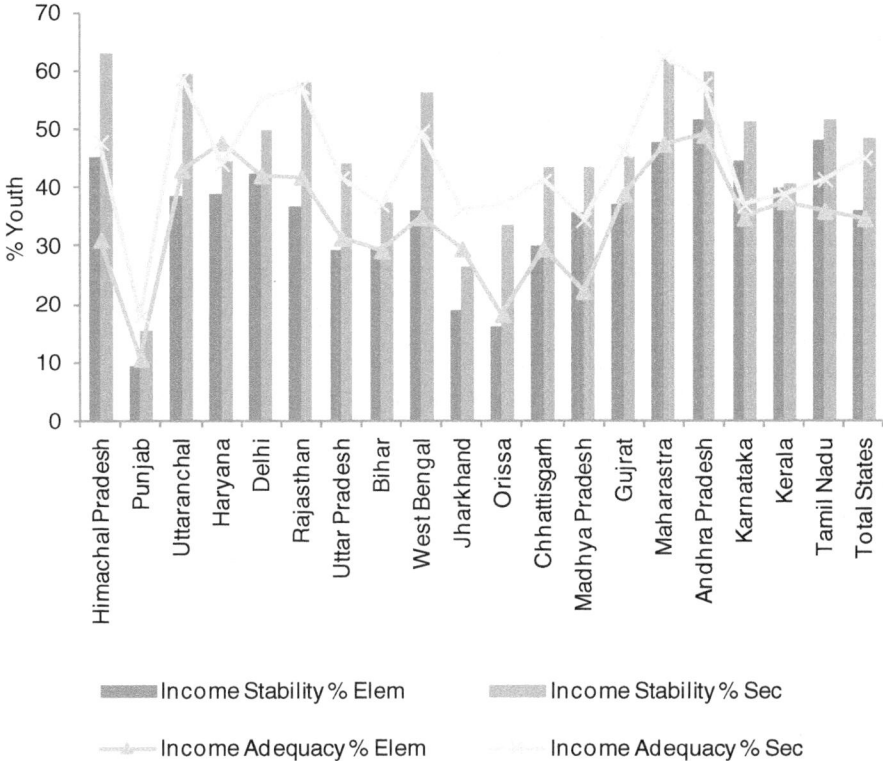

Fig. 9.22   Percent distribution of youths having confidence on job stability: by school education.
Source NBT NYRS survey data 2009–10

Figure 9.23 shows that more youngsters with secondary education are owning life insurance and health insurance policies than those with lower level of school education (Fig. 9.23).

It is evident from the above discussion that huge benefits can be accrued from secondary education at both individual and household levels which in turn can bring overall change in the lifestyle and status of households in terms of better occupations and income levels. At the same time, it also brings changes in the mindset of household members by providing them greater confidence about job stabilities and fulfilling basic family needs. In addition to this, it promotes savings within households and investments in intangible assets like insurance policies for family members.

Limitations of the Models: Although efforts have been made to consider most of the indicators at various dimensions to explain the model and its implications effectively at the state level, there might be certain indicators which are left uncovered and may have impacted the outcomes. Moreover, the analysis is limited to the major states in India. It excludes the north-eastern states, union territories and Jammu & Kashmir.

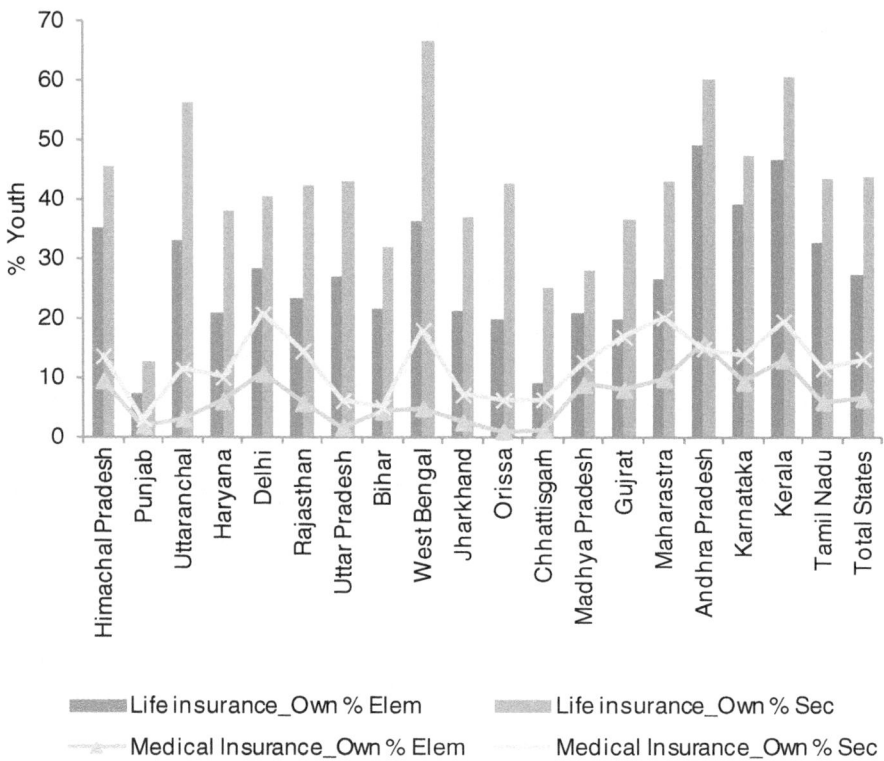

Fig. 9.23 Percent distribution of youths owning safety assets by school education. Source NDT NYR3 survey data 2009–10

9.6 Summary

On the whole, the chapter reveals that although progress has been made by states over the years in secondary education sector, the level of progress is slow and uneven. The findings indicate that the states incurring higher expenditure on education show higher attendance ratios as well. However, GER doesn't seem to flow with the expenditure pattern incurred by states. This is because in few states private schooling plays a major role compared to government-aided schools, hence, they have made huge private investments in secondary education which is actually raising the gross enrollment ratios in those states. Hence, it suggests that both public and private investment are equally important in raising up the bar of secondary education participation rates in India.

The state profiles further shows that it is not necessary that states which have done well in economic performance or social performance are also performing well on the education front. The analysis indicates that attainment of secondary education bear important relationship with various outcomes at both macro and micro levels. The macro model reveals that secondary education has direct impacts on economic growth, demographic transition, and demographic-health performances of states, whereas in case of social and health outcomes, it bears indirect impact. Along with this, it also shows that these impacts are much stronger in case of secondary education attainment as compared to elementary education attainment levels. Thus, it makes secondary education even more important area of concern not only at national level but for states as well. The micro model on the other hand found that youths with secondary education not only show significant relationship with regular salaried jobs but also with households in higher income quintiles. The result also shows that secondary education provides higher level of confidence to youngsters, in terms of job stability and in meeting basic needs of the family, than those who have pursued elementary education. The findings further suggest that secondary education helps in changing the mindset of people towards higher savings and safe future.

The chapter reveals that although progress has been made by states over the years in the secondary education sector, the level of progress is slow and uneven. The analysis in this chapter brings eye-opening results and suggests that the benefits attained from secondary education are huge at both micro and macro levels but cannot be achieved fully due to huge disparities existing at various stages in this system. Therefore, states need to make certain policies effective not only to minimize the differences in order to achieve balanced participation from various sub-populations but also to improve the quality of services. States need to re-design their education policies looking at their capabilities and inefficiencies in order to reap maximum benefits and grow in a balanced way.

References

Ammermueller, A., & Dolton, P. (2007). *Pupil teacher gender interaction effects on scholastic outcomes in England and the USA*. Centre for European Economic Research (ZEW), Discussion paper no. 06-060.

Census of India. (2001 and 2011). *Registrar general of India*. Government of India.

CSO. (2014–15). *Real growth rates of states—GSDP % at constant prices & other parameters released on 25 Oct 2011*. Directorate of Economics & Statistics of respective State Governments and for All-India.

CSO. (Various Years). *Statistical abstract of India*. New Delhi: Government of India.

Das, A. (1999). Socio-economic developments in India: A regional analysis. *Development and Society, 28*(2), 313–345.

Dee, T. S. (2007). Teachers and the gender gaps in student achievement. *Journal of Human Resources* (University of Wisconsin Press), *42*(3).

Government of India. (2011). *Report on family welfare statistics in India*. Statistics Division, Ministry of Health and Family Welfare.

Government of India. (2011–12). *Employment and unemployment situation in India*. NSS 68th Round 2011–12, MOSPI.

Government of India. (Various Years). *Economic survey of India*. Ministry of Finance, GOI.

Government of India. (Various Years). *Economic survey of India*. New Delhi: Oxford University Press.

Government of India. (Various Years). *Selected educational statistics*. MHRD.

Government of India. (Various Years). *Statistics of school education 2010–11 and 2014–15.* Ministry of Human Resource Development, Bureau of Planning, Monitoring & Statistics, New Delhi.

Kingdon, G. G. (2005). Where has all the bias gone? Detecting gender bias in the intra-household allocation of educational expenditure in rural India. *Economic Development and Cultural Change, 53*(2), 409–452.

Kingdon, G. G. (2007). *The progress of school education in India*. GPRG-WPS-071, March 2007, Global Poverty Research Group, ESRC Global Poverty Research Group. Website: http://www.gprg.org/.

Malhotra, S., & Singh, S. L. S. (2006). Linkages between poverty, education, health and development in India. *The Indian Economic Journal*, 364–390.

MHFW. (2013). *Estimates of total fertility rate (TFR), family welfare statistics in India: 2006–2010.* Sample Registration System (SRS), GOI (released on April, 2012).

NBT. (2009–10). National youth readership survey data used for analysis. Data collected by NCAER under National Action Plan for Readership Development of the Trust Initiative of National Book Trust (NBT), India.

Planning Commission. (2011). *DCH data book*. May 18, 2011. http://planningcommission.gov.in.

Shiva Kumar, A. K. (1991). Human development index for Indian states. *Economic and Political Weekly, 26,* 243–245.

Tilak, J. B. G. (1979). Interstate disparities in educational development in India. *Eastern Economist, 73*(2), 140–146.

Part IV
Determinants of Quality of Education: Empirical Results and Discussion

Chapter 10
Profile of Sample Population: An Overview

Abstract This chapter provides an overview of the sample population to have an insight about the quality of secondary education in schools in a more comprehensive way. The information provided in this chapter is purely based on the primary survey data collected from 41 sample schools in Delhi by interviewing students, teachers, and key informers. The chapter is divided into four sections—the first section discusses the in-depth profile of sample schools in terms of facilities available in general, types of courses offered, enrolments, teachers and their qualifications, etc.; the second section elaborates the characteristics of teachers in sample schools; the third section deals with the socio-demographic characteristics of student respondents who are presently studying in selected sample schools in lower and senior secondary level of education; while the last section summarizes the major findings.

Keywords Government schools · Private schools · Socio-demographic characteristics · Teachers' characteristics · Class size · Family background · Students' characteristics

10.1 Profile of Sample Schools

To measure the significance of schools on performance and learning outcomes of students, the information on the quality of resources and infrastructural facilities was gathered from 41 sample schools covering both private and government-owned schools from all over Delhi. This section elaborates the profile of schools in terms of geographical patterns, ownership type, enrolments, teachers and their qualifications, courses offered, facilities provided to both students and teaching staff. This will also help in studying the regional differences in the quality of education provided in schools in Delhi.

© Springer Nature Singapore Pte Ltd. 2018
C. Jain and N. Prasad, *Quality of Secondary Education in India*,
https://doi.org/10.1007/978-981-10-4929-3_10

10.1.1   Enrolments and Performance of Sample Schools

This section provides a brief description on enrolment rates, class structure, and average performance of students in sample schools according to regions and type of school ownership.

School Ownership: The average number of total student enrolments in the selected school sample, constituting First–Twelfth standards, is around 2,162. The average student enrolments are higher in private schools at 3,021 compared to 1,612 in government schools indicating the growing importance of privatization of school education in Delhi. Of these, on an average 39% of the total student enrolment in schools is of secondary enrolments with approximately 34% in private schools and 38% as in government schools for secondary level enrolments. The survey findings further show that despite lower student enrolments, the average class size is much higher in government schools at nearly 63 students per class, while this is just at 45 students per class in private schools. This could be due to lack of sufficient classrooms in government schools. In contrast, pupil–teacher ratio reflecting the number of students per teacher is lower in government schools compared to that of private schools, thus revealing lack of sufficient teaching staff in private schools. One reason justifying this argument could be that in government schools, there is a large number of contract teachers in addition to permanent teachers due to which PTR is comparatively lower. On the other hand, the performance of students passing out the Twelfth Standard exam in the last academic year suggests that the results are far better in private schools over the government schools results (Table 10.1).

Regions: The regional distribution of responses shows that total enrolment in schools is highest in the North followed by West and East. In the South enrolment rates are the lowest. The pupil–teacher ratios are quite higher in schools in the North and East as compared to West and South. However, in terms of percentage share of secondary enrolments out of the total enrolments, East and West holds 38% share of secondary enrolments, while the North and West holds 35% share of secondary enrolments in total enrolment approximately. The average class size is the highest in the East with 65 students per class followed by the West and North, while in the South it is the lowest. Table 10.1 shows that the North outshines all other regions in terms of average performances of students in the Twelfth Standard, while the East reflects the lowest passing percentage among all. The trend is almost similar at the school ownership level as well. In case of both government and private schools, while the passing percentage of students is the highest in the West and North regions, the East has performed the poorest amongst all.

Table 10.1 Average performance of sample schools by regions and ownership type

Trainings/Workshops	North	South	East	West	Overall
Government schools					
Average enrolments in schools	2,303	655	1,652	1,991	1,612
Average PTR in school	25.6	16.6	25.2	27.4	23.8
% Share of secondary enrolments	37.7	37.0	41.3	38.0	38.8
Average secondary class size	63.3	45.5	74.0	65.0	62.9
Passing % in XII CBSE 2012–13	93.5	89.1	86.3	93.0	90.0
Private schools					
Average enrolments in schools	3,392	2,570	3,206	2,917	3,021
Average PTR in school	59.7	48.9	49.9	40.0	49.6
% Share of secondary enrolments	33.0	33.0	33.4	36.5	34.0
Average secondary class size	43.8	47.5	48.3	41.5	45.3
Passing % in XII CBSE 2012–13	99.8	99.4	98.5	100.0	99.4
Total schools					
Average enrolments in schools	2,848	1,421	2,170	2,328	2,162
Average PTR in school	42.6	29.5	33.4	32.0	33.9
% Share of secondary enrolments	35.3	35.4	38.7	37.5	36.9
Average secondary class size	53.5	46.3	65.4	56.5	56.0
Passing % in XII CBSE 2012–13	96.6	93.2	90.4	95.5	93.7

Source Primary survey
Note Figures in table represents the findings of the surveyed schools only

10.1.2 Curriculums and Teachers Qualification in Schools

This part of the chapter presents the description of a variety of subjects/courses offered to students and the minimum qualifications required for teachers at different levels of school education.

Subjects Offered: Fig. 10.1 shows that a variety of subjects are offered to students at both lower and senior secondary levels of education in private and government schools. Almost all schools in Delhi provides compulsory subjects like English, Math, Natural Science, Social Science, and Hindi at the lower secondary level. However, in case of optional subjects, few schools offer Sanskrit and Computer Science as well. The data reveals that only 4% of government schools are giving the option of choosing computer science as an optional subject in lower secondary education, while it is much higher at 62.5% in case of private schools. This reflects the lack of sufficient resources in government schools. At senior secondary level, the situation of government schools in terms of offering a variety of subjects is quite poor. There are very few government schools which are providing science education, including medical and non-medical streams to students, while majority are limited in offering arts and commerce as fields of study. In contrast, almost all private schools are offering commerce as a stream of study to students, followed by arts and science subjects. The non-availability of the preferred

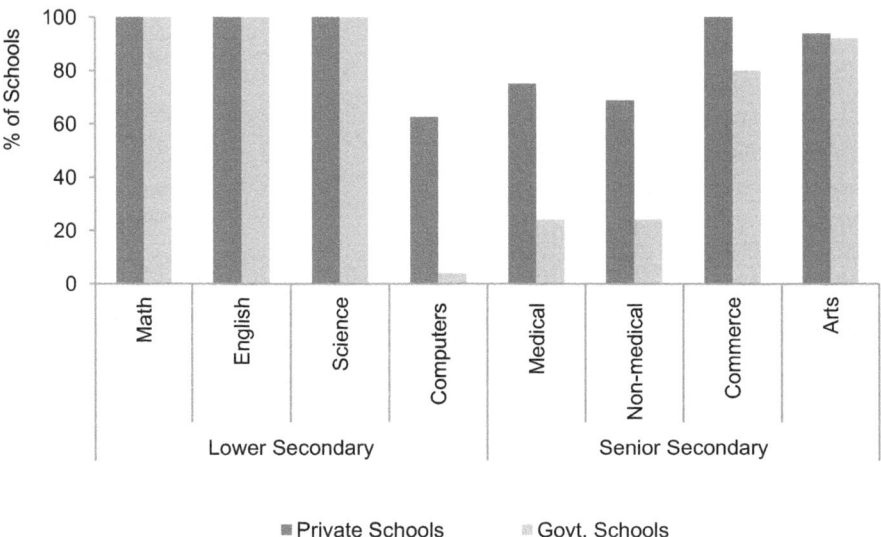

Fig. 10.1 Percentage distribution of schools by subjects offered and teacher qualifications: by school ownership type

field of study can lead to many consequences; particularly, in the case of government schools, this could be one of the reasons behind higher dropouts after middle or at lower secondary levels. Those who continue pursuing higher secondary education in government schools either need to shift the schools due to non-availability of subjects or choices or have to continue with available options unwillingly which leads to poor performance. In fact, this is one of the key reasons why private schooling is in high demand, even among poor income classes.

Minimum Qualification of Teachers: Larger proportion of private schools hire teachers at the primary level of education with graduation and teacher training degree, while in case of government schools, the minimum qualifications of teachers are completion of higher secondary education and a teacher training degree. For middle-level classes in both types of schools, graduate teachers with a B.Ed. degree from a recognized university are mostly hired. At the secondary level, however, 46% of the total schools have teachers with masters and B.Ed. degree from reputed universities, while 24% of schools have teachers at secondary level with graduation and B.Ed. degree. Overall, the data shows that at the lower secondary levels, schools hire teachers with graduate and B.Ed. degrees but at the senior secondary level, almost all schools take teachers with at least a Master's degree. Survey further reveals that proportion of teachers at the secondary level with higher qualifications (MA with B.Ed. or M.Ed.) is higher in government schools as compared to private schools in Delhi. Overall, in Delhi at the secondary level of education, almost all schools irrespective of their type of ownership, hire well-qualified teachers.

10.1.3 General Facilities and Basic Provisions Available in Schools

School Facilities: Almost all sample schools in Delhi are equipped with fire safety measures, of which 95% schools confirmed that such services are in working condition (Fig. 10.2). However, in government schools, fire safety measures were not functioning. In most cases, the staff is unaware about how to operate these measures in case of emergency; hence, it is evident that proper training sessions are not provided in schools. Nearly 94% private schools conduct regular health check-up camps for students; only 64% government schools carry out such camps and that too are infrequent. While 75% of private schools have their own transport facilities for students, government schools usually do not offer such amenities. In providing medical facilities too, private schools are on upper edge as compared to government schools.

General Provisions in Schools: The general provisions are further divided into three sections: for the staff, students, and for all. About 50% of private schools follow their own salary norms, while the remaining 50% follow government norms. In case of government-owned schools, all schools follow government-fixed salary norms only. The increment on the salaries of teachers in government schools is done annually, while this proportion is 81.3% in case of private schools. Regarding promotional strategies, government-owned schools have uniform system throughout as per the notice of Directorate of education, while private schools follow their

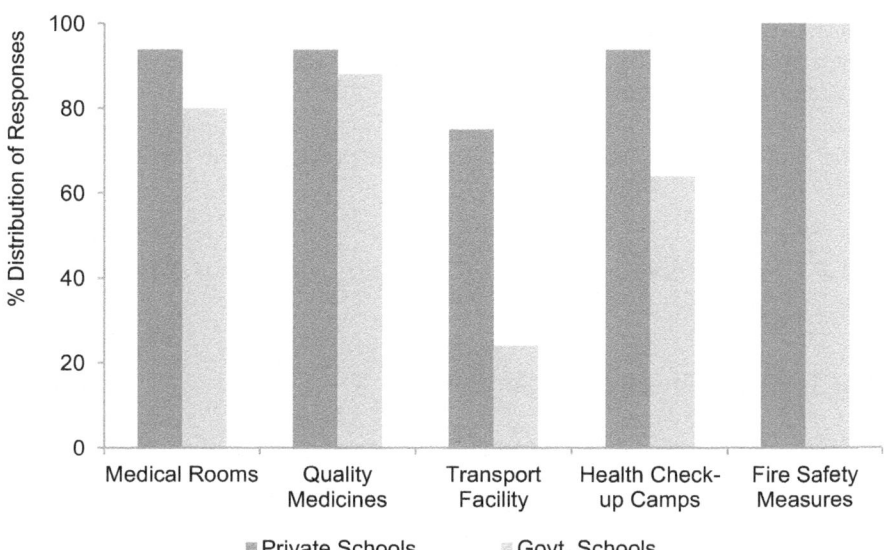

Fig. 10.2 Percentage distribution of responses by facilities in schools: by ownership type

own strategy. Most private schools promote teachers on the basis of years of experience, while remaining one-fourth schools follow government policies.

Within student-related provisions, the most important are related to admission norms. Only 75% private schools follow reservation policies at the time of admissions set by the government, whereas the remaining follows their own. About 76% government schools and 87.5% private schools have facilities for teaching handicapped students. Unlike most private schools, government schools provide free uniforms, books, and fee discounts to students, thereby serving the low-income group. Almost all sample schools have hospitals located nearby. However, in case of emergencies, more than 80% sample schools provide first aid and send students back home. Most schools take responsibility for physical safety of students but only within school premises, while few private schools take the responsibility of student safety till they reach home. In government schools, the safety of students is a major issue.

10.2 Teachers' Characteristics and Backgrounds

To have a better understanding of issues like quality of education in schools, performances of students, and factors affecting efficient teaching abilities, about 160 teachers are interviewed face-to-face. For a comparative analysis, on the basis of type of ownership of schools, the sample of teachers is equally distributed between private and government schools. About 71% teachers teach in co-ed schools, while 11% in boys' schools and 18% in girls' schools. This section will elaborate the profile of teachers presently teaching lower and senior secondary classes in sample schools. The information in this section is based upon the responses taken from teachers in schools through primary survey. The section will also highlight the socio-demographic profile of the teachers along with their educational backgrounds. In addition to this, their teaching profiles, professional development characteristics, and the non-teaching activities undertaken by them will also be discussed.

10.2.1 Socio-demographic and Teaching Profile of Sample Teachers

10.2.1.1 Socio-demographic Characteristics

Table 10.2 presents the demographic and social characteristics of the teachers in the sample. Nearly 67% teachers in our sample are females, while remaining 33% are males. The average age of male teachers is 42 years, while for female teachers it is 39 years. Nearly 55.6% teachers are above 40 and a larger proportion of the sample teachers are married. About 72% of the teachers have passed out their highest

Table 10.2 Percentage distribution of teachers by socio-demographic characteristics

Particulars	% of teachers
Gender	
Male	33.1
Female	66.9
Age categories	
Up to 30 years	23.8
30–40 years	20.6
40–50 years	43.1
>50 years	12.5
Average age of teachers (in years)	*40*
Marital status	
Unmarried	11.3
Married	86.9
Widow/Widower	1.9
Highest educational qualification	
Graduate without teacher training	2.5
Graduate with teacher training	43.8
PG or above without teacher training	10.0
PG or above with teacher training	43.9

education through English medium, while remaining through Hindi medium. The findings further shows that in total, nearly 46% teachers are graduates, while 54% teachers are postgraduates or possess higher degrees. Although majority of the teachers hold training degrees as well, there is still a certain percentage of sample teachers (12%) who are teaching without any training degree. As far as their area of specialization is concerned, wide variations are reflected. Majority of the teachers (that is 56%) have Mathematics, English, and Commerce as their specialization area in their highest education level, while 20% have specialized in science and engineering subjects.

10.2.1.2   Teaching Characteristics

Almost 67% teachers are teaching in English-medium schools and 33% in Hindi medium. Teaching experience ranges from low experience, that is, 10 years of familiarity (constituting 35% of the sample teachers) to high experience, or teachers with more than 20 years' (nearly 26%) practice. Survey results further show that 61% of the surveyed teachers take up lower secondary classes, while 28% teach senior secondary students only and the remaining 11% address both levels of secondary education. The findings indicate that teachers of lower secondary classes take a higher number of classes per week, on an average, compared to those who teach senior levels of secondary education. However, the burden is higher on those who are teaching both levels of secondary education simultaneously.

10.2.1.3 Professional Development Characteristics

The ability of teachers to function effectively in their jobs depends not only on their level of educational attainment but also on the training they receive to enhance their teaching abilities. The survey findings indicate that in government schools larger proportion of teachers acquire training to enhance their skills than private school teachers. In government schools, the proportion of teachers who have acquired training in the last five years accounts for 75% of the sample, while in private schools it is only 56%. Among those who have attended training, nearly 22% of the teachers in government schools do not find these training beneficial, while this proportion is just 9% in case of private schools. Teachers who have not attended any training during the last five years have mentioned various reasons: for them the training is non-beneficial; they did not have adequate time to undertake the training; though applications were few, many didn't get a chance; the training provided is not related to their area of interest (Fig. 10.3).

Along with training, the other important factor that enhances efficiency and enthusiasm among teachers is to teach subjects of their own choice/specialized area. The survey finds that a certain proportion of teachers are teaching subjects that are not from their area of specialization. The proportion of such teachers is higher in government schools compared to private ones.

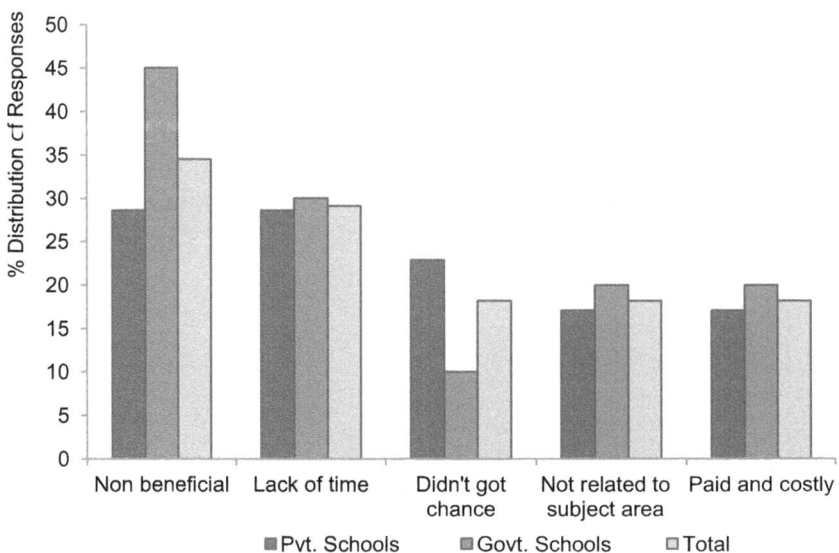

Fig. 10.3 Percentage distribution of responses for not attending trainings

10.2.2   Non-teaching Profile of Activities

In addition to teaching responsibilities, teachers are also involved in many other activities related to admissions, curriculum designing, functioning of school, managerial activities, etc., which lay an impact on their teaching capabilities. The reason being that more a teacher is involved in non-teaching practices, lesser the time he/she is able to devote in teaching practices. Among non-teaching practices, the most prominent practices are marking papers and organizing school activities, as mentioned by almost 86 and 77% of the sample teachers. Nearly 29% teachers are involved in handling school publications, while 26% help in setting examination papers. Other important activities undertaken by teachers are designing course structure and time table planning (33.2% of teachers).

10.3   Students Characteristics and Backgrounds

Along with teachers, perspectives of students on their schools, teaching quality, and performance levels have also been canvassed. For this, about 512 students from senior secondary sample schools were interviewed. The distribution of students among regions, school ownership types, and levels of education are equally represented. This section gives description on the individual characteristics of the students such as demographic and social characteristics, family characteristics, education profiles, and general characteristics related to their part-time interests/hobbies of students. Information regarding dropout students and reasons for dropouts is also presented in this section.

10.3.1   Socio-demographic Profile of Students

Table 10.3 presents the demographic and social characteristics of students.

Gender: To have a better understanding of performances and learning behaviours of both male and female students, quota was fixed on gender distribution and because of this, out of 512 student samples, 50% are boys and 50% are girls.

Age: The age profile of students suggests that nearly 59% students in secondary education belong to the age-group of 15–17 years, while 37% are in the category of up to 15 years. The sample also covers about 3.7% students who are in the age group of 17–20 years. This could be due to either late admission in school or dropout or repetition of classes.

Social Caste/Religion: Nearly 53% of students come from 'General' category, while remaining 47% of the students are of 'Non-General' category. The distribution of students across various religions illustrates that about 85.5% are Hindus, 10% are Muslims, and 4% are of other religions including Sikhs, Christians, Parsis, Buddhists, Jains, etc.

Table 10.3 Percentage distribution of student sample by socio-demographic characteristics

	Govt.	Private	Total
Gender			
Male	50.0	50.0	50.0
Female	50.0	50.0	50.0
Age (in years)			
Up to 15 years	37.9	36.3	37.1
15–17 years	55.9	62.5	59.2
17–20 years	6.3	1.2	3.7
Social caste			
SC	14.2	14.5	14.3
ST	11.3	7.3	9.3
OBC	25.9	20.2	23.0
General	*48.6*	*58.1*	*53.3*
Religion			
Hindu	82.4	88.7	85.5
Muslim	12.9	7.4	10.2
Sikh	2.0	2.7	2.3
Christian	0.8	–	0.4
Others[a]	1.6	1.2	1.4
Total Students	256	256	512

[a]Others include Buddhist, Jain, Parsi and Atheist

10.3.2 Family Characteristics

Table 10.4 presents the family characteristics of the students in terms of their family size, type of family, household ownership, and major source of household income.

Household Characteristics: About 81% of the surveyed students come from nuclear families and the remaining 19% are from joint families. On an average, the household size is 4 members per household. About 73% students reside in their parent's own house, while less than 24.5% in rented accommodation. Those living in rented accommodation constitute a larger proportion in government schools.

Major Source of Household Income: The major source of household income varies significantly according to type of school ownership. Nearly 37% of the sample students studying in government schools belongs to the salaried class with salary earnings being the major source of household income, while this proportion is 55% in case of students studying in private schools. The next highest source of income is wage earning for government schools students, while for private school students, it is business/trade. Overall, majority of students in the sample comes from the salaried class followed by business families.

Income Characteristics of Household: The findings indicate that there is significant difference in the household income distribution of students studying in private and government schools. Nearly 70% students in private schools come from top two quintiles, while those studying in government schools constitute 66.5%

Table 10.4 Percentage distribution of students by family characteristics

	Govt.	Private	Total
Family type			
Joint	22.7	15.6	19.1
Nuclear	77.3	84.4	80.9
Household size categories			
Up to 5 members	85.5	88.7	87.1
5–10 members	13.3	10.5	11.9
>10 members	1.2	0.8	1.0
House ownership type			
Rented	34.3	14.5	24.5
Own house	63.7	83.5	73.4
Major source of household income			
Wage earner	35.2	1.6	18.4
Salary earner	37.1	54.7	45.9
Business/Trade	12.9	27.7	20.3
Self employed	12.5	13.7	13.1
Others	2.3	2.3	2.1
Income adequacy to meet family basic needs			
Adequate	36.8	64.7	51.0
Somewhat adequate	35.9	18.9	27.3
Inadequate	10.8	2.9	6.8
Don't know	16.5	13.4	14.9
Household income distribution by quintiles			
Q1	31.0	4.0	17.6
Q2	35.5	6.9	21.2
Q3	20.6	19.4	20.0
Q4	10.5	38.5	24.4
Q5	2.4	31.2	16.8

share in the bottom two income quintiles. When asked about the adequacy of family income to meet the basic needs, almost 37% students from government schools and 65% from private schools mentioned household income to be adequate.

10.3.3 Educational Profile

Table 10.5 presents the educational characteristics of students in terms of their education type, medium of instructions, and fields of study. Basic school characteristics like distance from school and mode of travelling, etc., is also covered here.

Type of Education: In private schools, all students are studying in co-ed pattern, but in government schools, 44% of the sample students are from co-ed schools, while the remaining 55% are from separate boys' and girls' schools.

Table 10.5 Percentage
distribution of students by
educational characteristics

	Govt.	Private	Total
Education type			
Co-ed	44.5	100.0	72.3
Males	30.1	–	15.0
Females	25.4	–	12.7
Field of study (only XI–XII)			
Science	19.5	32.8	26.2
Commerce	43.0	51.6	47.3
Arts	37.5	15.6	26.6
Instructions medium			
Hindi	62.5	–	31.25
English	37.5	100	68.75
Distance from home to school (in km)			
Up to 1 km	42.2	40.2	41.2
1–3	39.8	37.9	38.9
3–5	9.8	16.8	13.3
5–10	3.1	3.9	3.5
>10	4.7	1.2	2.9
Average time to reach school			
Up to 15 min	44.5	46.1	44.9
15–30 min	45.3	45.7	45.5
30–45 min	5.9	7.4	6.6
>45 min	3.9	0.8	2.3

Study Field and Medium of Instruction: Out of the total sample, representation of students in lower secondary and senior secondary levels of education is equal. At the senior secondary level, while a larger proportion of students (government and private schools) are studying in commerce streams, there is a variation in arts and science students between the two school types. While in private schools, the proportion of science students at the senior secondary level is higher, in the government schools, the proportion of students in the arts stream is greater. Another important finding that the survey has highlighted is that few government schools in Delhi are providing English as the medium of instruction to students. On the other hand, all private schools are English medium. With the growing demand of English-speaking manpower in the Indian job market, students passing out from government Hindi-medium schools find it really difficult to adjust themselves in such an environment and feels less capable compared to others who have passed out from English-medium schools. Due to this, firstly, private schools are gaining more importance as compared to government schools, and secondly, the business of English-speaking courses is flourishing in Delhi.

Distance from School and Time Taken: Nearly 41% student respondents are attending schools located within a distance of 1 km from their home. Thirty-nine percent of the student respondents have their school within 3 km from home, 13%

within the range of 3–5 km, and 6.5% more than 5 km away. The major modes of travelling to school in case of government school students are walking, cycling, and public transport. In the case of private schools, it varies between walking, cycling, travelling in private cars/vans or school buses. Regarding time taken by students to reach school, about 45% of the students in all have mentioned that it takes up to 15 min to reach school from home. Almost equal proportions of students have mentioned the travelling time to be roughly between 15 and 30 min daily, while less than 10% students travel for more than 30 min to reach school.

10.3.4 Dropouts' Profile

This section presents the information about those students who have either dropped out or have repeated the same standard or class more than once. About 7.4% of the total sample students have not pursued their school education in continuation throughout, which means that they have either dropped out or have repeated the same session more than once. The proportion of such students is higher in government schools as compared to private ones. Among those who have either dropout/repeated, 24% have mentioned health problems and 18% have stated family financial constraints as the reason behind their dropout. About 10% students have explained the reason as their dislike to attend school, whereas another 10% had to dropout as they had to start working to support their family.

In many cases, it was found that females had to dropout to attend household chore activities and to look after younger siblings in the family (8%). There were even cases where migration of family came out as one of the reasons behind repetition of the same standard (8%). On the whole, the findings clearly indicate that factors related to the family plays a greater role in dropouts or repetition rates of students as compared to other school factors. Apart from this, individual health status of students also matters a lot.

10.4 Summary

The chapter gives comprehensive profiles of sample students, teachers, and schools covered in the study. It has clearly highlighted the differences between private and government schools. The findings of the survey suggest that government schools have higher share of secondary enrolments out of total school enrolments and have lower pupil–teacher ratios due to large recruitment of teachers. Private schools on the other hand reflect better class structure in terms of lower class size at secondary level and higher percentage of student pass-outs from senior secondary examinations. It was also found that private schools are offering wider variety of subjects to students at both lower and senior secondary level of education with English as the medium of instruction compared to government schools. In case of transportation facilities and organization of health check-up camps for students, private schools are much ahead of government schools. However, in terms of staff-related provisions like job security to teachers, annual increments, good salary structure, and promotion strategies, government schools are on a better place compared to private schools. It is also found that teachers teaching in private and government schools in Delhi are well qualified and experienced. However, as far as training is concerned, larger proportion of teachers in government schools have attended training compared to private schools. In case of students, while majority in private schools belongs to well-off family who fall in the category of top three income quintiles and have salary earnings or business as the major source of household income, students from government schools on the other hand, come from families falling in bottom two income quintiles deriving major source of household income from wage earning and salary earning. It is found that government schools reflect higher proportion of students with dropouts or repletion rates compared to private schools.

Overall, results suggest that from a teacher's perspective, government schools provide better pay structure, job security and promotion compared to private schools. However, from the student's point of view, facilities are better in private schools as compared to government schools. It is worth noting that by offering better facilities, 'English' as the medium of instruction, co-ed education, and wider selection of fields of study, private schools are in high demand in Delhi. The overall enrolments rates in private schools are much higher as compared to government schools despite their high fee structure. The preference for private schooling is observed even in lower income quintile households who wish to provide better education to their children.

Chapter 11
Understanding Factors Affecting Student Outcomes and Learning Behaviour

Abstract On the basis of discussion in earlier chapters, we have understood the importance of improving the quality of secondary education in India, due to its socio-economic implications impacting society and individual as a whole. But the main question arises on how to improve the quality of secondary education? Although at the macro level we have identified various deficiencies in Chaps. 8 and 9 that need to be relooked in order to improve the system, it is equally important to identify various obstacles at the micro level, that is, at school, by student or teacher to achieve overall improvement in the quality of education. It is equally important to understand their perspective as well to bring this change. But before looking at various factors that determine the quality of education, it is important to understand the way in which we can measure and try to improve the quality of education. It is pertinent to mention that by the expression 'improving the quality of education', we mean improving the performance and achievements of students by providing them best learning and growing environments. Hence, this study will measure the quality of secondary education in terms of student performances, their achievements, and overall satisfaction level. Available literature shows that schools, family environment, and teachers do play an important role here, but to measure the exact impact, a detailed analysis is required. To locate the determinants of student outcomes and performances, this study has conducted a survey to capture student perspectives on school environments, family culture, types of resources and infrastructural facilities available, and exposure to mass media. It also covers information on teacher's background and teaching methods and practices adopted, the findings of which are discussed in this chapter. In addition to this, the perceptions of students on their self-performance, development, schooling, teaching quality, and self-evaluation are also discussed here. The chapter further elaborates the factors which are affecting the performance and learning outcomes of students and thereby act as major obstacles in achieving quality education at secondary level. The first section of this chapter describes various characteristics related to schools, family and other background of students that may have possible impact on learning outcomes and achievement of students. The perceptions of students on different issues have been covered in the second section. The third section presents the exploratory model for

© Springer Nature Singapore Pte Ltd. 2018
C. Jain and N. Prasad, *Quality of Secondary Education in India*,
https://doi.org/10.1007/978-981-10-4929-3_11

identifying the factors affecting performance of students. The findings of this chapter have been summarized in the last section.

Keywords Learning outcomes · Logistics regression · Education quality · School resources · Teaching practices and methods · Receivers operating curve

11.1 Understanding Factors Influencing Student Performances and Behaviours

The available literature gives indications that among various factors having impact on student achievement levels, the most important ones are related to school, family, and teachers. This might include factors like the quality of school resources and infrastructure facilities, family background and education level of parents, teaching methods and practices. In addition to this, there are other actors also that influence the learning outcomes of students including, mass media exposures, self-motivation level of students, health considerations, and their future aspirations. In this section, we have made an effort to discuss each of these in detail.

11.1.1 School Resources and Quality

It is commonly presumed that formal schooling is one of the important contributions for the development of individual skills and human capital. The UNESCO's Global monitoring report highlights that schools have a special place apart from parents, individual abilities and friends, not only because education and creation of skills are among their prime objectives, but also because they are the factor most directly affected by public policies (UNESCO 2005). Schooling helps children to develop creatively and acquire the skills, knowledge, values and attitudes necessary for responsible, active and productive citizenship. The available literature reflects significant impact of school quality on the achievement level of pupils. For instance, after controlling household background variables, Case and Deaton (1999) find strong and significant effects of pupil–teacher ratios on enrolment, educational achievement, and on test scores for numeracy. In the Indian case, Sipahimalani (1999), Drèze and Kingdon (1999) reported that school quality matters a lot in explaining school participation even after controlling household characteristics. Few qualitative studies indicates that student academic achievement improves with improved building condition, lighting level, air quality and temperature and acoustics, although there is limited quantitative evidence available on some of these factors (Owoade 2012). Another study confirm that the quantity of schooling matters strongly, both for standard academic knowledge and less academic 'life skills' but further suggest that, conditional on a child's level of schooling, having better educated parents or a higher level of household resources have only modest or statistically insignificant benefits for academic performance (Glick and Sahn 2009). To have a better clarity on the connection between quality of schooling and learning outcomes of students, information on types and conditions of facilities provided by schools, classroom structure, kind of events organized is gathered through primary survey, the findings of which are presented in this section.

Class Structure: Survey finds that on an average the total number of students per class, number of sections for each class of study, and teachers are higher in the lower secondary level of education as compared to the senior secondary levels. There are nearly 65 students per class in lower secondary classes, while this is 57 in case of senior secondary classes. The distribution of schools by ownership types reveals that the average class size is higher in case of government schools as compared to private schools. However, the average number of sections for each class of study is higher in case of private schools as compared to government schools, thereby reflecting the lack of adequate classrooms in the latter leading to lesser number of sections per each class of study and larger class size. As far as number of teachers is concerned, government schools reflect higher provision of teachers' availability compared to private schools at the secondary level of education.

School Facilities and their Working Conditions: The survey findings reveal that private schools are far better in providing various basic facilities to students in their schools as compared to government schools. Private schools outshine government schools particularly in providing smart class technique, stores to purchase books and uniforms, canteen facilities, and covered windows in classrooms. The facilities related to sanitation, for instance, cleanliness, lightening, and water supply in toilets are lacking in government schools as evident from the response of a large proportion of students. A significant proportion of students in government schools have mentioned lack of water purifiers in their schools; while this proportion is lesser in case of private schools. On the overall responses, the most lacking facilities in schools are provision of smart class techniques, canteens, safe drinking water, and stores to purchase books/uniforms and hygienic sanitation facilities.

As far as conditions of these facilities are concerned, the responses reflect lack of maintenance in most cases. However, in government schools conditions of the available facilities are much lower than in private schools. The results reflect that while in case of private schools, the bottom category constitutes facilities related to sanitation, playground and bulletin boards, in case of government schools the problem is more serious as the lowest ratings goes for condition of sanitation facilities, basic classroom facilities including conditions of benches/chairs/tables/window panes and safe drinking water. This clearly reflects that most of the secondary schools although have provision of various facilities for students, the conditions are not good especially in case of basic facilities. The poor quality of these facilities can, in turn, affect the health of students which can further lead to increased absenteeism rate and lower performance levels. Research at International level also suggests that poor school infrastructure threatens academic performance and health (Amsterdam 2009).

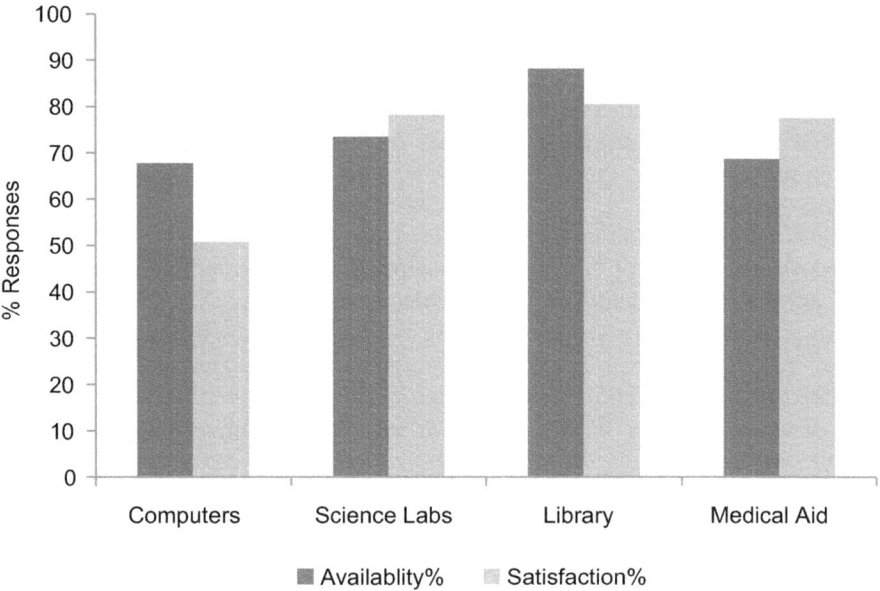

Fig. 11.1 Facilities available in schools and satisfaction level (percentage responses)

Figure 11.1 further explores the provision of computers, science labs, libraries, and medical aids to students studying in secondary schools. More than 30% of the respondents show lack of computer and medical facilities in their schools. This proportion is less than 30% in case of science labs. The largest proportion of favourable responses has gone for library facilities which are there in most of the secondary schools in Delhi. As far as satisfaction with the kind of guidance provided for various facilities is concerned, the highest satisfaction is reported for library services, followed by the guidance in science labs and medical services. It is quite clear that computer facilities available in schools are not up to mark as reflected by survey. Moreover, even in case where computer facilities are available for students, nearly 50% of the students are not satisfied with the kind of guidance provided to them. This also points towards recruitment of more trained faculty for computer science. Not only this, there is also need to equip more computers in schools for students with updated software, so as to provide them at least with the basic knowledge and expertise to students in this field.

Schools Initiatives in Organizing Various Events: Apart from imparting knowledge on regular prescribed syllabus to students, schools are equally responsible for nourishing the non-academic talents of students (like sports, painting, dancing and other extra-curricular activities) for their overall growth and development. For this, schools need to organize various events including competitions on various themes from time to time during each academic year. Not only this, schools should also encourage students to participate in these events or competitions. The

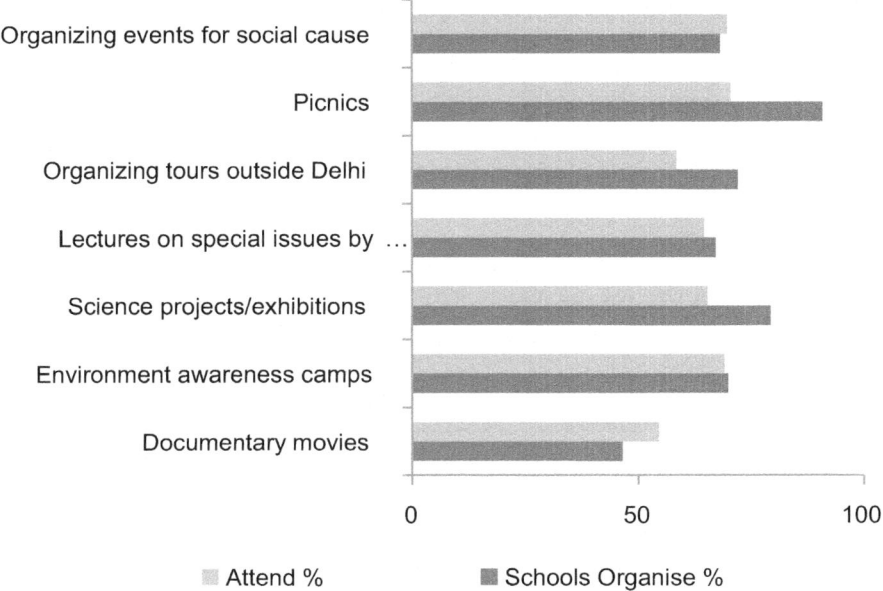

Fig. 11.2 Schools organising special programmes and participation rates

participation in these kinds of activities not only makes students multi-talented, but also increases their morale and confidence level.

Findings show that although majority of the students have given positive responses on the different kinds of events organized by their schools, the partici- pation rates are not so impressive. Among various events organized by schools, the most popular ones are annual day, sports, cultural shows, debates, paintings, and essay competitions. The participation rates of students reflect that majority of the students participate in events like sports competitions, followed by inter-house essay and painting competitions. The participation rate in activities like annual day, drama, debate, poems, etc., is comparatively lower. The major reasons for not participating, as mentioned by respondents are their disinterest, health problems, and low confi- dence level, as well as lack of opportunities as complained by a certain proportion of students. Nearly 55% students in government schools and 67% in private schools have blamed the schools for not encouraging students to participate in curricular activities and events. Hence, it is the responsibility of teachers to recognize talents and involve students in various activities/tours/exhibitions organized by the school and enhance their general awareness.

The findings reveal that among various special programmes organized by schools, the top rated programmes are annual picnic, science exhibitions and out-of-town tours (Fig. 11.2). These are followed by environment awareness camps and events organized for social cause which have got positive ratings from nearly 70% student respondents. Only 46% students have mentioned that their school organizes documentary movies on different themes for them.

In addition to the above-mentioned non-academic activities, schools also take initiatives towards organizing extra classes for weak students. The provision of these extra classes helps students in improving their academic performances. Survey findings show that nearly 58.4% student respondents report that their schools do not organize any extra class for weak students, while 41.6% schools organize such types of classes. Among those, who have mentioned that there schools don't provide any extra class, about 68.6% of students have expressed the need for such classes. However, schools where such extra classes are provided, only 50% of the students attend such classes. Now, within this category of students who are attending the extra classes, nearly 67% have repondend that the extra classes were very beneficial to them, while 21% have felt that extra classes are somewhat beneficial. Glick and Sahn (2010) clearly points out the need for alternative measures to improve the skills of lagging children in schools. On whole, the survey reveals that the extra classes are beneficial to students, hence more and more schools should try to provide it so that they can get an additional opportunity for clearing their doubts.

Ratings on Quality of Schooling

Satisfaction ratings for physical safety of students, followed by cleanliness in schools and overall facilities available in school are the lowest as expressed by students studying in senior secondary government schools (Fig. 11.3). In the case of private schools, physical safety of students, school atmosphere, and overall facilities obtained the lowest rating. Students in private schools have given the highest ratings for cleanliness. Two categories which have got the next highest ratings in both private and government schools are safety against fire and teachers along with their teaching methods. Overall, physical safety, school facilities, and cleanliness are the major areas of concern in secondary schools in Delhi as reflected

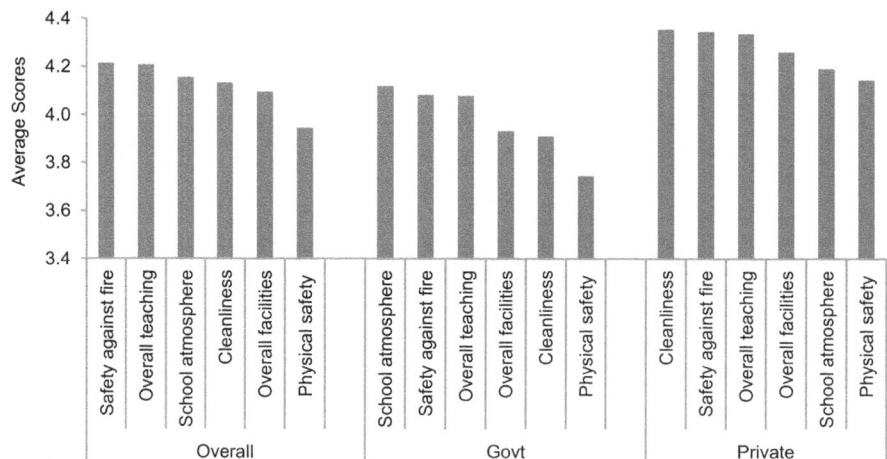

Fig. 11.3 Overall satisfaction with schooling and related factors (average scores)

by the low satisfaction ratings given by respondents. On the whole, survey results point towards the need for adopting greater measures for physical safety of students in schools. The overall facilities no doubt need to be improved further especially in terms of their maintenance.

11.1.2 Family Background and Parents Education

Literature shows that family background and the composition of peer groups in school had a much larger impact on educational outcomes and on subsequent economic success than did variations in the characteristics of the schools themselves (Coleman et al. 1966). Hence, to understand the family characteristics of students various questions were asked regarding their family culture and well-being, parents' education, income and occupational patterns, etc., the findings of which are discussed in this section.

Household Educational and Occupational Pattern: The distribution of the student responses on their household patterns by types of schools reflects wide differences. While in case of government schools, larger proportion of students belong to families where the highest educational attainment (judged by the head of the household) is lower secondary level (26.2%), followed by graduation (16.8%), and senior secondary (15.6%), in case of private schools, the larger proportion of students come from families with at least graduation or post graduation and higher degrees as the highest educational attainment level (Table 11.1). Overall, the study

Table 11.1 Education and occupational pattern of head of household (% of responses)

	Govt.	Private
Head of the household		
Father	97.3	98.0
Mother	2.0	2.0
Others	0.8	–
Highest education of head of household		
Illiterate	3.9	1.2
Primary	6.3	3.9
Middle	15.2	7.8
Lower secondary	26.2	6.6
High secondary	15.6	16.4
Graduate	16.8	29.7
Post graduate+	8.6	23.4
Occupation of head of household (major one)		
Wage earner	34.4	2.0
Salary earner	37.1	53.9
Business/trade	12.5	28.1
Self employed	11.7	13.3

reveals that most students in government schools belong to low educated families as compared to those studying in private schools.

The occupational pattern reflects that about 45.5% students have come from salaried families, followed by business class families constituting 20% of the total share. Nearly, 18% of students belong to families having wage earnings as the main occupation of the head of household, while 12% of students mentioned that the head of household is self-employed. Again, there are differences in the occupational pattern of student households between government and private schools. While, those studying in government schools, the heads of the household are mostly occupied in salary-earning and wage-earning jobs, while in case of private schools, they are involved in salaried professions or in business/trade. Further, 54% of private school students' households and 37% government school students' family have salaried jobs as the major source of income. The difference in the occupational pattern of households between private and government school students clearly reflects the differences in the economic status of their households.

Family Well-being: Family well-being refers to the financial status of the household, that is, the various consumer durable items that the family owns in general. The survey shows that nearly 94% households own television; 80% have mobile phones, 81% has cable connection, nearly 55% owns two-wheelers and 42% has four-wheeler (Fig. 11.4). Less than 40% of the student's households own desktop computer, while this proportion is lower in case of laptop or tablet ownership. More than one-third students gave positive responses for internet facility at home. The survey further reveals that majority of the students, especially in government schools, don't have computer facilities at home due to which they have to depend upon other sources like schools or friends for usage of computers/internet

In addition to consumer durable ownership, the study has also captured details of ownership of various assets/durable items by households in facilitating students in creating better learning environments at home. The results show that only 50% of the students have their own separate rooms for study at home. Nearly 40% of students own good collection of books. Majority of the students own only the prescribed syllabus books, while 28% of the total sample has a collection of non-syllabus books as well. This indicates that majority of the students refer to syllabus books only. Another important fact that has come up through this study is that nearly 62% of the students are facilitated with tuition support.

Family Support to Students: The kind of support students receive from their family members, to a large extent, depends on the education of family members. About 71% of the students have reported that their family members help them in their studies, while the remaining 29% have to depend on tuitions. As far as non-family members are concerned, which includes friends, relatives, or neighbours, less than one-third students take help from them, while majority do not.

Decision-Making Power and Financial Independence: In majority of the households, students jointly take decision with their parents on various issues such as deciding college/school, joining additional educational course, buying study material and computer/laptops, whereas in cases like choosing field of study or

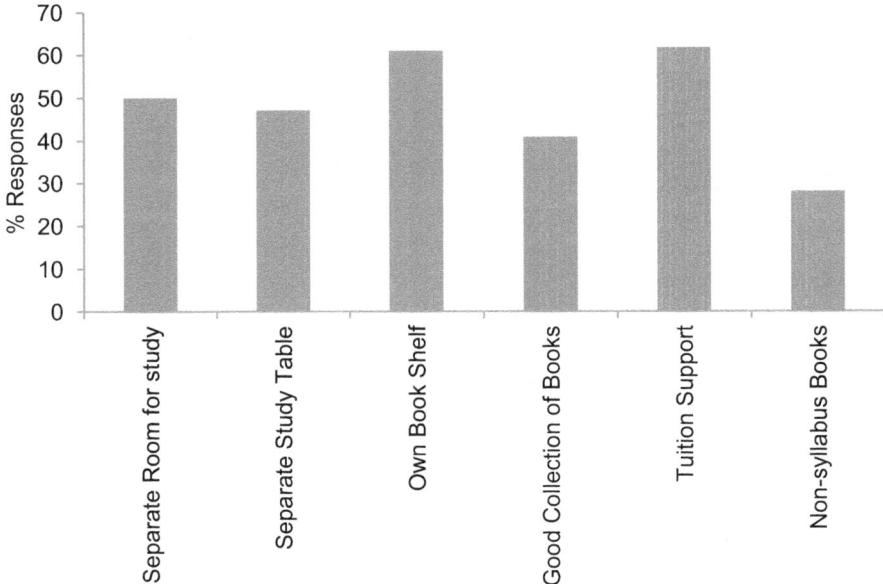

Fig. 11.4 Percentage responses on types of facilities related to studies

joining hobby course of choice, larger proportion of students have liberty to take self-decision. Overall, the results reveal that in most households either students are motivated to take decisions on their own or asked to consult their parents on various issues, which further increases their knowledge, self-confidence, and feeling of belongingness to the family. These factors somehow psychologically affect the learning outcomes of students and make them more confident.

Family Bonding: The type of relation or bonding that students have with their parents and other family members bear a huge implication on the learning level of students. It is generally seen in schools, that students who have problems at home are often disturbed and are not able to concentrate on studies which affects not only their health but their performance as well. An attempt has been made here to capture the level of bonding between parents and students. Survey shows that only 52% students are confident that their parents are satisfied with their academic scores, while this proportion is 64% in case of non-academic activities. As per the survey findings, only 53% of the respondent students seek help from their parents to solve their problems (Table 11.2). As far as level of interaction between students and parents is concerned, it is found that larger proportion of students interact with their parents on issues like their own achievements, about teachers, facilities available in school and about different topics discussed/taught in class. However, the issues which students don't like to discuss much with their parents include conflicts with other students and their own failures and examinations. The survey somewhere gives indications about the widening gap between parents and student relations.

Table 11.2 Parents–students interaction and participation in school events (% of responses)

	Always	Sometimes	Rarely/never
Parents dealings with students			
Parents treat fairly	82.0	14.8	2.1
Parents are unhappy/disappointed	24.0	47.7	28.3
Get along well with parents	60.2	28.3	11.3
Count on parents to solve problems	53.7	34.4	10.9
I am source of pride for them	78.3	17.2	4.1
Want to be similar to parents	63.3	27.9	7.2
Parents are satisfied academically	52.3	36.3	9.4
Parents feel proud with extra-curricular participation	63.9	29.5	6.3
Parents participation in school events			
Participation in school event	59.0	29.1	10.7
PTM meetings	59.0	21.5	18.0
Attend functions	42.4	37.1	19.1

As far as participation of parents in school activities is concerned, the most important amongst all is attending parents–teachers meetings (PTM). However, survey shows that only in 59% student's households, parents attend the PTM meetings on a regular basis. About 21.5% students responded that their parents sometimes attend these PTM meetings, while 18% shows that they never or rarely attend the same. The main purpose of organizing this meeting is to have a face-to-face interaction between student, teacher, and parents so that various obstacles/hurdles which are affecting the performance of students at school or at household level may be removed in order to improve the overall performance and learning by students.

11.1.3 Teaching Methods and Practices

Teachers play an important role in the achievement of students. Therefore, it is important to understand the quality of teaching in schools. Students are the best sources for revealing the quality of teachers in schools and also about various teaching aids, methods, and practices used by them to make their teaching effective and interesting. Hence, student respondents are interviewed about the various teaching methods teachers use in classrooms and how far students are satisfied with the overall quality of teachers and teaching methods.

Teaching Methods and Practices: The findings reveals that only 46% of the students feel that their teachers explain them the entire chapter thoroughly, while more than 28% express that only the main topics are explained in classroom (Table 11.3). Almost 22% of the respondents report that their teachers only read the chapters without explaining them properly. As far as provision of notes is

Table 11.3 Teaching practices and methods

Particulars	% of responses
Teaching methods	
Only read without explaining	21.6
Explain only main topics	28.4
Explain thoroughly	46.2
Others	3.8
Teachers focus in classrooms (multiple response)	
Reading chapters	58.4
Writing on blackboard	50.2
To develop better understanding of the topics	50.2
Checking papers/copies etc.	42.6
Covering syllabus	41.8
Maintaining active participation in class	40.0
Non syllabus discussion	37.9
Punishing and scolding students	28.5

concerned, students gave mixed responses. About 37% of the students say that their teachers encourage them to prepare their own notes rather than using notes provided by the teacher. In more than 30% cases, teachers provide readymade notes to students, while less than 30% students mention that teachers dictate the notes in classroom.

When students were asked about the teacher's main focus while being in classroom, majority responded that teachers keep on reading chapters in classroom, followed by those who mentioned 'writing on blackboards'. Only 50% students say that the main focus of their teachers is to develop better understanding of the topic among them, while 40% feel that their teachers try to ensure active participation by all students in classrooms. Checking copies in classrooms or simply covering the syllabus are also the focus areas of teachers as reflected by more than 40% of the respondent students. The results also reveal that in nearly 42% of the cases, teachers try to cover fewer topics in classroom and more as homework. When students are asked about teacher's reaction on raising questions in class, larger proportion of students mentioned that their teachers answer their questions in a proper manner, while 24% students say that they their queries are answered minor degree of accuracy. More than 36% students are of the opinion that teachers try to avoid answering their questions in classrooms. This clearly reflects the lack of confidence and knowledge in teachers.

In addition to this, students are also asked about the presence of teachers in classroom during their class. About 45% students respond that their teachers come in class well on time, while 55% report that teachers either come late or leave the classroom early. The findings clearly indicate the need for more supervision in secondary schools. There is further need to improve the quality of teaching methods and practices adopted. Our results show that the strength of such teachers whose

Table 11.4 Percentage of responses of students on teachers initiatives and attitudes

Statements	Agree
Our teachers keep us informed	88.9
Teachers encourage us to appear in various activities	85.2
Able to solve our conflicts with other students	82.8
Feel comfortable in discussing my personal problems	67.6
Very satisfied with the overall teaching atmosphere	65.0
Satisfied with my teachers	71.8
Teachers are approachable and friendly	72.2
Teachers are respectful towards students	72.0

main focus is to create better understanding among students, maintain active participation in classroom, and encourage students to prepare own notes as the basis of their understanding level is less in secondary schools. Most teachers are either busy in completing the syllabus or checking copies or writing on backboards.

Teachers Initiatives and Attitudes: Table 11.4 presents the findings on various initiatives taken by teachers and their attitudes. More than 80% students have responded that their teachers inform them about various competitions ahead, encourage them for various activities and take initiatives in resolving their conflicts with other students. However, 67% students have mentioned that they feel free in discussing personal problems with their teachers. Nearly 72% students have responded that there teachers are approachable, friendly, and respect students, while the remaining are either uncertain or dissatisfied on this statement.

Overall, nearly 65% students are satisfied with teaching atmosphere in schools, and 71% with their teachers. This shows that there is a significant proportion of students who are not satisfied with teachers and the teaching atmosphere in secondary schools which need to be addressed.

11.1.4 Students Characteristics and Self-motivation

If students feel de-motivated and do not take interest or initiative towards their studies, then even good facilities at schools and home become meaningless. However, it is seen that the level of motivation in students is much influenced by the kind of atmosphere provided to them at schools and home. The better the environment provided to them, the higher will be their motivation level to perform better. Hence, to have better understanding on the motivational factors of students, the study undertakes various issues like rate of absence/presence rate of students, areas of study, self-study methods, and their own performance and satisfaction level.

Students Absenteeism: Fig. 11.5 presents the findings on presence and absence rates of students at secondary level of education. By presence rate, we mean percentage share of classes attended by students each day out of total classes allotted.

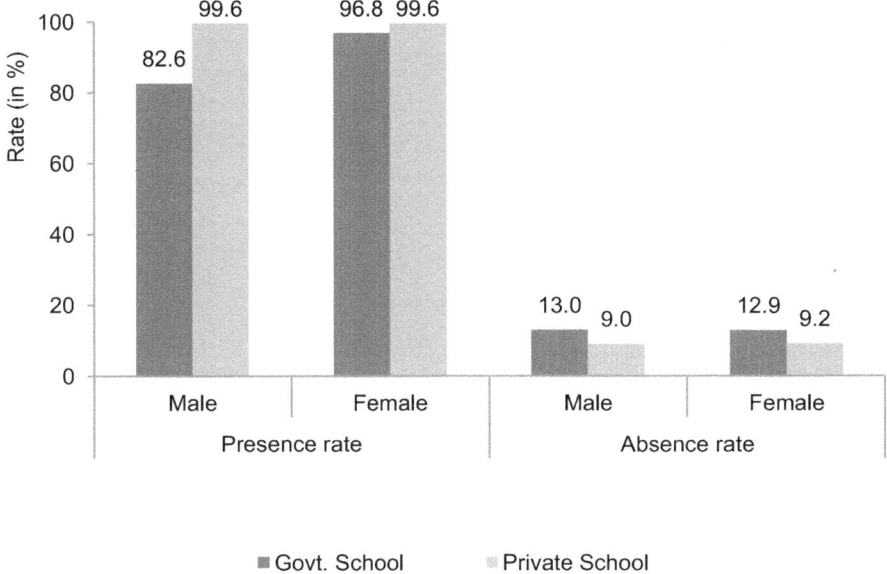

Fig. 11.5 Presence and absence rate of students in schools (average %)

By absence rate, we mean percentage share of days students go to school each month. Figure 11.5 shows that on an average, the presence rate in private schools is higher as compared to government schools. In private schools, while it is almost near to 100%, in case of government schools, the average presence rate of students per day is 89.7%. In private schools, the average presence rate is almost similar for both genders, however, in government schools, the findings shows that boys attend on an average 82.6% of classes per day, while girls attend 97% classes each day. This reveals that more discipline and rigidity need to be maintained especially in boy's government schools.

Regarding absenteeism rate, the average percentage is higher in government schools as compared to private ones. When asked about the reasons for absenteeism, majority of the student mention being unwell, followed by attending family functions or household chore activities. In few cases, students mention school-related factors as reasons for absenteeism, for instance; they don't feel like going to school or being not prepared for assignment/exam.

Subject Preferences: Motivation to perform better to some extent depends on the subjects/streams chosen by students. Therefore, in this regard, Table 11.5 presents the results on subjects and sub-streams chosen by students at senior secondary levels and also reflects expectations of students on choices of subjects at the lower secondary level. It shows that majority of senior secondary students in the sample have chosen commerce as their major field of study, while science and arts constitutes almost similar shares of nearly 26%. Among those who have taken science, the major fields of study are medical science and non medical science. For

Table 11.5 Percentage of responses on subject choices and expectations

		Lower secondary	Senior secondary
Field of study	Science	52.3	26.2
	Commerce	31.3	48.8
	Arts	14.8	25.4
Sub-streams	Medical	57.5	55.2
	Non-medical	16.4	29.9
	Engineering	25.4	13.4
	Commerce with Math	72.5	64.8
	Commerce without Math	27.5	35.2
Reasons for choosing field of study	Interest	55.9	56.6
	Better job opportunity	21.9	24.2
	Parents desire	7.0	4.7
	Peer group influence	2.3	3.9
	Influence by renowned people	2.7	3.9
	Others[a]	7.4	6.6

[a]Others include factors like interest in research, family background, influenced by quality of teachers

every medical student, it is important to study Biology as a subject, whereas non-medical students must study either engineering or mathematics or computers as core subjects instead of Biology. However, those who have chosen commerce, around 65% also study mathematics as one of the compulsory subjects. When asked about reason to choose the selected field of study, majority responded that they have chosen it due to their interest in this field. Nearly one-fourth of the students have chosen the selected field of study for better job opportunities. Only 5% of students have taken it to fulfill parents' desire. The results somewhere reflect that now students at the secondary level of education are more conscious about choosing subjects at higher level of education. They just don't go simply by what their parents expect or what their friends choose. The results show that they have their own interest and their own mindset regarding career options which influence them most while choosing subjects. The expectations of lower secondary students, on the other hand, reflect higher demand for science stream, followed by commerce. Within the science stream, majority of the students are likely to choose medical subjects followed by engineering, while in commerce field, more than 70% of the students are likely to choose mathematics as a compulsory subject. In case of lower secondary level, students have marked their preferences of subjects for senior secondary levels.

Study Methods: Survey results reveal that only 53% of sample students do regular studies at home, while others study near to exam. About one-fourth of the respondent students simply memorize the topic either with little or no clarity at all. The survey findings further show that in case of difficulty, only 57% of the students approach their teachers for solving their queries, reflecting the wide gap between teacher–student relation and interaction level in senior secondary schools in Delhi.

It is generally seen that due to inabilities of students in solving their subjective queries in school, most of them opt for tuition support. The findings reveal that almost 61.7% students have joined private tuitions for various subjects. When asked about the reasons for joining tuitions: 51% students explain 'to seek better clarity'; less than 25% report tuitions as an additional support/revision; while around 19% mention that they are not able to understand the subjects in school at all. The subjects which are mainly considered for tuitions, as reported by students, are mathematics, followed by English, science, accounts, economics, and physics. Students consider these subjects to be tough, therefore, schools should consider providing extra classes to students particularly in these subjects. It is found that the pressure of school and multiple tuitions is so high that in most cases, students don't even get any leisure time or self-study or other activities/interests, leading to stress and other health-related issues, thereby affecting their overall performance.

11.1.5   Mass Media Exposure

Mass media is defined as means of communication that reach and influence people. Although it is blamed for most societal ills, it has huge benefits also. It plays very important role in creating awareness about society, health, environment, technology, science, and everything. Young students today are exposed to a plethora of mass media channels which helps them in updating themselves from time to time on various issues. There are hundreds of newspapers, books, magazines available in the market. Almost every home has television nowadays and internet is fast becoming preferred choice among students. The mobile on the other hand, has also emerged as a means of accessing information on move. To gain insight into the media choices that students studying in senior secondary schools opt for, the survey has decided to capture information on the exposure of various mass media sources available to students. The findings are presented in Table 11.6.

The survey findings indicate that the most popular source of information to students is television (77.7%), followed by books (77.1%), newspapers (54.3%), and internet (41.4%). Radio is the least referred source of information as reflected by 25.8% of students. Within the category of those who have access to various means of mass media sources, majority access them on daily basis except for internet and radio. Majority of students have also mentioned that the place of exposure is home especially in case of television and radios. However, in case of newspapers and books, schools also play an important role, as reflected in the survey. There are significant proportions of students who don't have internet facilities at home due to which they visit cyber cafes or friends. For television and radio, while most of the students prefer Hindi language, for sources like internet, English is the most preferred language. Newspaper and books on the other hand, reflects preference of both English and Hindi languages.

Table 11.6 Percentage of responses on exposure to mass media

	Newspaper	Books	Television	Internet	Radio
Frequency of usage					
Daily	72.3	74.4	83.7	43.9	33.3
Twice a week	9.4	12.2	6.6	14.6	15.9
Once a week	6.1	8.4	4.2	9.0	11.4
Once a fortnight	1.8	1.8	0.7	5.2	4.5
Once a month	0.4	0.5	–	2.8	3.8
Rare	6.8	1.0	2.4	8.0	25.8
Place of exposure					
Home	77.0	53.9	88.9	55.2	63.6
School/library	16.9	38.5	–	5.7	–
Other libraries	2.2	2.3	–	–	–
Neighbours/friends	1.4	1.5	9.7	9.9	16.7
While travelling	0.4	–	–	12.7[a]	3.0
Language preferred					
Hindi	44.6	48.4	79.5	11.8	68.2
English	51.4	47.1	13.2	70.8	14.4
Local	0.7	1.0	2.8	–	3.0
Level of confidence in mass media source					
High confidence	71.9	71.4	46.9	50.0	33.3
Somewhat confident	22.7	25.1	48.3	31.1	45.5
No confidence	2.5	1.5	2.8	1.9	9.8

[a]Cyber cafes

The survey further explores that students who refer newspapers as major source of information, use it mostly for referring information related to movies/entertainment followed by sports news, current affairs, and news related to economy. The political and religious columns are least preferred by secondary students. In case of students who refer books most, the highest preference is for comic books, novels, fantasy books, thriller stories, and science fiction. Television, which is the highest preferred source of media among secondary students, is referred for watching daily news, sports, science/technology, daily soaps/reality shows and thriller shows. The survey shows that larger proportion of students at the secondary education level, reflects higher confidence in newspapers and books as sources of information compared to television or internet.

The other mass media sources of information which have become quite popular in recent years among secondary students are the internet and mobile facilities. These sources not only act as source of information to students but also give them an opportunity to stay connected with the rest of the world. The survey shows that those students who have access to internet facilities, mostly use the same firstly for social networking, then to download videos, prepare school assignments, e-mailing, reading books online, and chatting. One-third of the sample students use mobiles which also serve as a popular source of mass media. Among those students who have their own mobile phones, nearly 53% have internet facility on mobiles and more than 90% of them are using various applications as well.

11.1.6 Health Considerations

In the earlier sections, we have already seen that majority of the students have cited health problems as one of the major reasons behind their high absenteeism rates. Therefore, through this survey the researcher has attempted to understand the health profiles of students. Overall, survey shows that 11% students get unwell quite frequently, while 22% gets ill only sometime. Those who rarely get ill constitute about 53% of the total student sample while the remaining has no health problems. The survey also reports that it is found that the students who are found indulging in food outside quite frequently have greater health issues compared to those who rarely or never eat outside. Research shows that frequent intakes of junk food affect the health of individuals. Moreover, most medical practitioners have also informed that students should include more of dairy products and green vegetables in their diets which bears positive impact on health and thus can improve their overall performance. Lack of proper nutrition among children is one of the major factors behind poor performances. Table 11.7 clearly reflects that nearly three-fourth students like to eat junk food. Moreover, there are more than 20% of the sample students, who either don't consume fresh and green vegetables or don't take dairy products.

Nearly 82% students have accepted the fact that their health problems adversely affect their academic performances. Not only has this, but nearly 35% students had complaints of loss of concentration during class lectures. Nearly 68% students suffer from some inferiority complexes which affect their overall confidence level. Hence, adverse health or psychological issues have direct relation with motivation and performances of students.

Table 11.7 Percentage of responses in favor of health statements

Health statements	Agree	Uncertain	Disagree
Health adversely affecting studies and performance	81.8	6.4	10.7
Highly concentrated during class lectures	64.8	29.8	5.3
Wash hands before and after taking meals	86.3	9.6	3.7
Suffer from inferiority complex	67.6	13.3	18.8
Eat fresh fruits and vegetables	79.9	12.1	6.8
Take dairy products in my diet	77.3	15.0	6.8
Like eating junk food	64.1	21.3	14.3
Aware about 'organic food'	74.6	17.0	7.8

There is no doubt that improvement in health conditions of students can surely improve their scores as well. Schools can play a great role in improving the health conditions of students. We have seen that conditions of safe drinking water, sanitation facilities, and canteen facilities are not up to the mark in most schools. Thus, unsafe drinking water, unhygienic sanitation conditions and poor quality of food provided in canteens can pose serious health issues to students. It is the responsibility of school authorities to provide clean, hygienic, and quality atmosphere to students that can improve their health conditions and can reduce their absenteeism rates. These efforts can not only promote healthy learning environments in schools but can also improve the overall quality of education.

11.1.7 Future Aspirations

Future aspirations of students in terms of pursuing higher education and career options were also captured by survey. Responses by students on their career choices reflect that they are well familiar with various career options available in the job market for them in future. The most popular career options as desired by students are that of a teacher, followed by doctor, lawyer, engineer, and scientist. Few students even show their desire to join managerial jobs or professional jobs like CA/CS or police services/army after completing their education. The interesting point to note here is that apart from these basic career options available which most of the students are generally aware about, students also respond on certain special career options which have gained huge popularity and importance in recent years especially in metropolitan cities like Delhi which include options like politics, fashion designing, acting, various artists, etc. Despite the fact that nowadays students have access to various mass media sources and are familiar with these new career choice, they largely lack information on various competitions that need to be cleared for pursuing the career of their choice. Hence, schools should try to organize various career counselling programmes for students, especially at lower and senior secondary levels of education, so that they can plan accordingly.

As far as expectations for achieving the highest level of education is concerned, the top two preferences are for doctorate degrees (27%) and professional courses (26.6%), followed by graduate and diploma (22%) and then post graduation (10.5%) degrees. Those who don't want to pursue education after schooling constitute just 5% of the total respondents. The survey also shows that about 80% students are quite confident that they would be able to achieve the highest education level as desired considering various family limitations, while the remaining 20% are not sure about it.

11.2   Quality Ratings by Students

This section explores ratings by students on the conditions of quality of various facilities or services provided by schools. The result shows that the highest ratings were given for the overall education atmosphere in schools; followed by quality of textbooks; facilities given at home; and quality of teachers in schools. The lowest ratings have been given to quality of computer facilities, followed by library services, school infrastructure/facilities, and examination system. The lowest ratings on the quality of these facilities clearly demand the need for improvement (Fig. 11.6).

11.3   Exploratory Model-Identifying Factors Affecting Student Performance

Nowadays, many of the research studies concentrate on evaluating whether a causal link exists between student achievement and behaviour on the one hand, and the overall condition of schools and its resources, teachers, family influences, etc., on the other. In one such study, researchers (Wang et al. 1993) have tried to review the influence of educational, psychological, and social factors on learning level of students. They have ranked various factors that can influence student achievement (from high to low): student characteristics; classroom practices; home and community educational contexts; design and delivery of curriculum and instruction; school demographics, culture, climate, policies and practices; state and district

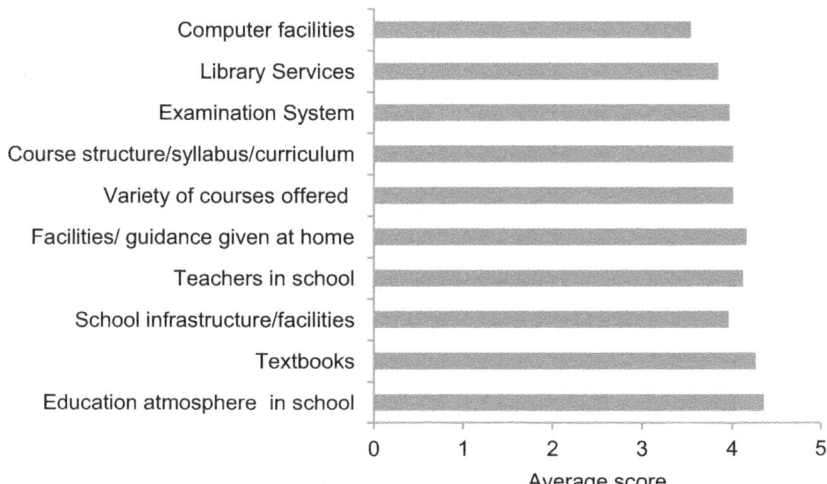

Fig. 11.6 Average scores by students on quality ratings

governance and organization. In another study conducted in primary schools in Georgia in the United States, Fourth Grade students in non-modernized buildings recorded poorer results in basic skill assessment than those in modernized or new buildings (Plumley 1978). Similarly, Eighth Grade students accommodated in new or modernized buildings, scored consistently higher in mathematics and vocabulary assessments. Almost similar study was repeated in 30 elementary schools where teacher's attitudes to school buildings also significantly improved in new and modernized buildings (Chan 1979). The results from these studies emphasized that variations in life expectancy and level of maintenance of school buildings impact the learning and behaviour of students differently. Till date, no relationship has been established between school size and student achievement that can be generalized or correlated but few studies do indicate an effect on behaviour. Although, up to elementary level of education, lot of primary based research has been conducted, however at the secondary level, these are quite a few. To fill up this gap, an attempt has been made in this book to identify various factors which can influence student outcomes and overall performances at the secondary level of education.[1]

11.3.1 Methodology and Data Considerations

As mentioned earlier, the objective is to generate a model that could define the various factors which ensure the possibilities of achieving distinctions by students in secondary education. To develop this model, the sample of all students was divided into two categories: those who have obtained distinctions in the previous academic year and those who did not. Viewing the type of analysis to be conducted, the current study binary logistic regression model was used. Binomial (or binary) logistic regression is a form of regression which is used when the dependent is a dichotomy and the independents are of any type.

The student outcomes and performance level can be well measured quantitatively in terms of their academic scores in examinations. Hence, to measure student outcomes and performances, we have considered students with distinctions as our response variable. Various factors related to school resources and facilities, teachers and teaching methods, family backgrounds, self-motivational characteristics of students, and exposure to mass media to test the impacts on student outcomes were considered. To perform this analysis, all variables were converted into dichotomous variables with 0 and 1 as values, while giving '1' to the scale of interest and '0' to non-interested responses. Here, dependent variable was 'Students with distinctions in the last academic year' against whom discussed variables were to be tested. Thus,

---

[1]The major findings and methodology of the exploratory model for determining the factors affecting student learning outcomes have been presented in Third International Asian Population Association (APA) Conference held in Kuala Lumpur, Malaysia from 27 to 30 July 2015.

our dependent variable will take only two-value; *1—If the student has got distinction in last academic year and 0—Otherwise.*

11.3.2   Model, Results Interpretation and Validations

Binary logistic regression model finally came up with 18 factors, which were having the maximum impact on dependent variable. The results are summarized in Table 11.8.

The overall correctly specified group percentage is 74.6% with the cutoff point of 0.5 by default, indicating the accuracy of the model. The Wald Statistics is also significant at 0.042% reflecting the goodness-of-fit model. The results show that school-related factors, family influences, self-motivational factors, and exposure to mass media have significant impact on likelihood of scoring distinctions by students, thereby reflecting higher outcomes and performances. Within *school-related*

Table 11.8 Binary logistic regression—determinants of students outcomes

Step 1(a)	B	S.E.	Wald	Sig.	Exp (B)
School related factors					
Cleanliness in schools	0.664	0.365	3.307	0.07**	1.942
Quality of school infrastructure/facilities	0.758	0.320	5.611	0.02*	2.133
Less variety of courses offered in school	−0.956	0.348	7.546	0.01*	0.385
Poor library services	−0.526	0.324	2.636	0.10**	0.591
Well qualified teachers in schools	0.946	0.340	7.721	0.01*	0.388
Teachers attitude friendly and supportive	0.840	0.332	6.391	0.01*	2.315
Less extra class organized	−0.734	0.329	4.975	0.03*	0.480
Family characteristics					
Quality of facilities and guidance at home	0.993	0.368	7.290	0.01*	2.700
Adequate family income	1.123	0.238	22.212	0.00*	3.073
Parents never attend PTM meetings	−0.965	0.400	5.820	0.02*	0.381
Mother education graduation and above	1.015	0.261	15.079	0.00*	2.759
Occupation of household head-salary	0.589	0.346	2.904	0.09**	1.802
Occupation of household head—business/self employment	0.583	0.358	2.648	0.10**	1.791
Exposure to mass media					
Read newspaper daily	0.381	0.238	2.551	0.09**	1.463
Surf internet daily	−0.498	0.276	3.262	0.07**	0.608
Self-motivational factors					
Have joined additional courses	−0.401	0.247	2.629	0.10**	0.670
Does regular studies at home	0.544	0.233	5.430	0.02*	1.722
Less time to prepare for exams	−0.486	0.181	7.229	0.01*	0.615

*Significant at 5%; **Significant at 10%; Model accuracy 74.6%; Wald statistics significant at 5%

category, factors like cleanliness in school, well-qualified teachers, their friendly and supportive attitude with students, and quality of school infrastructure/facilities have positive impact on student who have achieved distinctions. However, poor school library services and less variety of courses offered in school bear negative influences. Schools that organize less extra classes for students are also likely to affect the scores of students negatively. This reflects that there is need to improve the quality of library services in schools along with introducing more variety of courses to provide better choice of study streams. Presently, lower satisfaction of students on variety of courses offered in schools and library services has resulted in negative impact on student outcomes. The result further suggests improvement in the quality and frequency of extra classes organized in schools in terms of its timings and contents.

Within the broad classification of *family characteristics*, mother's education plays an important role. The results show that graduate or higher qualified mothers are more likely to influence outcomes of students positively. However, parents who never attend PTM meetings have negative impact on student performances. Households with salary earning as major source of income shows greater likelihood of increasing the scores of students compared to business families. Along with these indicators, factors like adequacy of household income and guidance and support given by parents to students also shows positive and significant impacts on student outcomes. As far as *exposure to the sources of mass media* is concerned, only newspapers and internet reflect significant impacts. The results show that those students who read newspaper daily have positive impact on outcomes, while those who surf internet daily are negatively related. This is due to the fact that most students do misuse internet facilities by wasting time on chatting, playing games or social networking. Among *motivational factors*, joining of additional courses along with school studies or having less time to prepare for exams have negative impacts on student outcomes, while students who does regular studies at home shows positive impacts.

11.3.3 Validation of Model

A measure of goodness-of-fit often used to evaluate the fitness of a logistic regression model is based on the simultaneous measure of sensitivity (True positive) and specificity (True negative) for all possible cutoff points. First, we calculate sensitivity and specificity pairs for each possible cut-off point and plot sensitivity on the y-axis by 1-specificity on the x-axis. This curve is called the receiver operating characteristic (ROC) curve. ROC curves evaluate the accuracy of a model that predicts dichotomous outcomes. The area under the ROC curve measures the accuracy of the model (Fig. 11.7). The area under the ROC curve ranges from 0.5 to 1.0, where an area of 1 represents a perfect model, while an area of 0.5 represents a worthless model. A rough guide for classifying the accuracy of the model

Fig. 11.7 ROC curve showing accuracy of the model

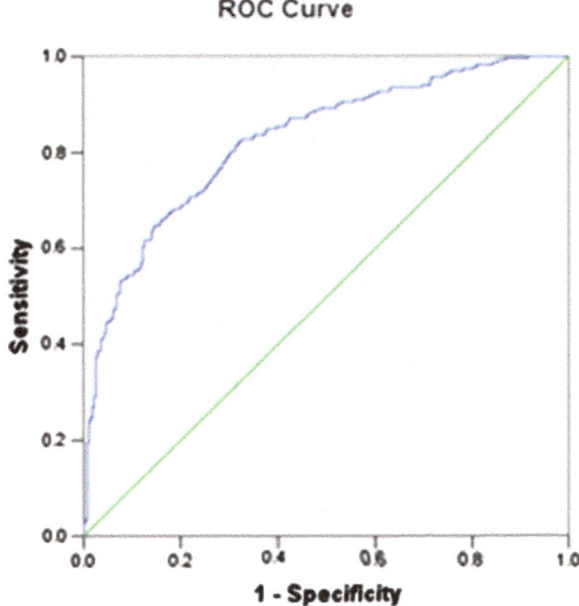

suggests that results above 0.90 are excellent, 0.80–0.90 are good, 0.70–0.80 are fair, while below this level it is poor or fail.

On plotting the ROC curve, the area under ROC came out to be 0.826 which implies that the model correctly classified 82.6% of the total observations. This shows that our model is perfectly classifying student outcomes in terms of distinctions achieved during the last academic year.

11.4 Summary

The chapter clearly distinguishes between quality of resources available in private and government schools. In providing almost all types of facilities the survey shows that private schools are ahead of government schools. However, study suggests that lack of resources or infrastructural facilities in schools is not that a big issue, especially in private schools and to some extent in government schools. It is found that most of the facilities, although available in schools, their usage become almost meaningless due to lack of proper maintenance. Thus, survey results strongly suggest the need for improving the quality of available resources in schools by employing regular and timely maintenance and supervision. The chapter further explores the need for improving the quality of teaching methods and practices adopted in schools. Moreover, it has been proved that behaviour of teachers have an impact on student outcomes. Therefore, there is need to develop more friendly and supportive attitudes towards students by their teachers which can improve their morale and motivation levels. Another problem that has come up is about large class size and high pupil–teacher ratio. Due to large class sizes and lower teacher strength, the quality of learning and performing for both teachers and students get affected. Even the logistic regression model also reflects the similar views. It shows that the indicator 'lower class size' shows insignificant results but has positive impact on student outcomes and behaviours. Survey also reports the dissatisfaction reflected by majority of students in both private and government schools for computer facilities and guidance given for its usage, which points towards need for improvement. More and more schools should be equipped with new technology computers, along with well-qualified computer staff, and latest software to promote better learning among students. In addition to this, the usage of smart class is also not optimum due to shortage of time and hurry of completing the curriculums.

The chapter discusses the development of logistic regression model that identified various factors affecting the students' learning outcomes. At the school level, the quality of school resources, well-qualified teachers, and their friendly attitude towards students strongly influence the overall performance and learning outcomes of students. Although most schools have well-qualified, disciplined, and knowledgeable teachers at the secondary level of education, a healthy teaching atmosphere in terms of student–teacher interaction, teachers' friendly attitude towards students and their support is somewhere missing which is important in motivating students psychologically. In addition to this, the family also plays a great role in providing better study atmosphere at home to students. The model shows that mother's higher education attainment, family support, and guidance really matters a lot in increasing the confidence level among students and thus improving their performance level. Not only has this, but family income level and parents participation in school activities and monthly meetings with teachers also show significant impacts on student outcomes. The finding further indicates that amongst various available mass media sources, the most popular sources of information are television, books, newspapers and internet, while radio is the least preferred.

The findings suggest that schools should provide sufficient support to students by organizing extra classes for weak students and for poor students coming from financially weaker sections of the society. In addition, schools should also provide guidance to students regarding the various career options available after completing senior secondary level of education and should also guide students that despite limitations how they can achieve their targets. These efforts will not only motivate students but will also improve their level of performance, thereby reducing dropout rates.

However, before implementing any policy that seeks to make improvements in the access, quality and equity of secondary education needs to recognise the complexities that there are differences between elementary and secondary schools in terms of size, organisation, relationship to their communities/parents, and ways of assessing quality, therefore, one should not assume that patterns in elementary education will work in secondary schools (Bruns et al. 2011). On the whole, the overall findings emphasize the need for more collaborative efforts from all fronts—that is, school, teachers, and family in achieving the quality standards in secondary education.

References

Amsterdam, C. E. (2009). *School Infrastructure and Teaching and Learning Experiences in South Africa*. Paper presented at the annual meeting of the 53rd Annual Conference of the Comparative and International Education Society, Francis Marion Hotel, Charleston, South Carolina.

Bruns, B., Filmer, D., & Patrinos, H. A. (2011). Making Schools Work: *New evidence on Accountability Reforms*. Human Development Perspectives, Book Published by IBRD, World Bank, Washington D.C.

Case, A., & Deaton, A. (1999). School inputs and educational outcomes in South Africa. *Quarterly Journal of Economics, 114*(3), 1047–1084.

Chan, T. (1979). The impact of school building age on pupil achievement: Greenville County, US Department of Health Education and Welfare, National Institute of Education.

Coleman, J., et al. (1966). *Equality of educational opportunity*. Washington D.C.: Government Printing Office.

Drèze, J., & Kingdon, G. G. (1999). School Participation in Rural India. *The Development Economics Discussion Paper Series*, London School of Economics.

Glick, P., & Sahn, D. (2009). Cognitive skills among children in senegal: Disentangling the roles of schooling and family background. *Economics of Education Review, 28*(2), 178–188.

Glick, P., & Sahn, D. (2010). Early academic performance, grade repetition, and school attainment in senegal: A panel data analysis. *World Bank Economic Review, 24*(1), 93–120.

Owoade, A. I. (2012). A comparative assessment of physical condition of infrastructures in public and private primary schools in Shomolu Local Government Area of Lagos State, B.Tech Project submitted to the Department of Urban and Regional Planning, Lautech, Ogbomoso, Nigeria.

Plumley, J. (1978). The Impact of school building age on the academic achievement of selected Fourth Grade Pupils in the State of Georgia: D.Ed. Dissertation, Athens, Georgia, University of Georgia, 2005.

Sipahimalani, V. (1999). *Education in the Rural Indian Household: A gender based perspective*. Working paper series.

UNESCO. (2005). EFA global monitoring report. *The impact of education quality on development goals*, Chapter 2 (pp. 40–78).

Wang, M. C., Haertel, G. D., & Walberg, H. J. (1993). Towards knowledge base for school learning. *Review of Educational Research, 63*, 249–294.

Chapter 12
Teachers Perspective on Quality of Teaching in Schools

Abstract Research across the globe consistently demonstrates that teachers are important factors in determining the learning and achievement level of students. Hence, improving the quality of teaching and its process may be one of the effective means of raising pupil achievement levels. By quality in teaching, we mean possessing competencies to teach effectively. However, making teaching most effective is not just a one-dimensional term as it depends upon a number of ways in which other resources work in combination. Hence, it becomes important to discuss those dimensions which affect the quality and competencies in teaching. Improvement in these dimensions can help in enhancing the expertise and motivation of teachers towards achieving the common goals of quality secondary education and better learning outcomes in schools. Therefore, in this regard an attempt has been made to examine the teachers' perspectives on various issues which are limiting their competencies and teaching abilities, thus restricting them in adopting efficient teaching practices and methods. This chapter thus provides better understanding on existing teaching environments and practices in schools, working conditions, problems faced by teachers in achieving their professional goals, and perceptions on various issues by elaborating on the important factors at school level, student level, and teachers self-evaluation. The chapter is further divided into six sections; the first section provides details on facilities available in schools and their working conditions; second section elucidates on the characteristics of teaching practices and aptitude; the third section discusses the extent of teacher–student interactions; fourth section discusses various factors affecting teaching abilities; the fifth section deals with perceptions of teachers; while the last section summarizes the major findings of the chapter.

Keywords Working conditions · Teacher–student interaction · Teaching practices · Teaching abilities · Factor analysis · Teachers perception

© Springer Nature Singapore Pte Ltd. 2018
C. Jain and N. Prasad, *Quality of Secondary Education in India*,
https://doi.org/10.1007/978-981-10-4929-3_12

12.1 Working Conditions of Teachers

Research at the international level suggests that poor school infrastructure and inadequate resources threatens academic and health performance of both students and teachers. It is associated with high absenteeism and reduced productivity levels. It is evident from one study in which survey of teacher absence in rural India in 2003 conducted in 3,700 schools in 20 major states of India found that, on average, 25 per cent of teachers in government primary schools were absent from school on a given day and even among teachers who were present, only about half were found engaged in teaching (Kremer et al. 2005). Poor infrastructural facilities in schools range from sanitation problems to water problems and lack of medical facilities. This section documents the inequitable distribution of school infrastructural facilities in Delhi across regions and type of school ownership.

Table 12.1 presents the proportion of responses on the types of facilities available in schools across four regions in Delhi. With respect to classroom and related facilities like fans/tube light, drinking water, separate toilets for boys/ girls/ teachers, the majority of teachers, that is, more than 90% across all regions have confirmed the availability of such facilities in their schools. In the North, nearly 18% of the respondent teachers said that schools lacked in proper electricity supply, while in South and East regions have marked the lowest responses with regard to classrooms having window panes. As far as sanitation facilities are concerned, the results show that although schools in Delhi possess separate toilets for both boys and girls and for teachers as well but are lacking behind when it comes to provision

Table 12.1 Types of facilities available in schools: by regions and school ownership (% of responses)

Facilities	Regions				School type	
	North	South	East	West	Govt.	Private
Proper classrooms	97.8	97.1	97.5	97.5	96.3	98.8
Fans/Tube lights	93.3	100.0	97.5	100.0	97.5	97.5
Electricity supply	82.2	97.1	95.0	100.0	95.0	91.3
Covered windows	91.1	88.6	85.0	92.5	87.5	91.3
Safe drinking water	93.3	94.3	95.0	95.0	98.8	90.0
Separate toilet for boys and girls	95.6	97.1	97.5	95.0	93.8	98.8
Separate toilet for teachers	97.8	97.1	97.5	95.0	98.8	95.0
Water supply in toilets	73.3	82.9	77.5	100.0	82.5	83.8
Lighting in toilets	60.0	62.9	80.0	92.5	73.8	73.8
Cleanliness in toilets	26.7	20.0	57.5	85.0	50.0	45.0
Canteen	42.2	52.8	40.0	52.5	38.8	53.8
Staff room/s	80.0	88.6	87.5	90.0	90.0	82.5
School transport facility	46.7	54.3	45.0	50.0	22.5	75.0
Science laboratory	84.4	85.7	87.5	97.5	81.3	71.3
Library	77.8	80.0	87.5	97.5	92.5	78.8

of facilities like water supply in toilets or lighting and cleanliness issues related to toilets. These facilities are considered to be the most basic ones which every school should possess, especially in a capital city like Delhi. Nearly 27% teachers in the North have mentioned about the non-availability of water supply in toilets in their schools. This proportion is 22.5 and 17% in case of schools located in the East and South. An important problem is related to lighting in toilets, which is well reflected in case of schools in the North and South. Another major issue is regarding cleanliness in toilets. About 73% teacher respondents in the North and 80% in the South show lack of cleanliness in school toilets which has huge adverse impacts on the health of staff members and students.

Canteen facilities are lacking in schools which is an area of concern among all regions. Findings suggest that majority of schools in the East followed by North and West lack canteen facilities as well as school transport facilities. Due to non-availability of school transport, teachers are forced to make their own arrangements for commuting to schools which is obviously more costly for them and even time-taking in some cases. When asked if lack of canteens or transport facilities in schools actually make any difference to their professional life, few male teachers responded that

> There are certain times when they don't carry their lunch with them and have to order it from nearby shops due to lack of canteen facilities in schools, which do affect their health conditions and leads to higher absenteeism or low productively levels.

Even few female teachers mentioned that:

> Due to non-availability of canteen facilities in schools, they are forced to cook their own food in the morning at home and on top of that commuting through public transport due to non-availability of school transport facility makes them so tired that by the time they reach school they don't feel like teaching any more.

About 23% of the surveyed teachers in the North and 20% in the South have mentioned about lack of library facilities in schools. Regarding science laboratories, except for West, all other regions have got less than 90% of responses which shows that more than 10% of teachers have mentioned lack of science laboratories in schools. On an average the findings indicates that among all four regions, the availability of school facilities are still better in schools located in West region followed by East and South.

Table 12.1 presents the availability of these facilities in private and government schools in Delhi. However, results show that there is not much difference in the provision of these facilities between both types of schools expect for a few cases. More than 90% of the teachers in both types of schools reveal the presence of most of the facilities in their schools with respect to proper classrooms, fans/tubes, electricity supply, drinking water, separate toilets for boys and girls and teachers, except in case of window panes where the proportion of positive responses is 87.5% in government schools. Nearly 17% teachers in both types of schools show lack of proper water supply in toilets. The extent of this problem is even more severe in case of lightning and cleanliness in toilets. However, the difference between private and government schools is well reflected in case of facilities like canteens, school transport, science laboratories, and library. While in providing canteens and school transport facility, private schools are ahead of government schools, in terms of provisions for science laboratory and library, government schools are ahead of private schools.

Another interesting fact which has come out of this study is regarding conditions of these facilities in the surveyed schools. The survey findings show that although most of these facilities are available in schools, on an average the conditions are not very satisfactory which clearly implies the lack of proper maintenance. Figure 12.1 presents the average scoring on conditions of various facilities in both private and government schools. Average responses of teachers show that the conditions are worst in case of canteens, followed by cleanliness in toilets, staff room, water supply in toilets, and safe drinking water. This implies that the basic facilities of food, water, and sanitation are in poor state in schools which need attention from policymakers. Few female teachers in government schools even mentioned:

> The conditions of toilets in schools are so poor that most of the time they try to avoid using it due to fears of getting infection. Although school management has appointed sweepers to clean the toilets, they fail to perform their duties due to lack of supervision.

On the issue of safe drinking water, few teachers say:

> Due to non-availability of water purifiers, most of them have to carry their own water bottles as there have been frequent cases of water-borne diseases. Moreover, schools, where water purifiers are available, don't care about servicing them.

Even staff rooms, where teachers are supposed to sit during free periods, also lack proper maintenance. The result shows that the condition of most of these facilities in government schools is lower than that of private schools except for libraries where the condition is better in government schools. The significant difference between the conditions of facilities in private and government schools is recorded in case of classrooms, window panes, safe drinking water, water supply, and cleanliness in toilets. Overall, it gave a clear vision about the kind of environment or working conditions where teachers are forced to pursue their jobs and then they are even expected to perform their best. In addition to these facilities, teachers were also inquired about other provisions available in schools like first-aid kits, computers, fire safety measures, teaching aids, and sufficient reference books in library (Fig. 12.2).

Figure 12.2 shows that larger proportion of teachers in private schools as compared to government school have mentioned the availability of these facilities in their schools. When questions were asked from teachers on the working conditions of fire safety measures or medical facilities, majority of the teachers told:

> Although their schools have provisions for fire safety measures, they never have had the mock trainings for its usage. Hence, in case of emergencies they don't know how to handle them. Moreover, they are not even sure if these facilities are still in working conditions or not.

As far as the condition of the medical first-aid kits are concerned, most teachers, especially in government schools mentioned that:

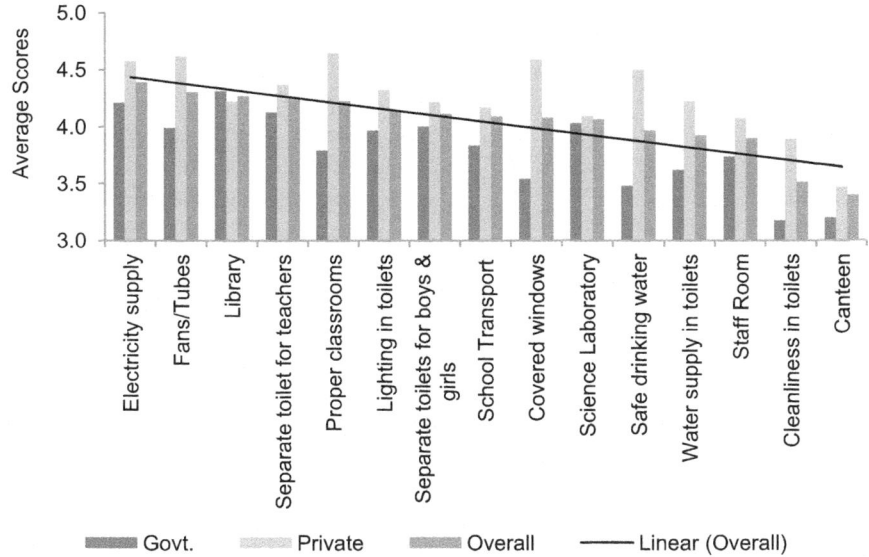

Fig. 12.1 Average scores on conditions of available facilities by school ownership

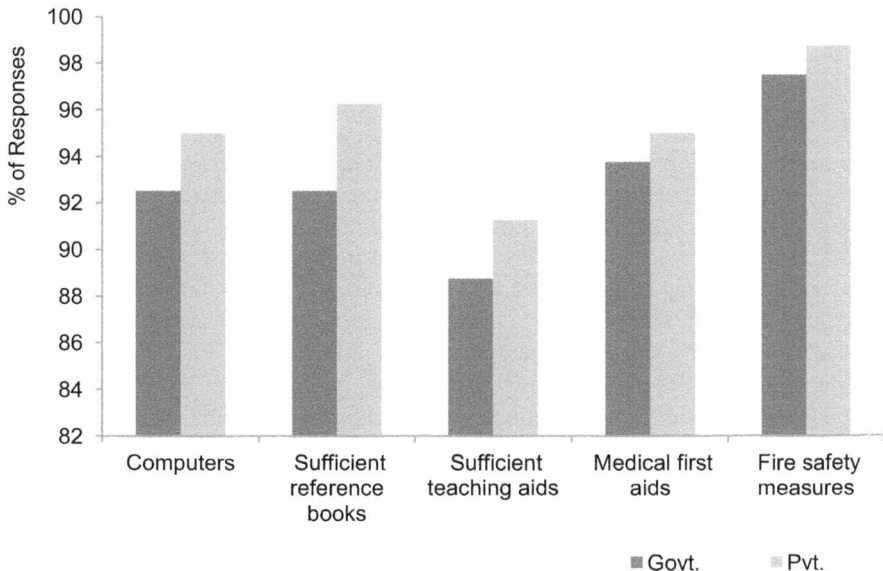

Fig. 12.2 Percent distribution of respondents by additional facilities in schools

They are not sure about the quality and expiry dates of medicines provided by the school. Hence, they try to avoid it as much as possible. In case of students also most of the times they either prefer to take them directly to the nearby dispensary or send the child back home.

In case of libraries, although the condition is better in government schools, in terms of sufficient reference material, private schools are ahead in the race. Figure 12.2 highlights that among all, the availability of sufficient teaching aids have got the lowest responses from teachers. The lack of sufficient teaching aids can have serious implications on teaching abilities. Creemers's (1994) model of educational effectiveness, argued that it is the school factors that create the conditions in which effective teaching and learning occur. Therefore, teachers' behavior could be affected by the school factors.

On the whole, the responses of teachers reflect that the conditions of various facilities available in schools are not up to the mark. The result suggests the need for more facilities in schools, especially government-owned schools, while pointing that mere allocation of funds or provisions of these facilities in schools is not an end in itself. What requires the most is regular maintenance of available facilities in order to have efficient utilization of the available resources. At the same time, it should be seen that schools are more equipped with modernized and upgraded teaching aids to support teachers in adopting the best teaching methods and practices which can further enhance the learning environment in schools.

12.2   Teaching Practices and Aptitudes

At all levels, teaching is increasingly being considered as a real profession and not simply as a talent. This recognition thus necessitates a sound professional training, acquisition of skills well beyond those related to subject knowledge, and adoption of best teaching practices. The criteria for initial training, recruitment, integration, and in-service training concern all teachers particularly those in the secondary level. Some subjects that teachers were initially trained in are disappearing. This is because new learning areas are emerging. Health promotion, HIV/AIDS prevention, sex education, and life skills training, which in the past rarely or never appeared in schools, now imply different approaches to teaching and learning, based on strong human relations and interpersonal skills. Consequently, teachers need to be redeployed to accommodate the changing roles and functions within the teaching system. Campbell (2004) refers to to teachers' job competencies as the impact that classroom factors (e.g. teaching methods, teacher expectations, classroom organization and use of classroom resources) have on students' performance. The literature makes clear that the robotic approach to teacher development produces neither the teaching skills nor the attitudes required for improving classroom approaches and student learning. It stresses that if teachers are to become reflective practitioners and users of active teaching and learning methods, they must participate in professional development programmes that advocate and use such models.

Within this perspective, the survey attempts to capture the responses of teachers about their professional development, connection between specialization and teaching subjects, and on various teaching methods and practices adopted by them. The responses reveal that nearly 34% of the surveyed teachers have not attended any training in the last five years. The proportion of such teachers is quite high in case of private schools. When asked about the reasons for non-participation in professional development trainings or workshop, majority responded that they were not beneficial in their day-to-day teaching or were not related to their area. This shows that most of the trainings which are being organized by various government or non-governmental organizations for professional development of teachers merely wasted the resources. The results indicate that training programmes/workshops neither provide any linkage between theory and practice, nor do they benefit them in improving their teaching skills or learning of new technologies. A significant proportion of teachers in surveyed schools in Delhi consider these programs as sheer wastage of money, resources and time. Almost similar proportion of teachers also mentioned 'lack of time' as one of the major factors for not attending trainings, particularly in case of private schools. As already discussed above, majority of the private schools lack sufficient teaching staff and that which is available with them is burdened with a number of non-teaching activities which hardly provide them any extra time for their own growth and professional development. Few teachers couldn't attend these trainings as they were expensive.

A study by Sungoh (2010) clearly highlights the incompetence of existing training programmes that fails to provide adequate opportunities to teachers to develop competency to face the varied type of situations in the real teaching life as training organisers are not aware of exiting problems of schools. According to this study, the gap between training institutions and schools, stagnates the growth of content and methodology and further weakens the contact with academic discipline. Hence, there is a need for redesigning these training programmes so as to provide greater linkage between theory and practice, enhance knowledge and make them more beneficial in terms of content and usability in day-to-day school activities. Workshops should be able to upgrade teachers with latest teaching methods and aids which can enhance their teaching skills. At the same time, care should be taken to ensure that the duration of such trainings should be kept short and affordable to have greater participation from teachers. These trainings should provide the kind of platform to teachers where they can interact, have brainstorming sessions, and share knowledge on various issues.

Another important factor which has come up in this survey is with regard to teaching of specialized subjects. Although survey shows that majority of the teachers are teaching subjects of their specialization area, there are certain proportion of teachers who even teach non-specialized subjects. This can have great impact not only on teaching abilities of such teachers but also on the learning and achievement level of students as well.

Teachers were also asked about the various teaching methods/aids practiced by them most frequently. Figure 12.3 presents the percentage distribution of responses on various teaching methods used by teachers to promote better learning among

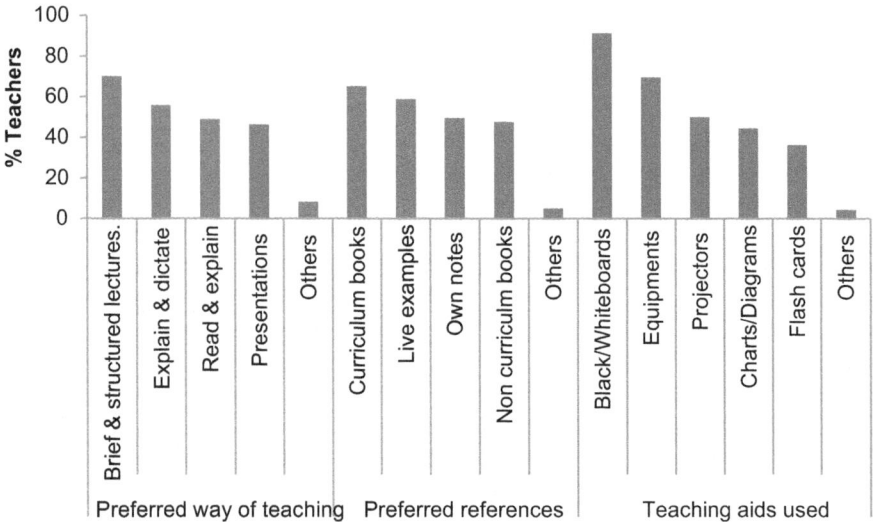

Fig. 12.3 Percentage distribution of teachers by preferred teaching practices

students. The results show that among various modes of teaching in secondary schools, the most preferred method is to provide brief and structured notes, as adopted by nearly 70% teachers, followed by explanations on the topics, and dictation of notes thereafter (56%). Less than 50% teachers prefer to read the topics from books and explain the difficult parts. The use of presentations is, however, the lowest preferred way of teaching among all options

As far as the most preferred references are concerned curriculum books are referred by nearly three-fourth teacher respondents followed by references from live examples. Nearly 47% teachers have also mentioned using non-curriculum books. The usage of curriculum books as the most preferred method of references and non-syllabus book as the lowest preference clearly indicates lack of sufficient teaching reference books in school libraries due to which the majority of teachers are forced to restrict their teaching to curriculum books only or to live examples.

In case of teaching aids, blackboards/whiteboards is the most popular option as responded by more than 90% teachers, followed by the use of equipments that is more or less restricted in the teaching of science; the use of flash cards is not so common a practice among teachers. Projector is another teaching aid which is used by just 50% teachers for imparting knowledge to students. These findings some-where reveal that majority of the schools still lack the provision of sufficient modernized teaching aids due to which teachers are still making use of outdated technologies. Although teaching is now supported by smart class technique in most of the secondary schools in Delhi, however, such facilities are limited to private schools only, and fail to contribute much towards the learning and achievements of students. The reason behind the same is that, when teachers were asked about the impact of smart class teaching on learning level of students then few teachers replied:

> There is no doubt that smart class has made teaching much easier and interesting due to its diverse knowledge contents, however, most of the teachers are not able to discuss or show all of its contents, diagrams, or visual pictures to students due to lack of time. Teachers told that they are given limited time period in which they have to cover the entire syllabus, conduct exams, prepare results, and check textbooks, hence, it is not possible for them to take up in-depth and visual description of each and every topic provided through smart class technique.

Clearly, time factor is the most important reason behind inefficient utilization of smart class technique in secondary schools. Overall, the existing pattern of teaching practices used in secondary schools indicates that most of the teaching is in abstract. Thus, in majority of the cases, teachers either just keep on talking and repeating the same things to students in class, or reading the fixed referred curriculum books, or dictating their old notes which were prepared several years back without updating them with information on new discoveries/inventions or latest events happening in those areas. The main reason behind this is lack of sufficient equipments and teachings aids like projectors or smart classes in schools. Moreover, even in schools where these kinds of facilities are available, the usage is not up to the mark which further makes the availability of such teaching aids meaningless. Lack of necessary skills in using teaching aids and lack of time to cover the syllabus are two most important reasons behind inefficient utilization of these resources.

Hence, it is important that school management should make efforts in employing the best and latest teaching aids and methods in their schools which will not only add-up the abilities and skills of teachers but will also promote healthy learning among students that can further improve the overall performance and quality teaching in schools. Governments should also provide more funds to schools in this area. In addition to this, teachers also require acquisition of skills that are much larger in scope than those necessary to simply transmit knowledge. Overall, the adoption of best teaching practices in the secondary education system requires re-designing of curriculums which are more interactive and can promote active participation of the teacher and learner in the learning process. Along with this, schools should focus more on using best teaching methods, aids, and equipments for imparting knowledge to students and should provide training to their teachers for the maximum utilization of the assigned teaching aids.

12.3 Teacher–Student Interactions

The image of the teacher as a specialist in a specific subject who stands alone in front of the class is still a reality today in many contexts, particularly at the secondary level. However, this perception of the role of teachers no longer matches the demand of teaching and the expectations that are made with regard to the education of young people. Even if the teaching profession has preserved an element of permanency, regardless of time period or education level, many elements have changed and are continually changing: knowledge and ways to access it, the influence of the media and of ICTs, societal demands, the social environment, the students themselves, etc. According to Perry (1994) the necessary conditions for quality teaching include the performance of the teacher that requires professional expertise. A professional's level of capability is not static but constantly changing partly because of rapid changes in the environment caused by new technical, social or institutional claims, but also because the individual's personal development continues and new job demands arises.

Today, teachers are moving away from being 'transmitter of knowledge' to more towards becoming a 'mediator in the construction of knowledge', a facilitator and, even at times, a social worker. He or she must also foster the development of social skills and create a learning environment that will encourage young people to learn to live together and to become responsible citizens. However, for creating such an environment within schools, the basic ingredient required is strong relation between students and teachers which can further promote healthy interactions between them. Hence, in this regard, the study has tried to capture the various initiatives made by teachers in promoting their interactions with students.

Although majority of the teachers have responded in favour of the various initiatives taken by them to promote their interactions with students, the average scores calculated on the basis of their responses on the five-point scale reflect the exact picture on which initiatives are preferred by the teachers most. The results also highlight the level of comfort that students feel with their teachers while discussing various issues (Table 12.2).

Table 12.2 shows that among the various initiatives taken by teachers to promote their level of interaction with students, 'encouraging students to participate in various class level discussions', 'giving live examples from day-to-day life', and 'discussion with students related to exams, etc.' scores the top most ratings. Initiatives like 'informing students about various study/career options' and 'keep asking questions to maintain interest' scores the fourth and fifth position in terms of teachers initiatives. Initiatives like 'discussion with students on various competitions' record the lowest average scores from teacher's perspective.

Table 12.2 Average scores on teacher initiative to promote interaction with students

Teachers initiatives	Average scores
Encourage students to participate in discussion	4.71
Give examples from their daily life	4.46
Students discuss queries related to subject, exams, results etc.	4.35
I keep informing students about various study/career options available	4.30
Keep asking questions to maintain interest	4.26
Encourages and inform students about various competitions	4.26
Students discuss problems related to family/friends/personal etc.	4.24
Students discuss issues related to exploitation etc.	4.22

Note Average scores calculated on the basis of responses on the five-point Likert scale

On the student front, the results reveal that larger proportion of teachers feels that students are comfortable with them in discussing their queries related to exams, subjects, or results. When it comes to discussion on problems related to family and friends or issues related to exploitations, these initiatives score the lowest ratings among all. The results suggest that teachers have to go a long way to promote healthy relation with their students. They need to develop more faith and confidence among students towards themselves so that their interactions are not just limited to school curriculums or examination queries but extend beyond that. Teachers should take more initiatives to have a friendly approach with students so that they feel free to discuss all those issues which restrict their growth and development. There is need for more healthy interactions on various dimensions which can create better learning environment for both.

12.4   Factors Affecting Professional Growth and Abilities of Teachers

One might expect that teachers themselves are committed to improving the quality of education, have a professional ethic, and feel responsible for their own continuous professional development both as a right and a duty. However, often gap is observed between the expectations of the parents or society and the way in which teachers believe that they should practice their profession. Lydiah and Nasongo (2009) observed that head teachers' who used teamwork by ensuring parents, teachers and students were involved in the running of the institutions enhanced performance of their schools. At times teachers feel isolated, overworked, live in precarious conditions, and face difficult classes; we need to remember that teachers also need a decent status, support, and recognition of their irreplaceable role; they need this from public officials, parents, students, and society as a whole. They also need to create a community amongst themselves and be able to count on the support of effective and responsible professional associations. One of the studies conducted for Nigeria shows that teachers' beliefs, community support, initial teacher education and opportunities for professional learning are important for improving the quality of science teaching and learning and this is an important contribution to knowledge (Ogunmade 2005). Hence, it is important to study all those factors which are considered to be important by teachers in achieving their professional growth and at the same time see how far schools have been able to deliver those factors by measuring the satisfaction level of teachers. This method will not only highlight the positive strengths of schools in maximizing the professional growth of teachers, but will also point out the critical areas where schools need to work ahead. The improvement of those factors where satisfaction of teachers is low despite being important can definitely play a great role in enhancing the morale of teachers which can further boost up the lost enthusiasm among teachers towards their teaching profession. This section is further divided into two sub-sections; the first section discusses various factors that are important for the professional growth of teachers, while the second section identifies the obstacles in rendering efficient teaching abilities.

12.4.1 Importance–Satisfaction Scale

Since all the factors were marked important or most important on the five-point scale by teacher respondents in both private and government schools, an effort has been made to differentiate between factors that lie higher or lower in importance on the measurement scale. For this, the average scores were calculated for each factor on the basis of their responses on a Five-point scale; thereafter, a priority list was prepared reflecting the highest important factor followed by next highest, and so on. Similar exercise has been done in case of satisfaction scale. Figure 12.4 identifies the various factors which they consider to be most important by teachers for their professional growth and their satisfaction level, thereby identifying the gaps in importance and satisfaction.

The results show that teachers consider job security to be the most important factor in their professional growth followed by gaining quality experience, student's performance and satisfaction and promotions. Indicators like awards and training opportunities have the least ratings here. However, on the satisfaction scale, the average scores are lowest in case of indicators like students' satisfaction, self-development, and quality experience, while on job security and salary increments the satisfaction scores are the highest. Overall, the gap between importance and satisfaction is highest in case of student performance and satisfaction, quality experience and self-development indicators, indicating that although these factors rank high on importance scale they ranks low on satisfaction.

To improve the quality of teaching, schools need to focus their strategies in enhancing the morale and motivation level of teachers. It is important to make them feel enthusiastic about their profession so that they can use the best teaching practices and aptitudes in order to create healthy learning environment. However, this is possible only when school authorities are giving them equal opportunities to achieve their professional goals.

12.4.2 Factors Affecting Efficient Teaching Abilities

An education system that aims to offer quality education for all young people should be able to count on teachers who are well trained and adequately paid. Further, they should be capable of independently following the evolving processes and structure of knowledge, and take into account the growing interdependencies at both the global and local levels that impact schools. Many countries are suffering from a serious shortage of qualified teachers. There are numerous obstacles that

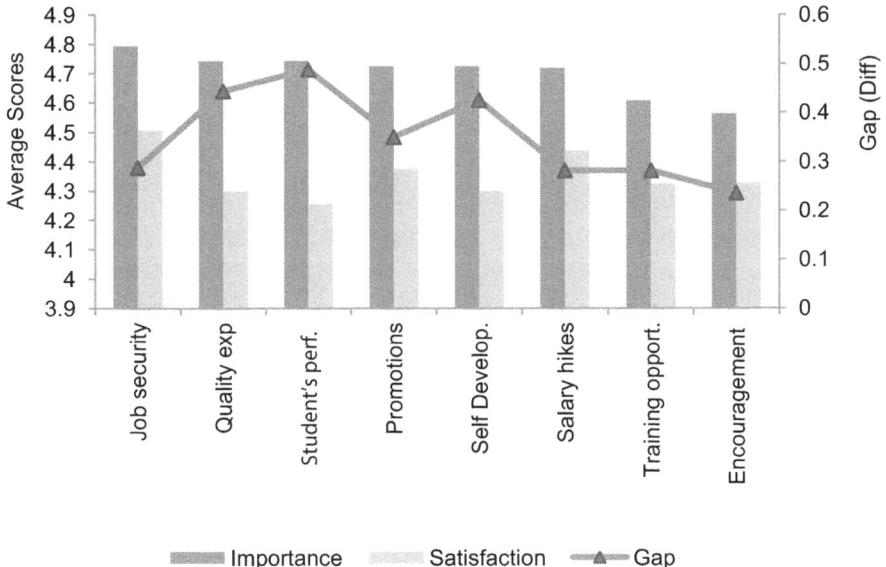

Fig. 12.4 Important-satisfaction scale for teachers

frequently challenge the presence of well-trained, competent teachers in classrooms, for example, low wages, precarious social status, poor working conditions, heavy workload, large class sizes, limited prospects for professional advancement, etc. Many systems are bearing witness to an aging secondary teaching staff, which further accentuates the cultural distance between students and those who are responsible for their education; female representation is often very unequal as well. Moreover, the attractiveness of the teaching profession to competent young people is lessening in favour of higher revenue professional opportunities. All over the world, too many young people are leaving the formal education system having lost the motivation to learn, and consequently, the desire to teach. In certain countries, teachers are leaving their profession early on, in favor of more advantageous working conditions and career prospects. In other countries, as a response to the shortage, there is a call even for teachers who have not had adequate training.

To have a better understanding on the various obstacles that affect the quality of teaching, an attempt has been made to apply the *Factor Analysis* technique.[1] This method reloads factors into structures with similar themes and provides clarity on what kind of factors affect teaching abilities the most. The findings of factor analysis technique are presented in Table 12.3.

---

[1]The major findings and methodology of this model have been presented in the paper entitled 'Factors Affecting Teaching Abilities, Practices and Motivation—Evidences from Senior Secondary Schools in Delhi' at 2nd International Conference on Education (ICEDU) organized by TIIKM held in Bangkok, Thailand during 21–22 April, 2016.

Table 12.3 Factor analysis results: identifying factors behind inefficient teaching abilities

Variables	Comp 1	Comp 2	Comp 3	Comp 4
	School factors	Teaching factors	External factors	Non-teaching factors
Large class size	0.83			
Lack of students motivation to learn	0.82			
Lack of school resources and facilities	0.80			
Lack of adequate teaching material/aids		·0.84		
Lack of professional trainings		0.77		
Interference from senior teachers		0.65		
Lack of time for planning lessons		0.51		
Polices interferences			0.80	
Interference from parents			0.67	
Frequent changes in curriculums, structure				0.83
Huge work load of additional responsibilities				0.73

Notes Extraction method: principal component analysis. *Rotation Method* Varimax with Kaiser normalization. (a) Rotation converged in 6 iterations

Interpretation of Results:

- The value of KMO statistics is 0.86 which indicates that it is adequate and we should be confident that factor analysis is appropriate on these data sets.
- Bartlett's test measures show significant results which indicates that there is some relationship between the variable we are hoping to include in the analysis.
- SPSS identifies 11 linear components of which four factors have been extracted that together explain 80% of variance in data. The rotated component matrix table shows that 'school factors' bear the greatest influence on teaching abilities with 24.54% of its explained variance, followed by 'teaching factors' with 24.50% of explained variance. The third and fourth highest components are 'external factors' and 'non-teaching factors' with nearly 15% of explained variance each.

Major Findings:

The model has come up with four broad factors having maximum influence on quality teaching. These factors are discussed here in detail:

- *School Factors:* The findings show that lack of proper school facilities are the greatest obstacles in efficient teaching abilities. Within school component, the most important factors that restrict efficient teaching are larger class size, followed by lack of student motivation, school resources, and facilities.

- *Teaching Factors:* This constitutes the second most important component which affects teaching abilities almost with similar weight as school factors do. Within this category, lack of sufficient teaching aids and professional trainings are the most crucial ones. In addition, lack of opportunities for personal development and interferences from senior teachers/staff also affect their abilities.
- *External Factors:* In addition to the above factors, there are certain external factors which affect the quality of teaching like policy changes-related grading system, examination system, recruitment of teachers, etc.
- *Non-teaching Factors:* The findings also capture the implications of non-teaching factors on teaching abilities. This includes frequent changes in curriculums and the burden of additional responsibilities of non-teaching work.

Overall, this section clearly distinguishes between various factors which have a strong bearing on teaching abilities and thus act as major obstacles in the path of quality teaching. Among all, undoubtedly the most crucial factors are school and teaching-related factors.

12.5 Perceptions of Teachers on Various Quality Issues

This section elaborates the perceptions of teachers on various quality issues related to schools, teaching, examination systems, results, and peer group teachers and the qualities that a good teacher must possess. In this regard, Table 12.4 presents the average scores as given by teachers on various quality issues related to schools and resources. Findings reveal that quality of textbooks has the highest ranking, followed by quality of general admission procedures, quality of examination system and school infrastructure. Quality of classroom facilities and grading/marking system has the lowest rating. This indicates that although overall infrastructure of school with respect to school building, playground, etc., is in good condition as responded by teachers, the resources and facilities within schools like condition of classrooms, etc., lack quality. Table 12.4 also throws light on the new grading system which was introduced in schools in Delhi few years back. The results reflect that teachers are not satisfied with the quality of new grading system and thus this indicator scored the second lowest rating.

Table 12.5 presents the average scores as given by teachers on the quality of peer group teachers. It shows that the highest average scoring for rating the quality of peer group teachers goes in favour of qualities like well qualified and well versed subject knowledge. A large proportion of teacher respondents also feel that the peer group teachers are friendly with other faculty members in school and are well disciplined/mannered in nature.

Table 12.5 further shows that the peer group teachers' quality traits of helpfulness and supportive nature share the fifth position. while respondent teachers'

Table 12.4 Teachers perception on quality of schools and related services

Quality statements	Average scores
Quality of textbooks	4.55
General admission procedure in school	4.38
Examination system	4.36
Quality of school infrastructure	4.34
Variety of courses offered	4.27
Marking/Grading system	4.23
Quality of classroom facilities	4.11

Note Average scores calculated on the basis of responses on 5 point Likert scale

Table 12.5 Teachers perceptions on quality of peer group teachers

Peer group qualities	Average scores
Well qualified	3.76
Well versed through the knowledge of subject	3.52
Friendly with other teachers as well	3.36
Disciplined/Well mannered	3.35
Helpful and supportive	3.33
Confident and highly motivated	3.29
Very friendly with students	3.25
Respect students	3.20

Note Average scores calculated on the basis of responses on 5 point Likert scale; however there were no responses in 'strongly disagree' category

perception of other teachers in their schools showing respect to students or being friendly with them stands at the lowest ranking. This clearly reflects the high communication gaps between teachers and students. However, few teachers have even responded that their peer group teachers lack confidence and motivation, hence this quality trait comes at the bottom three ratings.

Thus, although majority of the teachers at the secondary level of education are well qualified and well versed with their subject well-mannered and maintains good communication or relation with other teachers in the group, they lack confidence while teaching and fail to maintain healthy interaction with students. The study emphasizes that in order to create better environment in classroom, it is very important for teachers to maintain healthy relations with students and respect their feelings so as to provide them with the best solutions to their queries.

In addition, the respondents were also asked to explain what they meant by 'quality teaching'. For this, options were given to teachers and they were requested to rank those options on the basis of their views/opinions. For instance, they should give rank 1 to the most important criterion and rank 11 to the least one, and so on. On the basis of the responses of teachers, the findings are presented in Table 12.6. The idea has been derived from one of the study conducted in Nigeria, where results

Table 12.6 Teachers perception on qualities of good teaching

Qualities	Ranking	Mean	Std. Dev.
Teaching skills (presentation, explanation etc.)	1	2.79	2.30
Knowledge base of subject matter	2	2.84	2.57
General knowledge base	3	3.42	2.74
Enthusiasm and devotion to teaching	4	3.64	2.80
Organization (effective learning environment)	5	3.83	2.69
Ability to motivate students	6	4.43	3.16
Appropriate utilization of teaching tools	7	4.48	3.03
Demonstration of teaching situation	8	4.92	3.03
Interaction between students and teachers	9	5.05	3.60
Ability to assess and evaluate students' and their work	10	5.20	3.49
Approachableness	11	5.60	4.24

revealed that knowledge base of subject matter, teaching skill and subsequently, general knowledge base were regarded as the most important factors (Iolube 2005).

Table 12.6 shows that the top five traits for being a good teacher includes qualities like possessing efficient teaching skills, knowledge base of the subject matter, general knowledge base, enthusiasm towards teaching, and ability to create an effective learning environment. Next in line come quality traits like ability to motivate students and ability to utilize teaching aids effectively. However, factors like student–teacher interaction, ability of teachers to evaluate students and their work, and approachability of teachers form the lowest rating for being a good teacher. This clearly points out that teachers in secondary education still do not bother much about maintaining healthy interactions and relation with students. One study (Austin et al. 2003) argued that construction of a classroom relationship is a visible consequence of the structuring of classroom learning. Lack of these quality traits among teachers at the secondary school level reflects on the poor learning environment within classrooms and thus low level of teaching.

12.6 Summary

The chapter, while highlighting various issues related to the working conditions of teachers and kind of support or facilities provided to them by schools, also discusses the factors that affect the teaching abilities and practices in schools. The findings in this chapter reveal that there are four broad dimensions that affect teaching abilities and practices in secondary schools—school factors, teaching factors, external factors, and non-teaching factors. The simultaneous improvement in all these broad dimensions can definitely improve the overall quality of teaching.

The survey reveals that making provision of basic facilities like drinking water, separate toilet for boys and girls, etc., is not a big issue as most of the schools, especially in a capital city like Delhi already have these; however, the biggest challenge is to have proper functioning and regular maintenance of these facilities which is missing in both private and government schools. The study further shows that schools should also focus on providing adequate modernized teaching aids to teachers and training which they need to practice in their day-to-day teaching. In addition to this, teachers should also be given opportunities for their professional growth in terms of training workshops or conferences that can help them in increasing their morale and expertise and lead to the creation of healthy teaching and learning environments in schools. An important factor which has come up in the findings is the huge load of additional responsibilities that teachers have to bear due to which they are neither able to concentrate on their teaching nor do they get sufficient time for doing lesson planning, which affects their teaching abilities. Hence, it is important to recruit better qualified managerial staff in schools which can look after non-teaching activities, thereby reducing the burden on teachers.

The chapter also throws light on certain factors that are limited to teachers' behaviours and attitudes which need to be changed. Interaction of teachers with students is found to be missing in the present scenario, as indicated by survey results. Due to lack of proper interactions with teachers, students hesitate to discuss their problems which, in turn, lead to lower learning levels and outcomes.

On the whole, it is a multi-dimensional process where everyone including the government, school administrations, teachers, and students need to work in collaboration with each other to improve the quality of teaching and learning processes, which in turn can improve the quality of secondary education in schools. While government should redesign certain policies to ensure timely implementation and delivery of funds, resources, and support to secondary schools and ensure supervision, schools on the other hand should try to utilize the allocated resources and funds in efficient ways. In addition, schools should take more initiatives in recruiting trained teachers, providing them with best working conditions and facilities and opportunities for professional growth, and encourage them through awards and deserving remuneration. Teachers also need to take initiatives to improve the quality of knowledge imparted to students by making the best use of available teaching aids and methods. Finally, there is need to create an environment in schools where students feel motivated to learn and participate in various activities, as lack of motivation in students has come up as one of the major factors which restrict teachers to adopt the best teaching practices in secondary schools.

References

Austion, H., Dwyer, B., & Freebody, P. (2003). *Schooling the child*. London: Routledge Falmer.

Campbell, J., Kyriakides, L., Muijs, D., & Robinson, W. (2004). *Accessing teachers job effectiveness: Developing a differentiated model*. London and New York: Routledge Falmer.

Creemers, B. P. M. (1994). Effective instruction: An empirical basis for a theory of educational effectiveness. In Reynolds et al. (Eds.), *Advances in School Effectiveness Research and Practice* (pp. 189–205). Oxford: Pergamon.

Iolube, N. P. (2005). School effectiveness and quality improvement: Quality teaching in Nigerian secondary schools. *The African Symposium: An On Line Journal of African Educational Research Network, 5*, 17–31.

Kremer, M., Muraldhiran, K., Chaudhury, N., Hammer, J., & Rogers, F. H. (2005). Teacher absence in India: A snapshot. *Journal of the European Economic Association.*

Lydiah, L. M., & Nasongo, J. W. (2009). Role of the head teacher in academic achievement in secondary schools in Vihiga District. *Kenya, Current Research Journal of Social Sciences, 1* (3), 84–92. ISSN: 2041-3246.

Ogunmade, T. O. (2005). *The status and quality of secondary science teaching and learning in Lagos state Nigeria.* Research Thesis work submitted at Education and Social Science, Edith Cowan University, Perth, Western Australia.

Perry, P. (1994). Defining and measuring the quality of teaching. In D. Green (Ed.), *What is quality in higher education?.* Bristol: SRHE and Open University Press.

Sungoh, S. M. (2010). Quality issues in teacher education. *University News, 43*(18).

Part V
Summary and Suggestions

Chapter 13
Conclusion and Policy Recommendations

Abstract India aspires to become a knowledge hub with hopes to transform millions of young people across the world into educated global citizens. To attain this objective, the entire education system in the country has to become sound and robust by achieving excellence. An effective and innovative education system opens enormous opportunities for individuals, whereas a weak educational system can result in declining standards of living, social exclusion, and unemployment. To reap the benefits of education to the extent possible, policymakers need to address the dual challenge of increasing the quantity of education and assuring its high quality. It is generally seen that schools of high quality can lead to improved educational outcomes. Even from a public policy perspective, interventions in schools are generally viewed as more acceptable than say, direct interventions in the family. Although cognitive skills may be developed in formal schooling, they may also come from the family, peers, culture, and so forth. It is not wrong to say that successful learning involves enabling environments at schools, home, work, and everywhere. In this context, the concept of quality is not a unitary process but involves multiple perspectives. Considering the wide disparities at the regional and state levels in India, expectations from quality education may differ from one situation to another. Despite this, it is recognized that for growth to be inclusive, access to quality education must be broadened so that all sections of the population could benefit from new employment opportunities. For achieving the objective of rendering quality to education in India, initiatives are required at both micro and macro levels. For this, there is a need to understand and examine the factors affecting the education system and having a bearing on its quality standard. With this background, the study explains why there is a need to improve the quality standard of education in India, particularly secondary education, in terms of its strong linkages with socio-economic outcomes at the national and state levels. This study has analysed the present situation of secondary education at both national and state levels, identified the various gaps and disparities at various levels. Along with this, an effort has also been made to capture first-hand information from schools, students, and teachers in understanding the current scenario of education in schools, the existing problems faced by them, quality issues etc. This chapter summarizes the results of the study.

© Springer Nature Singapore Pte Ltd. 2018   211
C. Jain and N. Prasad, *Quality of Secondary Education in India*,
https://doi.org/10.1007/978-981-10-4929-3_13

13.1 Overview of the Empirical Study on Quality Improvement of Secondary Education

With an objective to identify important parameters for accessing the present status of quality of secondary education in schools and estimating its importance in terms of linkages with various socio-economic outcomes at the national and state levels and identifying the factors affecting students' outcomes and efficient teaching abilities, the study is undertaken to answer various specific research questions. The most important of these are: need to measure the quality of education; how to measure quality of education; factors affecting learning outcomes of students; and factors restricting efficient teaching practices. To answer these questions, the study is conceptually framed around three approaches. While the first two approaches analysed the current situation of secondary education at the macro level: national and state level, the third approach analysed the situation at micro level, that is, from the perspectives of schools, students, and teachers.

The book has been presented in five parts each one covering unique aspect of quality education at school level. The *first part* discusses the theoretical and conceptual framework of the study. It clearly defined the concept of quality of education and its origin followed by a discussion on available literature, thereby identifying the gaps. In the conceptual framework, the study adopts three approaches to measure the quality of education: firstly, analyse the situation at the national level while identifying gaps; secondly, recognize the disparities between states with different socio-economic characteristics, its linkages with socio-economic outcomes, and inter-state disparities; thirdly measure quality indicators based on primary data collection in sample schools. It also elaborates the rationale for undertaking the study, research questions, objectives, and hypothesis to be tested. While discussing the need for undertaking this research work, it has been emphasized that this study is new not only in terms of coverage area but also in terms of estimating its linkages with various socio-economic outcomes and generating new models for education. The *second part* describes the methodology of the study and procedures for collecting the empirical data. Both quantitative and qualitative research approaches have been adopted for conducting the study. A two-stage stratified systematic random sampling technique has been applied for the collection of primary data. The *third part* of this book presents the current scenario of development and expansion of secondary education in India (in terms of number of institutions, enrolments, and teachers) and the performance indicators like transition rates, dropouts, and completion rates to measure effectiveness of secondary education. It further discusses the management and financing pattern of secondary education. The development and performance of secondary education in major states in India and the existing disparities have also been discussed. The development of an exploratory model to understand the impact of secondary education on development indicators of states at macro and micro levels are further discussed here. The *fourth part* presents the findings based on the primary survey conducted in sample schools in Delhi. While the first chapter within this section presents an overview of the background characteristics of the sample population that promotes our understanding about the quality of secondary education in schools in a more comprehensive way, the next chapter provides in-depth description of students studying in secondary education on their performances, achievements, learning outcome, and their perceptions and views on various issues, while the last one elaborates all dimensions which affect the quality and competencies in teaching. These include teaching environments and practices adopted in schools, working conditions, problems faced by teachers in achieving their professional goals, and teachers' perceptions on various issues, student level, and teachers' self-evaluation. The summary, conclusions, and policy implications have been covered in the *fifth part*.

13.2 Major Findings and Policy Implications

The findings are presented here at three levels: national, state, and school level, based on the three approaches adopted in the study. These conclusions further provide answers to research questions which were posed in the beginning of the study.

13.2.1 Findings at the National Level

- Findings reveal that on expansion side, despite the fact that there is huge growth in number of institutions, teachers, and enrolments over the years, the number of secondary schools available per lakh population is still quite low which indicates that the goal of achieving universalization of secondary education in India is still far away.

- The performance indicators pose great challenges as they reveal slow growth rates in improving transition rates and promotion rates and reducing dropout rates.

- In terms of management; private players have played a major role in case of secondary education, whereas at the middle and primary levels of education, government and local bodies have played a significant part. Even on the financing side, private share of educational expenditure is significant in India for secondary education and has increased manifolds over the years. The public expenditure on other hand, as the percent of GDP and of public expenditure indicates, the education sector has always received low priority in comparison to other social sectors in the economy.

13.2.2 State-Level Findings

- Richer the state in terms of per capita GDP, higher is the expenditure on education. Moreover, the states that tend to spend more on education are characterized by higher attendance ratios among students. This is due to the fact that increased expenditures lead to better provision of facilities which increases attendance ratios in schools.

- In attainment of secondary education, huge disparities exist within states at various levels ranging from rural to urban, male–female as compared to elementary educational attainment levels. Moreover, it is not necessary that states which have performed well on economic or social fronts also perform well on the educational front. This to some extent points towards unequal distribution and inefficient utilization of resources.

- It was observed that inverse relationship exist between gross enrolment ratios and dropout rates. Lower the GER, higher are the dropouts. Lower GER was recorded for both girls and boys in states like Assam, Bihar, Jharkhand, and Rajasthan, accompanied by higher dropouts, while in case of states where higher GER were recorded, lower dropout rates were observed (Himachal Pradesh, followed by Delhi, Kerala, Haryana, Uttarakhand, and Tamil Nadu). It is ironical that the dropout rates are higher in case of boys from the First–Tenth standards compared to girls for most of the major states in India. However, girls' dropout rates are reported to be higher than boys, particularly in north-west states.

- States which have performed poorly despite development in the secondary education sector constitute West Bengal, Rajasthan, Assam, and Chhattisgarh, thereby implying misallocation or inefficient use of resources. States like Bihar, Odisha, Madhya Pradesh, and Karnataka fall in the poorest category with low performance level and low development in secondary education. These states seriously need to look into quality and infrastructural issues at the secondary level of education.

- At the macro level, secondary education has direct impact on economic growth, demographic transition, and demographic-health performances of states, whereas in case of social and health outcomes, it bears indirect impacts. In the matter of social and health indices, although the results were not significant, the impact is highest in case of secondary education compared to other levels of school education. This implies that at the state level too secondary education has huge implications compared to primary or middle levels of education.

- At the micro level, youngsters with secondary education has better chances of being employed in regular salaried jobs in comparison to those having elementary level of education. Further, such youngsters (having secondary level of education) are more confident about their job stability and about getting the jobs they have aspired for than those in other education levels. They are better off in terms of owing security assets like life insurance and medical insurance policies.

A large proportion of youngsters with secondary education make up the top four income quintiles, whereas those with elementary education falls in the lowest income quintile. Thus, the impact of secondary education at the micro level is higher on individual incomes, employment, and household well-being than those in other levels of school education at the state level.

13.2.3 Findings Based on Primary Survey in Schools

- Class size affects both teaching abilities and students' learning. It is found that government schools face the problem of large class sizes due to lack of adequate classrooms in senior secondary schools, while private schools shows higher PTR. Both these factors—large class size and high PTR—affect students' learning and teaching atmosphere.

- The variety of subjects offered to students is wider in case of private schools as compared to government schools. Moreover, it is found that smaller proportion of government schools are providing instruction through English language in comparison to private schools where almost all schools are in English medium. Private schools are much ahead of government schools in providing facilities like transportation and regular health check-up camps for students. The provision of better facilities in private schools is pulling the demand for admissions in private schools in Delhi. However, in terms of staff-related provisions like job security to teachers, annual increments, good salary structure, and promotion strategies, government schools are a better place compared to private schools.

- Schools are lacking behind in providing facilities like smart class techniques, canteens, safe drinking water, stores to purchase books and uniforms, and hygienic sanitation facilities, which in turn affect students' learning outcomes and behaviours. The classroom conditions are also in poor conditions particularly in government schools which not only affect students' learning outcomes but also teaching abilities.

- Among various provisions, it is found that conditions of computer facilities available in schools are not up to the mark.

- Majority of the students have given lowest satisfaction ratings to school indicators like physical safety of students in schools, quality of school facilities, and cleanliness in schools, which means that these areas need further improvement.

- In government schools, majority of the students belongs to lower educated families that constitute the bottom two income quintiles. Further, the heads of the household are usually salary earners and wage earners in case of government school students, while they are occupied in salaried jobs or in business/trade in the case of private school students. This reflects that unlike students of government schools those in private schools come from better-off families who have access to better facilities and support at home.

- The survey findings indicate that the most popular source of information to students is television followed by books, newspapers, and internet. Radio is the least referred source of information among secondary students.

13.2.4 Findings of the Exploratory Model: Factors Affecting Learning Outcomes of Students

- The result of the exploratory model, that is, binary logistics regression model reveals that school resources, teachers and teaching quality, family background, mass media exposure, and self motivational factors determine student outcomes to a significant extent. Within school-related factors cleanliness in school, well-qualified teachers, their friendly and supportive attitude with students, and quality of school infrastructure/facilities show positive impact on students. However, poor conditions of school library, poor classroom conditions, less number of extra classes for weaker students organized by schools, inefficient teaching methods, and less variety of courses offered in school shows negative relation which imply that there is need to improve the quality of these facilities in schools at secondary level of education.

- Within family characteristics, the mother's qualification influences outcomes of students positively. Education of heads of household show insignificant influence although positive results. Parents who never attended PTM meetings have negative impact on student performances. Households with salary earnings as a major source of income show greater likelihood of increasing the scores of students compared to business families. Along with these indicators, adequacy of household income and guidance, and support given by parents to students also show positive and significant impacts on students' outcomes.

- Newspapers and internet influence students' performances positively, whereas those students who surf internet daily shows negative impact on their performance.

13.2.5 Findings from Teachers' Perspectives

- The conditions of various facilities available in schools are not up to the mark particularly in case of canteens, cleanliness in toilets and staff room, water supply in toilets and provision of safe drinking water. Lack of these facilities leads to low motivation among teachers.

- Nearly one-third of the respondent teachers have not attended any training since the last five years. The proportion of such teachers is higher in case of private schools as compared to government schools. Fewer opportunities, huge work load of additional responsibilities, and lack of time are the few major reasons behind not attending such trainings.
- The top five factors that affect teaching abilities are lack of student motivation, large class sizes, inadequate school resources and facilities, less time for lesson planning, and inadequate teaching materials and aids.
- The findings of factor analysis indicate that school-related factors followed by teaching factors are the two most important components which affect teaching abilities the most; it shows almost 50% variance, while external factors and non-teaching factors shows 30% variance in teaching abilities. Hence, providing better teaching aids and improving school facilities can enhance quality of teaching to a significant extent. In addition to this, reduction in frequent changes in syllabus and policies related to school education along with lessening of additional burden of non-teaching work load can also improve teaching abilities to a great extent.

13.3 Policy Recommendations

In this global age, the word 'quality' in education has attained new definitions. Child being the focal point, quality initiatives in recent times have aimed at enhancement of skills that build competencies and values which form the character. Due to such shift in the ideology of education, teaching–learning process has become more interactive and child-centered. Institutions are looking at education as something that fosters a holistic development of the child not only in cosmetic sense but in real form. Respect for culture and heritage are an integral part of the curriculum transaction. At the same time, the necessity to be technologically oriented is never undermined in these organizations. The most important entity in the process of education is the teacher. Competencies and the character of a teacher are of utmost importance. Induction and in-service programmes orient a teacher towards updating and enhancing talents and skills. Soft skills to create a conducive work environment are essential too. The role played by the parents is crucial to the quality of education. Parents are instrumental in identifying, nurturing, and promoting their ward's potential and interests. It is a parent who should also coordinate and cooperate with the teacher in bringing about a desirable metamorphosis of the child's personality. The role of the management is vital in providing the paraphernalia of technical as well as emotional support. Based on the findings of the study, the following recommendations are made, which can be addressed by various stakeholders such as Ministry of Human Resource Development (MHRD), school principals, parents, teachers, and various research scholars.

Increased Funding and Investments: Although in absolute terms, the outlays might have increased over the Five Year Plans, in terms of percentage shares of public expenditure and GDPs, there are huge fluctuations in the pattern of spending. The goal of 6% investment in education sector is still unfulfilled. The private share of education expenditure on the other hand, although has increased manifolds over the years, shows unbalanced distribution and reflects huge disparities at various levels. Hence, considering the importance of secondary education, government should increase the share of secondary education in total expenditure outlay and also make efforts in seeking more private investment in this sector. It should be seen that mere allocation of funds should not be the end process but regular checks need to be done on how well the allocated resources are implemented at the school level. The outcomes from various schemes should also be measured from time to time to see how effective funds have been utilized.

Privatization of Secondary Education: Overall, about 60% of the lower and senior secondary schools in India are privately managed (both aided and unaided). It is essential, therefore, that the private sector's capabilities and potential are tapped through innovative public–private partnerships, while concurrently stepping up public investment by the central and state governments at the secondary level. The presence of private schools varies considerably across states, context-specific solutions need to be promoted. Considering the increasing demand for private-owned schools, the Twelfth Five Year Plan has made certain interventions in setting up more private-owned schools. However, the fulfilment of these targets demands strategy for timely implementation and regular monitoring.

Making School Education Affordable: Another factor which has come up in this study is the expensive nature of school education due to the huge demands arising for private schooling. It has been observed that not only low-income famIlles, but middle income households are also finding difficulties to afford private school education. Therefore, government should take policy decisions in fixing certain criterion for fees charged by private schools.

Improving Accessibility of Secondary Schools: It has been found that majority of the households have access to a secondary school within 5 km range, while this is 1 and 3 km in case of primary and middle schools. At the national level, on an average, availability of 150 secondary/senior secondary schools per one lakh population is quite low. Therefore, the number of secondary schools in India needs to be increased. To supplement the efforts in this direction, certain incentives should be given to private players to open more schools so that secondary schools can be easily accessible by students in both rural and urban areas within a range of 1 km.

Universalization of Secondary Education: The current GER for the combined secondary and senior secondary stages is woefully low. It has been empirically established that there are social, demographic, and economic benefits of attaining secondary level of education at both the national and state levels. Secondary education leads to improvements in health, gender equality, living conditions, and the overall well-being. Investments in secondary schooling have high marginal rates of return. Hence, there is a need to expand the capacity of secondary schooling significantly. Efforts towards increasing accessibility and making school education

would help in a large way to accelerate participation rates. Further, in line with primary education, the secondary education should be universalized and made compulsory for every child to make the base for secondary education larger.

Efforts to Improve Transition Rates and Reduce Dropout Rates: Findings reveal that the transition rates in India have not increased much since the last three decades. It was further found out that students' dropout is not merely because of poverty or financial constraints but also because schools do not respond to their special education needs. Policy measures aimed at mitigating the causes of low transition rates from primary to secondary education need to take into account the growing demand for secondary education. Supply-side interventions, such as increasing or improving the provision of schools and qualified teachers, as well as demand-side interventions, such as improving social and economic conditions of households needs the attention of policymakers. Out-of-school children and the barriers that prevent their participation in education should be better identified. Comprehensive profiles of out-of-school children, which identify key personal and household characteristics, as well as past and expected school exposure, can help policymakers to formulate interventions aimed at increasing primary and secondary school enrolment and graduation rates. Targets should be set not only to increase participation at the entry level of secondary education but also in widening the scope of upper secondary level education as well. Moreover, the content of upper secondary education should therefore be relevant to the demands of the labour market.

Need for Proper Counseling of Students: The ultimate target of polices designed for secondary level of education should not only be to increase the participation rates or reduce dropout rates, but also to create such a healthy and quality atmosphere in secondary schools where students can learn, perform, and develop a base for achieving their future targets. Students should be given adequate guidance at both lower and senior secondary levels of education so as to enable them to plan for their future studies and career options. This will not only put them on the right track after completing schooling but will increase enthusiasm and provide them confidence and motivation to perform better so as to achieve their future targets.

Need to Foster Equity in Access to Secondary Education: There are large inequalities in access to secondary education by income, gender, social group, and geography. While private provision in secondary education should be fostered wherever feasible, the government will have to take the prime responsibility of providing access to secondary education to the disadvantaged sections and bridge the rural/urban, regional, gender and social group gaps.

Balanced Growth of Secondary Education: The study highlights unbalanced growth and expansion of secondary education at the state level. While few states are performing well, the others lack resources and perform poorly at school level education. It is also found that richer states spend more on education, while the poorer ones do not have adequate funds to allocate to this sector. Therefore, more funds should be allocated to poorer states by the central government so as to promote equal and balanced growth of secondary education amongst all states.

Improving Quality of School Resources: The major problem in most of the secondary schools is lack of basic facilities and infrastructural resources. Further, even where these facilities are available, they lack regular maintenance. Therefore, school authorities should enforce timely and regular maintenance of these facilities. Along with this, regular supervision and monitoring is also required. The faculties should be given training on usage of fire-safety measures in case of emergencies.

Upgradation of Existing Facilities: Efforts should be made to employ latest technologies in schools in libraries, science laboratories, and computer labs. It is the responsibility of schools to equip their students with latest technologies available in the labour market to make them more competent. Latest books on wide issues should be available in libraries for student's references. Science and computer labs should also be equipped with latest and modern equipments and software.

Maintaining Lower Class Size: Large class size is another issue that not only affects students' learning but also teaching abilities adversely. Hence, more classrooms need to be constructed in government schools so that students may be distributed in different sections to reduce the average number of students per class. Alternatively, depending upon the feasibility and need, schools may be run on two or three shifts.

Increasing Scope for Government Schools: Findings reveal that government schools lag behind private schools in providing most of the facilities to students. In such a scenario, mere opening up of more government schools may not be the best policy. What is required is to improve the quality of education in senior secondary government schools by providing good facilities. Presently, there are very few government schools providing English-medium education. Moreover, most schools provide either commerce or arts as fields of study. There is need to introduce English-medium education and science as a field of study in more government schools. Students should also be given chance to learn computers in schools itself so that poor students may also benefit. Government should promote special schemes to make government secondary schools more competitive. A separate fund may be allocated for this purpose. This will help in a long way in reducing dropouts and absenteeism rates in government schools and increase the demand for government schools.

More employment of Trained Teachers: High PTR is another problem that is affecting the student outcomes. This problem is quite prominent in private schools due to shortage of trained staff. Hence, schools should recruit more qualified and trained staff, if not on the regular rolls, perhaps on contract basis which can be made permanent later based on.

Provision for Extra Classes: It is found that majority of senior secondary schools in Delhi do not organize extra classes for weak students. Further, majority of the students believe that extra classes help them in improving their academic performances. Hence, survey suggests that considering the benefits of extra classes to students, more and more schools should try to provide it so that they can offer an additional opportunity to students when they can clear their doubts in much smaller gatherings and on various subjects.

Improving Teaching Efficiencies: Efficient teaching methods and use of proper teaching aids have positive implications on students' outcomes. Hence, government must invest in teacher education and accountability, curriculum reform, quality assurance, examinations reform, national assessment capabilities, and management information systems, which will require time and significant institutional capacity building to succeed on a national scale. In addition to this, on regular intervals, teachers' evaluation and monitoring should also be conducted so as to cross-check their performances. Students may be the best evaluators for teachers and their teaching methods.

Addressing Teachers' Problems: Schools should address various problems faced by teachers which restrict them in rendering their best teaching abilities. These problems include high workload of additional responsibilities, low motivation of students, non-availability of adequate reference books, lack of proper facilities in schools and efficient teaching aids. Apart from these, most teachers also show dissatisfaction with their growth and promotions, salary structure, job security and opportunities for trainings and professional development which reduces their motivation and enthusiasm for teaching. Hence, these problems should be taken on priority basis by school authorities and government to improve teaching quality in secondary schools.

Promoting Teacher–Student Interaction: Teachers should also take initiatives in improving and strengthening their interaction with students on various issues. This will help in creating better learning environment in schools which will further promote quality teaching. Teachers should encourage their students and keep on informing them from time to time about various career options and competition ahead.

Modification in Grading System: Findings reveal that most teachers and students are not satisfied with the kind of grading system introduced in secondary schools in Delhi. The present grading system has adverse impacts on the learning outcomes of students. It reduces their motivation and enthusiasm for studies as they are already confident that with the present grading system, most of them will clear the exam. Low motivation among students has further huge implications on inefficient teaching abilities. Hence, the present grading system demands modification.

Proper Inspection: Inspection and supervision across the world has been considered a process of assessing the quality and performance of schools by internal and external evaluations. Inspection and supervision systems need to be re-examined in the face of demands that schools should be made more transparently accountable for the outcomes and standards that they achieve and, therefore, responsible for continuously assessing their performance.

Family Support: The findings clearly reveal the positive impact of family background and culture on students' outcomes. Parents should try their best in developing a friendly relation with their children and should encourage and support them in every sphere of life which can psychologically motivate students to perform better.

To conclude, one can say that quality is the language of integrity that makes the child 'Fit for Life'. While dealing with educational change, the emphasis needs to shift from strategic planning to strategic thinking; from the management model of 'control and command' to networking and greater participation; from planned strategy to building sustainable capacity; and from transforming people to transferring opportunity. Making secondary schools and their teaching settings effective in India, therefore, would require creating the momentum for change through analyses of school culture—whether teaching–learning is taking place as part of a reaction or compliance, and whether the school is operating in isolation. Accordingly, there is a need to shift the school culture from reaction to defining clear purpose and focus; compliance to engagement of students, teachers, and other immediate stakeholders; and from an environment of isolation to an environment of collaboration.

Appendix

Box A.1 Conceptual Framework of Study

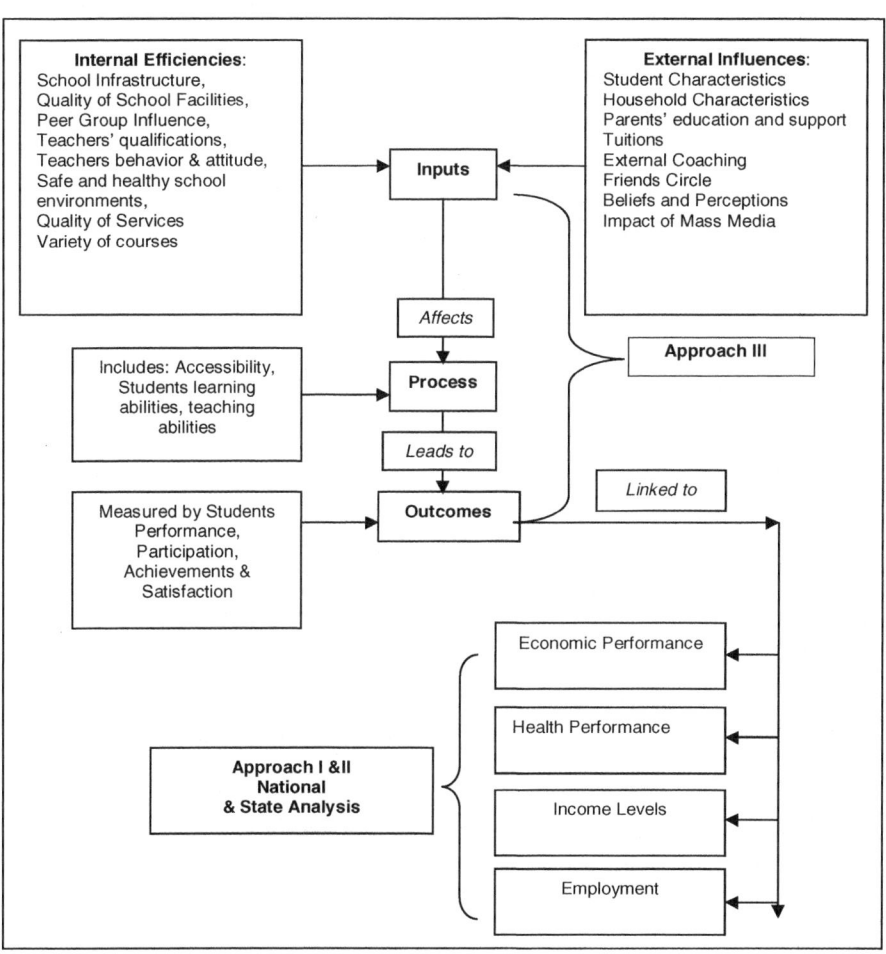

© Springer Nature Singapore Pte Ltd. 2018
C. Jain and N. Prasad, *Quality of Secondary Education in India*,
https://doi.org/10.1007/978-981-10-4929-3

Box A.2 Sampling Design

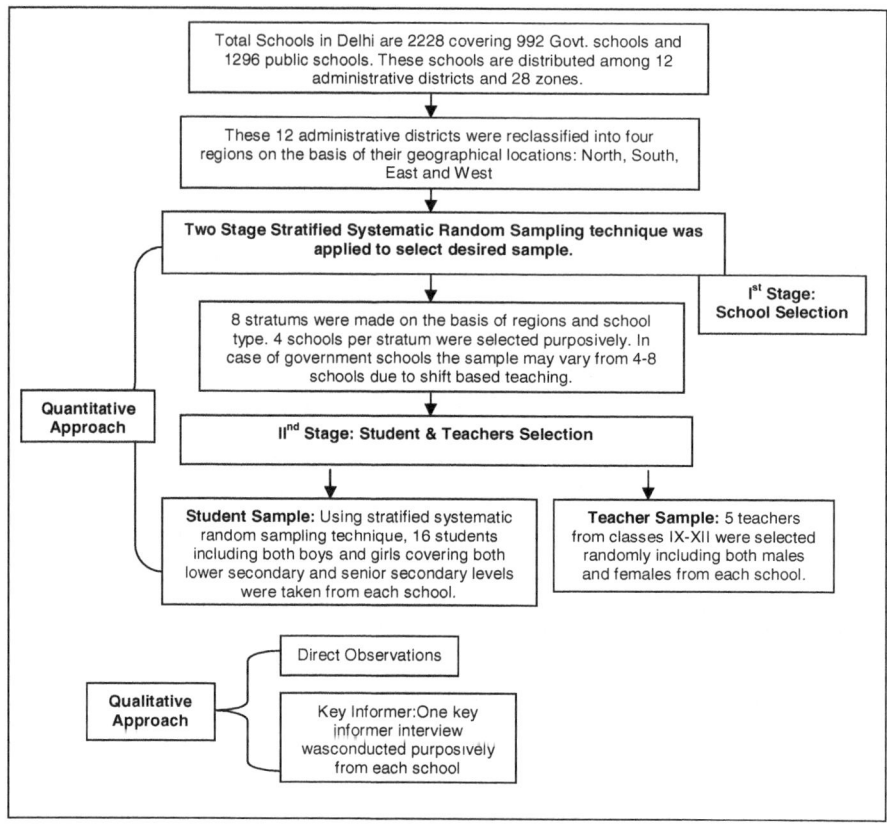

Box A.3 List of Indicators for Various Dimensional Indexes for Macro Model: State-level

S. No.	Index type	List of variables
1	Elementary education index (EEI)	• Public expenditure on elementary education as % of GSDP • Elementary schools/1000 population • Pupil teacher ratio in elementary schools • Elementary GER • Girls per 100 boys
2	Secondary education index (SEI)	• Public expenditure on secondary education as % of GSDP • Secondary schools/1000 population • Pupil teacher ratio in secondary schools • Secondary GER • Girls per 100 boys

(continued)

(continued)

S. No.	Index type	List of variables
3	Economic index (ECI)	• Per capita NSDP at FC constant prices (2011–12) • Public debt as % of GSDP • Real GR of states as % of GSDP • FDI proposals approved (in million Rs)
4	Social index (SCI)	• Urban population % • Mean age at effective marriage (females) • Poverty % • Literacy rate % • HIV prevalence rate adult • Employment in organized sector
5	Demographic index (DMI)	• Sex ratio (females per 100 males) • Life expectancy at birth • Exponential GR of population
6	Demographic health index (DMHI)	• Crude birth rates • Crude death rates • Infant mortality rates • Maternal mortality rates • Total fertility rates
7	Health index (HLI)	• Full Immunization of children (%) • Contraceptive use by any methods (%) • Percent of institutionalized deliveries • Percent of women with any ANC • Average population served per Govt. hospital

Printed by Printforce, the Netherlands